M000283930

PORTUGAL
THE IMPOSSIBLE
REVOLUTION?

PHIL MAILER

Portugal: The Impossible Revolution?
Phil Mailer
© 2012 PM Press
All rights reserved. No part of this book may be transmitted by any means without
permission in writing from the publisher.

ISBN: 978-1-60486-336-9
Library of Congress Control Number: 2011927959

Cover and interior design by briandesign

10 9 8 7 6 5 4 3 2 1

PM Press
PO Box 23912
Oakland, CA 94623
www.pmpress.org

Printed in the USA on recycled paper, by the Employee Owners of Thomson-Shore
in Dexter, Michigan.
www.thomsonshore.com

Published in the EU by The Merlin Press Ltd.
6 Crane Street Chambers, Crane Street, Pontypool NP4 6ND, Wales
www.merlinpress.co.uk
ISBN: 978-0-85036-648-8

CONTENTS

INTRODUCTION

The military coup in Portugal on April 25, 1974, ending nearly fifty years of fascist rule, was followed by eighteen months of intense social transformation that challenged every aspect of Portuguese society. What started as a military coup turned into a profound attempt at grassroots social change that made headlines on a daily basis around the world due to the intensity of the struggle and the presence of the right-wing, moribund Francoist regime in neighbouring Spain. There was much uncertainty at the time as to how these struggles might affect Spain and Europe at large.

This book is a personal description of these events from the day of the coup and its tumultuous aftermath up to November 1975, when another military coup reinforced liberal parliamentary democracy and brought Portugal into the mainstream of European capitalism.

Today, very few outside Portugal can remember these events. With the failure of the revolution, Portugal was quickly recuperated into the European Union and the whole experience was considered a tempest in a teacup barely worth mentioning.

But inside the country, the experience was profound: many companies were taken over by their workers; Neighbourhood Committees occupied empty houses and ran crèches and other community services. The police were rendered ineffective and the army (usually the last bastion of the state) divided into opposing factions, with the revolutionary left factions being in control of the state apparatus for quite some time.

The rhetoric of revolution was everywhere and there were hints as to what a modern revolution might entail. But in 1974, there was no Internet, no mobile/cell phones. The two main TV stations were state-controlled and there were only a half dozen radio stations in the country.

Workers tried to organise in this vacuum. The problems of self-organisation and political manipulation when workers were forbidden to carry any political party banners or trade-union banners at demonstrations are highlighted in the latter half of the book. The control of the media (television, radio, and newspapers, especially the Catholic Church radio station occupied at the time by the far-left) and their problems are also discussed in great detail. Throughout the book I have also sought to pay particular attention to the problems of rank-and-file soldiers organising within the army.

The split in Portuguese society after the 1974 coup was threefold: among the various state capitalist ideas (and parties), those who wanted to install liberal parliamentary democracy, and the various attempts of People Power to increase the direct influence of the workers from the bottom up. This latter effort by the workers is well documented here, mostly in their own words, in its struggle to develop organisational autonomy and economic self-management. In this, my account of the events in Portugal may differ from others of its kind.

Through five successive military governments, the Portuguese Communist Party (PCP) installed state capitalism throughout the country and the various far-left parties largely actively collaborated with this project. The Socialist Party, however, was divided between those who wanted to go along with the military governments and the Communist Party, and those who wanted a European-style liberal capitalism and thus conspired with the Right and extreme Right and the U.S. Embassy. The Social Democrats, situated to the right of the Socialist Party, were trying to find new clothes for the old regime.

Today's Portugal is the outcome of these struggles. The Socialist Party (PS) and the Popular Democrats (now PSD) are the power-mongers while the PCP remains the main left opposition group and is in control of the trade union movement. The far-left groups, with all the colourful acronyms you'll encounter throughout the book, are now all allied into the Left Wing Alliance (BE, Bloco de Esquerda) while the Maoists have thankfully mostly disappeared altogether.

In reediting this book of events that occurred over thirty-five years ago, it is sometimes difficult to imagine the intensity of the moments. As I reread my account, I had to frequently ask myself, *did this really happen?* But, yes, it did happen; I still have all the documents to prove it. For a younger generation, it may truly seem impossible! Maurice Brinton's afterword deals with that word in the title of this account in some detail. At the time of these events, there was endless discussion across continents as to whether there should be a question mark after the word "impossible." Such were the times. I still support the question mark.

At the time I wrote this book, state capitalism was considered to be as big a danger (if not bigger) to Portugal than private capitalism. This was the main emphasis of my analysis of the grassroots movement as well as political party analysis in this book, although neoliberalism and market economics became the dominant ideology in the Portuguese (and world) ruling class instead. This did not seem so obvious in 1974-75. Today, Portugal is a country fully integrated into modern capitalism with all the iniquities that implies.

At reissue, the book is essentially the same as the 1977 edition that was published jointly by Solidarity in London, Black Rose in Canada, and Free Life Editions in New York. I have omitted a chapter on Portuguese history, as I found it a bit too long-winded and statistical, obstructing the narrative; for those eager to seek further information, the subject has been dealt with amply and better elsewhere, in other books or on the Internet. I have edited some sections slightly, omitting parts that I felt went into too much detail and were not relevant today. I have omitted the twenty-six appendices originally at the back of the book as they, too, are available elsewhere. Maurice Brinton's introduction, which I feel continues to be a valid contribution, is now an afterword; I am indebted to him in so many ways for getting this book off the ground from the start. A few names have been restored to their proper Portuguese spelling, and a few errors about geographical location of factories and barracks have been rectified. Very little else has changed.

It is what it is. *Vamos ver*.

I would like to dedicate this edition to the memory *of Maria Teresa Viana* (1946-2010) who influenced it in so many subtle ways.

Phil Mailer
Lisbon, 2012

GLOSSARY

ADU	Assembly of (military) Unit Delegates
ALA	Free Association of Farmers
AMI	Group for Military Intervention; counterforce to COPCON set up by Sixth Government
ANP	Popular National Action; main fascist party before April 25
AOC	Association of Workers and Peasants, formed by Maoists in the chemical industry, to combat PCP-dominated Intersindical
CAP	Confederation of Portuguese Farmers
CC of MFA	Coordinating Committee of the Armed Forces Movement
CCP	Coordinating Committee originally, clandestine Movement of the Captains
CDE	Democratic Committees for the Elections Founded in 1969 for electoral purposes; originally composed of PGP, PS, and MAR, a group of progressive Catholics
CDS	Social and Democratic Centre; in fact a right-wing party which regrouped many of the fascists after April 25
CGT	Confederacão Geral do Trabalho; anarcho-syndicalist trade union federation, smashed by the fascists
CIAC	Centro de Instrução de Artilharia de Cascais (Artillery Instruction Centre in Cascais)
CICAP	Centro de Instrução de Conducão dos Automóveis do Porto (Military Driving School)
CIP	Confederation of Portuguese Industry; the organisation of the bosses
CM	Comissão de Moradores: Neighbourhood Committee

CODICE	Central Committee for Dynamisation; controlled by the Fifth (pro-PGP) Division
COPCON	Continental Operations Command; security force of the MFA, incorporating units most loyal to the original programme; set up July 1974; dissolved November 1975
CRAM	Federation of Autonomous Revolutionary Neighbourhood Committees
CRTSM	Revolutionary Councils of Workers, Soldiers, and Sailors; formed in April 1975 with the assistance of the PRP-BR
CT	Comissão de Trabalhadores; Workers' Committee, usually elected by a plenário (general assembly)
DCS	See PIDE Emissora Nacional, the national radio network
EPAM	Practical School of Military Administration (Lisbon)
FEC-ml	Communist Electoral Front (Marxist-Leninist) that brought together various Maoist groups sympathetic to Albania
FMU	Frente Militar Unida; political section of "Group of Nine" to warn of coups
FNLA	Angolan National Liberation Front
FPLN	Patriotic Front for National Liberation, formed in 1962, in Algeria, with General Humberto Delgado, Cunhal (PCP), and Tito de Morais (PS)
FRAP	Spanish Antifascist Patriotic Revolutionary Front
FSP	Popular Socialist Front, the result of a "leftist" split in the PS in January 1975
FUR	Frente de Unidade Revolucionária (Revolutionary United Front), including PCP, MDP, FSP, PRP, MES, LCI, and First of May group
GAPS	Grupo Atonomo do Partido Socialista, an independent group within PS
GNR	National Republican Guard, heavily armed paramilitary police force, one of the mainstays of the fascist regime; restructured after November 1975
Inter-Comissões	Association of Committees. This term was used to refer to several organisations: a) Federation of Shanty town Neighbourhood Committees b) Federation of Soldiers and Sailors' Committees c) A group of committees, emerging from Inter-Empresas

Inter-Empresas	Federation of Workers' Committees
Intersindical	Main Trade Union Federation, under control of PCP
IRA	Institute for the Reorganisation of Agriculture
LCI	Internationalist Communist League; Trotskyist
LUAR	League of Union and Revolutionary Action, a direct action group responsible for some spectacular bank robberies and bombings before April 25
MAHR	Movement for Revolutionary Homosexual Action Portugal
MDP	Portuguese Democratic Movement; political line usually indistinguishable, after April 25, from that of PCP; originally encompassed the CDE group
MDM	Democratic Women's Movement (PCP-oriented)
MES	Movement of Left Socialists, founded at the end of 1973 from the old GAPS; attracted many technicians into its ranks
MFA	Movement of the Armed Forces
MLM	Women's Liberation Movement
MPLA	Angolan Popular Liberation Movement
MRPP	Movement for the Reorganisation of the Party of the Proletariat, founded in 1970 by students and young workers who left the PCP; the noisiest Maoist group
MUD	Movement for Democratic Unity
PCP	Portuguese Communist Party, founded in 1921
PCP-ml	Portuguese Communist Party (Marxist-Leninist); a Maoist group formed in 1970; split after April 25 into two groups of the same name, one joining PUP and the other joining AOC; recognised by China as the "official" Portuguese Maoist group
PDC	Christian Democratic Party; an extreme right-wing party, which also regrouped many of the fascists after April 25
PIDE	International Police for the Defence of the State; in 1970 became DCS (General Security Command), the Portuguese political police
PM	Military Police, under control of COPCON until its dissolution
PPD	Popular Democratic Party, capitalist party of the Centre; had ministers in every Provisional Government, except the Fifth

PPM	Popular Monarchist Party
PRP-BR	Revolutionary Proletarian Party—Revolutionary Brigades; split from the FPLN in 1972, setting up the Brigades which were responsible for various attacks on troop-ships and military installations before April 25; founded the Workers' Councils movement
PRT	Revolutionary Workers' Party, Trotskyist
PS	Portuguese Socialist Party, founded in 1967; Affiliated to Second International
PSDI	Independent Social-Democratic Party (right-wing)
PSP	Public Security Police, the main police force
PUP	Party of Popular Unity, caused by a split in PCP-ml
RAC	Coastal Artillery Unit, stationed near Lisbon
RAL-1	First Light Infantry Regiment (stationed near Lisbon)
RASP	Artillery Regiment of Serra do Pilar (near Porto)
RCP	Rádio Clube Português, radio station, originally privately owned, nationalised after November 25
RIOQ	Operational Infantry Regiment of Queluz
RPA	Antifascist Popular Resistance, opposition nuclei in armed forces
RPAC	Popular Resistance against Colonialism (the MRPP soldiers)
RR	Rádio Renascença; owned by Church, later occupied by its workers; returned to Church after November 25, 1975
RTP	Portuguese State Television (two channels)
SAAL	Serviço de Apoio Ambulatório (Mobile Service for Local Support); Semigovernment agency working for Ministry of Housing
SADA	Support Services for the Development of Agriculture; a PCP front, within the Ministry of Agriculture
SDCI	Service for Detection and Coordination of Information
SEDES	Group of technocrats founded in 1970 following the so-called liberalisation policies of Marcelo Caetano
SUV	Soldados Unidos Vencerão (Soldiers United Will Win); A rank-and-file soldiers' organisation
UDP	Popular Democratic Unity. Regroupment of various Maoists
UEC	PCP student organisation
URML	Revolutionary Union of Marxist-Leninists; Maoist group

SOME COMMON PORTUGUESE TERMS
USED THROUGHOUT THE BOOK

autogestão	self-management
bagaço	a strong brandy
barracas	shanty town dwellings
burguesia	bourgeoisie, the ruling class
latifundio	a large agricultural estate
plenário	plenary session, general meeting
pluralismo	free association of trade unions
saneamento	purging of undesirable political elements
tasca	a working-class tavern
unicidade	one big union for all workers
unidade	unity of trade unions by choice

I THE FIRST WEEK

DAY 1: THURSDAY, APRIL 25, 1974

The 25th is a cold morning for April. At 7:45 a.m., the following radio announcement stuns hundreds of thousands of Portuguese into a realisation that a new phase in their history has begun:

> The Portuguese Armed Forces appeal to all the inhabitants of Lisbon to stay at home and to remain as calm as possible. We sincerely hope that the seriousness of the hour will not be saddened by personal injuries. We therefore appeal to the good sense of all military commanders to avoid any confrontation with the Armed Forces. Apart from being unnecessary, such action would only create or aggravate serious divisions between Portuguese people, which must be avoided at all costs. It is because of our concern to spare Portuguese blood that we are appealing for a civic spirit. All medical personnel, especially those in hospitals, should hold themselves ready to give help, though it is hoped this will not be needed. To all political and military forces, the Command advises maximum caution to avoid any action which may be dangerous. It is not our intention to shed blood unnecessarily, but if we meet provocation we shall deal with it.

It goes on to advise to

> Go back to your quarters, and wait for orders which will be given by the Movement of the Armed Forces. Commanders will be held responsible for any attempt, in any form whatsoever, to lead their subordinates into conflict with the Armed Forces We appeal to the forces of the GNR (National Guard) and PSP (Police)—and even to the DGS (Political Police) and Portuguese Legion—who may have been recruited under false pretences to remember their civic duty of maintaining public order. In the present situation this can only be

achieved if there is no reaction against the Armed Forces. Attention, all military and police units. Since the Armed Forces have decided to take your place in the present situation any opposition to the troops which surround the city will be dealt with drastically. By not obeying this advice you could provoke a senseless bloodbath, whose responsibility will be yours alone.[1]

8:15 a.m. My neighbour wakes me; there's crazy look in her eyes as she stands there in her pyjamas. She tells me not to go to school today: all schools are closed, the Army have taken over, shooting, everyone to stay at home. She speaks in broken Portuguese to help me understand, firing her fingers into the air.

I close the door thinking she's mad, turn on the radio and return to bed. Nothing: the usual ads. I can't believe it. I can't sleep though I need to. I try other stations. Marching music on the National Radio. Could she be right?

9:10 a.m. Already late, I arrive at school. No buses outside. I meet R, a teacher who is bursting with the news. D, the school fascist, is also there. We ask if it's from the Right or from the Left, or even from which forces on the Right: the generals or Spínola. The question remains unanswered all morning. No one knows.

10 a.m. Breakfast with R, a kind and good-hearted person, dying to find out but afraid to go into the centre of the city. Coffee. The radio is playing Zeca Afonso, a left-wing singer. Could it be true? An announcement:

> It has been reported to the Command of the Armed Forces that the civilian population is not respecting the appeal to remain at home, an appeal which we have already made many times. Although the situation may seem almost under control, since the ex-Minister of the Army has abandoned the Ministry and is in contact with the commanding officers of our Movement, we ask the population, once again, to stay at home and not endanger themselves. A communiqué will be broadcast shortly, to clarify the situation.[2]

I explain what I know of Spínola: his Nazi sympathies, his support for Franco during the Spanish Civil War, his decorations as a "war-hero" in the Portuguese colonies. His interview with the magazine *Vida Mundial*,

---

1   *Diário Popular*, April 25, 1974.
2   Ibid.

some weeks earlier, had outlined what he's written in his book *Portugal and the Future,* and for these views he's been sacked by Caetano.[3] His book called for an end to the search for a military solution to the war and for change within Portugal, along "democratic" lines. We talk about the revolt in March, when troops had marched from Caldas da Rainha, in the North, in what had seemed a farcical attempt at revolt at the time. Or was it a putsch by certain right-wing generals, dissatisfied with the "liberal" policies of Caetano, and wanting a return to a purer form of Salazarism? No one knows. Either way, it seemed the coup could only be from the Right.

At 10:45 a.m. I phone João, the son of Mário Soares. The phone is busy. I phone R, a worker in a bloodbank. She's on a twenty-four-hour call. Troops are on the streets outside. It's impossible to enter Lisbon except through Praça da Espanha. She knows nothing of what it's all about. I decide to go into Lisbon to see for myself, driving along the Marginal, which follows the river Tagus. The greatness of sixteenth-century history is far from my thoughts. I arrive at Infante Santo and am diverted by traffic police. Something is definitely on. I accelerate, arrive at the centre, and park the car. I can see nothing out of the ordinary except that all the banks are closed. I walk towards the lower part of the city. Troops and tanks in the Chiado, soldiers everywhere. The tanks look gigantic in the narrow streets, the machine guns threatening. It is impossible to enter. The troops are cautious but friendly. The crowds have a mixture of fear and hope in their eyes. Everyone is asking the same questions: "Who is it?" "What do they stand for?" It's 11:30 a.m. I've promised to lunch with C, at noon. She may have heard more. In C's house we listen to short-wave radio and pick up the walkie-talkies of the Forces. From her next-door neighbour, an old and already saddened Salazarist, we hear the news that Caetano and Tomás have sought refuge in Belém (the Presidential Palace) and the Quartel do Carmo (the National Republican Guard Headquarters) respectively.[4]

Someone phones to say that his car has been requisitioned, as a barricade. He is laughing on the telephone. There is a great feeling: the fascist dictatorship is crumbling. For the moment few can think further.

We go again into the city. There is still nothing definite. We go to San Sebastião and see the troops. Large groups are talking to the soldiers. The

---

3   Marcelo Caetano, Prime Minister, 1968–74.
4   Américo Tomás, President of Portugal, 1958–74.

troops have already become "forces of liberation." No one is yet specifically asking who is going to be "liberated." And from what? The confusion is immense. Can an antifascist coup really have taken place? Led by
a fascist? We search for precedents, and discover already how new the
features are of what we are witnessing.

We buy the newspapers. The headlines are startling: "Golpe Militar,"
"Amplo Movimento das Forças Armadas." Their accounts fill in some
details. At 11:30 last night, radio programmes were apparently interrupted and "Depois do Adeus" and "Grándola, Vila Morena" were played.
Shortly after midnight the College of Military Administration was occupied. At 3 a.m. the studios of the pop-radio station Rádio Clube Português
were occupied and other radio stations soon after. The airport fell. A little
later the Seventh Cavalry, Spínola's crack troops, moved into Praça do
Comércio, the great square in the lower part of the city. At 7 a.m. tanks
took up positions on the other side of the river, facing Lisbon.

We listen to the radio. At 10:15 a.m. the Quartermaster General,
Louro de Sousa, was detained. At 10:30 a.m., troops occupying Rua do
Arsenal joined in the revolt. At noon comes the announcement that the
armed forces are in control, both North and South. 1 p.m.: the political
police headquarters are surrounded and some political prisoners released.
4 p.m.: the centre-left CDE and most of the political groups applaud the
movement. Shortly after, Marcelo Caetano surrenders. He has been on the
phone to Spínola. 5:30 p.m.: prisoners from the Caldas da Rainha rebellion
are released, to cheers from the crowds. At 5 p.m. the television broadcasts
a statement saying that the Armed Forces Movement "has liberated the
people from a regime which has oppressed them for many years."

I take C home and go out again into Lisbon. The political police, the
PIDE, have resisted and refuse to surrender. There are crowds calling for
their blood. They want to storm the offices and burn them down. They are
unarmed. The PIDE have machine guns, pointing from their verandas. I
feel helpless and decide to leave. Later we learn that a PIDE had fired into
the crowd from a window, killing five and wounding fifty. The sailors fired
back. The PIDE are desperate. They have tortured their victims too much
and for too long to hope for mercy.

I return home and go to a tasca. We drink wine and wonder what it all
means. People are excited, fantastically excited. I go to R's for dinner. All
restaurants have been closed in compliance with the communiqués. We
cook dinner: an assortment of old vegetables. We are completely unprepared, like everyone else. We listen to the foreign stations to see if they

have any news. We can't really believe what we hear. As yet, no names have been given. The coup is completely anonymous. I phone a friend who lives near the radio station: the area is surrounded by troops and he can't get out. I phone another friend who is very tired, having been up since 6:30 a.m. that morning. I don't want to go home. I want to go to Lisbon.

I'm euphoric. A French girl who is present shares some of my enthusiasm. Everything is confusion. Spínola has moved from being a fascist that morning to being a "liberator" that evening. We try to gather our thoughts, to analyse. What class forces are involved? Spínola had married into one of the richest families in Portugal: the Melos. He was an "individualist." In Guinea-Bissau, he had often flown right into the scene of battle and commanded great respect from the troops who'd served with him. His monocle, his conservative ways, all that just didn't fit the role of a radical liberator. The ambiguities of "antifascism" were already apparent.

There are so many divergent interests. The middle class look to Europe and the EEC as the only future for Portugal whereas the *burguesia* of the "100 families" still has large undertakings in Africa, especially in Angola. Some sections of the middle class have their eye on economic expansion; others support a moribund Salazarist ideology which is a brake to expansion. In Africa, white "colons" face black Africans. But the greatest opposition of all is surely the one between all these elements and the working class.

It is marvellous: natural amphetamine. M and I leave together. We want to go out despite the curfew. We go to a friend's who lives near the radio station. The streets are blocked. We speak English. A smiling nineteen-year-old soldier calls his officer and we explain that we want to sleep in a house nearby. The young soldier, a rug over his shoulders and machine gun looking huge against him, escorts us to the house. All the way, he is smiling happily; he is feeling great, too.

Everyone there is asleep, dead from a day of movement and discussion, but we manage to find some blankets. Almost immediately, we fall asleep, too, exhausted.

DAY 2: FRIDAY, APRIL 26

We awake wondering what has happened during the might, sore from the floor, and with a terrible hangover. M makes coffee; I go to get the papers.

The headlines are startling. Spínola, the leader of the new Junta, has promised the "democratisation of politics" new elections as soon as possible, an end to all fascist institutions, and negotiations over the wars in

Africa. Caetano and Tomás have been exiled to Madeira. Some PIDEs have been captured, one with his trousers down, which makes us all laugh.

We go off to lunch and pore over the morning papers. The photos are telling. Masses of people are involved. This is clearly more than just a *coup d'état*. Already the old structures seem to be falling apart. We just aren't reading the same newspapers as yesterday, though the names, layout, and style are much the same. Nervously, faces on the streets are beginning to smile. Whiffs of freedom are rising over Lisbon and people are passing them on to one another in their speech and laughter. It is fantastic, shattering, growing.

Troops everywhere are giving the victory sign. We hear about Caxias, the notorious political prison: 170 prisoners have been released and about a hundred PIDEs put in their place. I'd had friends who'd been sent there, then beaten and tortured. The pictures in the papers are tremendous. Thousands had been to Caxias to welcome the prisoners. We hear that the Junta had only wanted to free a few of them, but that the crowds had noisily insisted on releasing the lot.

Organisations, which had been living hand to mouth, underground, are surfacing and making statements: the Communist Party (PCP), the Socialist Party (PS), CDE, LUAR. We pinch ourselves to see if it is really true. There is other news, but it doesn't interest us. Someone mentions that Mitterrand stood a chance in the French elections. So what? The pictures are spectacular, unfaked. Every photo seems an image of liberation. Could those be the same newspapers which only a few weeks before reported, in some corner of an inside page, that the police had attacked student troublemakers on an attempted demonstration, without mentioning the number beaten up? Free speech seems to be getting freer every minute.

A crowd is gathering near Rossio (a big Lisbon square). Troops come towards us. What will happen? They raise their fingers in a V sign. The crowd cheer like I've never heard cheers before. I have heard crowds shout in anger, but this is joy, unmitigated.

I can't make sense of this, nor can M. We are getting shivers. We remember Prague 1968, when people placed flowers in the gun barrels of tanks in gentle irony. But now people are giving carnations to the soldiers, like one gives to one's loved one on the night of Santo António, the patron saint of Lisbon. They are buying them newspapers, offering them beer, sandwiches. I clap, incredulously. I remember pictures of revolutionary troops during the Spanish Civil War, their hands clasped in a fist:

the Durruti Column. I try to think of the Kiev mutiny which led to the Spartacist revolt in Germany in 1918; of the rebellious troops in Russia in 1917; of the troops during the Paris Commune. My thoughts are running away with me.

It starts to rain heavily. Lightning lights up the sky. There are peals of thunder, like some grumble from the Gods. M comments that heaven is not on our side. We decide that nothing could happen until night, even if other forces are still holding out, even if the PIDEs are trying to reorganise. We feel tired and depressed by the rain. We go to a cinema for two hours to see a Paul Newman film and then head off again in the direction of Rossio. On the way, we cross a demonstration. I'd often dreamed of it. I'd seen photos of 1910, when the workers had marched up Avenida da Liberdade occupying its enormous width. And here it is, made real, right before my eyes. The Maoists are in front with their banners, but behind are all sorts of groups, with banners of their own. "We salute the Armed Forces," "Free Unions," "Power to the Workers," "The Right to Strike." It feels heady, despite the palpable contradictions.

I'd often walked this avenue conscious of the irony of its name (a residue from more liberal days), feeling oppressed as hell. And here, right in front of me, are several thousand people parading up its middle. Motorists cannot get through. They blow their horns—not in anger but joyfully, as is the custom at Portuguese marriage feasts. We are in the centre of the street, in a free demonstration. It is unheard of. We are still afraid of course, expecting the PSP squads (a special riot police force, created to deal with demonstrations) to erupt from a side street, at any minute. Emotions are so high that even traffic cops are embraced as "liberators," much to their embarrassment and confusion.

Tanks appear. The cheers grow louder than if Sporting FC had beaten Benfica. People run after the tanks and clamber all over them. The soldiers smile and raise their machine guns in the air.

For forty-eight years, there have been no demonstrations of joy in Portugal. Two generations have passed without being able to walk the streets freely: now fathers and sons are there together. An old man in rags, an old man for whom Salazarism hadn't done anything, carries the Republican flag. He is embraced so much I think he'd have a heart attack. I ask him if it was like this in the days of the Republic and he says it had never been so good. I, too, want to embrace him, he is so baby-like. He knew I was foreign from my accent. Which part of Ireland? The South, I answer. He claps my shoulder and tells me he remembers the Easter rebellion. He probably remembers 1917, 1918, and 1936 as well, though I don't ask. What beauty can be found in people at such times!

We arrive at the great statue of the Marqués de Pombal, sometimes known as Portugal's first (1755) dictator. It is now covered with May Day slogans: "Paz, Unidade, Liberdade, Democracia. Poder aos Trabalhadores."

We pass it and arrive at the CDE offices. We could have marched all night. Some aspiring politicians are trying to make speeches, but it is not the right day for that. Their every sentence is inaudible. The crowd just cheers, repeating the slogan of the day: "*O povo unido jamais será vencido*" (United, the people will never be defeated).

CDE commanded fairly wide-based support. They used the month prior to last November's elections for political agitation. Leaflets and some graffiti (quickly daubed out) appeared on the walls of Lisbon and the independent *República* was even able to get certain articles past the censor. Then, at the last minute, they withdrew their candidates, denouncing the elections as a farce.

The Maoists were already more active than others. This is annoying, as they are so unimaginative. Their clearest slogan is "Nem Marcelo, nem Spínola: Revolucão Socialista" — "neither Marcelo (Caetano) nor Spínola but Socialist Revolution." It is difficult not to have a certain respect for them, and for the Communist Party, too. They were among the bravest under the old regime, tortured and beaten, and yet returned night after night to put up their slogans on the walls, only to have them painted out by the police in the small hours of the morning. Yet the situation is already different: ideas which for decades had influenced people's thoughts about revolution were now to be tested. Those who had kept hopes alive started as heroes. If they were to remain heroes, they would have to measure up to the challenge of the new.

We meet a group of workers singing the Internationale and are astounded. How do they remember the words after all those years? We buy the papers again and go to the nearby Monte Carlo, a haunt of the so-called "night-people," a café that has been repeatedly raided by the agents of PIDE and by the police. The news has again overtaken our wildest hopes.

Headline: "Freedom for all Political Prisoners. Prison for all PIDEs." We are not reading newspapers any more, but political manifestos. Censorship has been trampled underfoot. In all the papers: the picture of Spínola, looking older and more tired than ever, taken from his television broadcast last night. The Junta presented an ominously detailed programme.

What contradictions does this "liberal" programme cover? Yesterday: a *coup d'état*. Today: already massive popular involvement. Something important is developing. A new spirit has invaded all public life. How far will the Junta allow it to go? How much will the Junta be able to control it?

We read about Caxias and about the joy of the political prisoners. We learn that they were awaiting their liberation an hour before it happened, informed of developments by Morse code signals, sent over car-horns. We see the photos of the machine gun bullets at the PIDE offices. We learn that a group of demonstrators has smashed the windows of a bank in the commercial district.

We meet G and others, in a café. They have been to Caxias; the place has been forced open. A PIDE was attacked by the crowd and barely saved by the Army from being beaten to death. He was carrying an infant and people had called out to "save the baby." The man is now in prison.

What to do? Four hours of sleep in two days. This is difficult to sustain, especially with little food. We decide to go to a tasca near my home in a working-class suburb of Lisbon. The atmosphere is electric. João greets us with "Long Live the Revolution." Some workers, who also happen to be soldiers, are in uniform. It is the first time I'd seen them like this. Others are full of spirit, in every sense of the word. Only one, very political, is sceptical. "What about the workers?" he asks. We listen. He went to his factory that morning—but only to talk, to discuss. The tasca has never been so lively. The radio is playing Portuguese music and everyone feels proud. Yes, sad fados are playing, but also the lively music of the exiles in France, the hope of thousands, perhaps millions. And yet, it is obvious that people haven't changed in a day and revolutions aren't made overnight. The owner, João, till now a racist, is calling for the independence of the colonies. In a loud voice, he shouts abuse at a government that for forty-eight years repressed and tortured the people into submission, sent their youth to be killed in a useless war, destroyed free speech and censored all publications, ruled brutally and bloodily, allowing neither strikes nor any other form of dissent, and whose subjects have been afraid to even utter its name. João rails against the old regime. But, when he comes to name it, João lowers his head to mine and his voice quivers ever so slightly. He whispers the horrific word: *Salazarismo*.

We go upstairs; we are sore, tired, but still excited. We listen to some Cabo Verde music: a sad music of a people near to destruction. Some refrains are soothing and near to what we feel. Great hope is the outcome of great despair. For a long time, we can't sleep, but finally doze off. I wake once, in the middle of a dream, and remember the day I went to listen to a clandestine radio in the deserted hills nearby; now, instead of listening to forbidden broadcasts, we are marching on Lisbon.

DAY 3: SATURDAY, APRIL 27

We can't be dragged from our dreams. We have gone too far in our talk and our thoughts. We wake up late. The TV is already on. The news is dreadful: no more demonstrations without permission, or that is how it sounds.

I speak to my neighbour. The fear and hesitancy is gone from her face. She has never drunk before but has already had three whiskies. She has already strolled out into the streets of Lisbon, to watch. She is happier than I ever thought possible. The first concrete thing she says, after expressing all her joy, is that her rent could not now be raised.

We make straight for the Chiado. The hunt for the PIDE is on. People who know where a PIDE lives, go there. Only the Army saves many from being lynched. That afternoon, in the Escola Politécnica, a PIDE is spotted by someone in the crowd as he tries to get away in a car. A cry goes out: "Death to PIDE." I understand the hatred. I knew a girl who had been seized in a demonstration, beaten and then had her hair shaved off. I knew that the PIDE had beaten up the wife of a university professor I'd met, a sixty-year-old woman. I, too, want to lynch the man. The Army barely rescues him. His car, the engine ticking over, is still there. A youth starts pushing it. Others help. The car is overturned, doused in petrol and, within minutes, is a flaming mass. The soldiers, our brothers, give the sign of victory. The Junta has no control over this little episode — it is only the natural revulsion to taking human life, common to soldiers, that saves that man.

We move on down to the PIDE offices again. I know my passport is in there, awaiting a work visa. I want the troops to storm the building and get it for me. We meet a worker to whom I gave a lift at Easter, on the road between Setúbal and Lisbon. We'd talked politics in the usual cautious way, without hope, without any real feeling for what we were saying. There had been nothing to give any hint of what he is saying now. "Spínola is no socialist. And socialism is the only answer to the present situation."

At the Brasileira, an old haunt of poets and artists, people are talking and discussing feverishly, but it doesn't seem as interesting as what is happening on the streets. After lunch at M's, we again march up and down the Avenida da Liberdade. It was as though people were showing off their own defiance: we marched to the top of the Avenue, didn't quite believe we'd done it, and then marched down again to prove it was really possible.

In Rossio, the Maoists dominated the situation. Their spray guns had been active. We meet a very middle-class English person who shrugs off the whole thing as if it were a Portuguese football match. I want to string him up there and then, but doubt that people would understand. We talk to a German comrade, full of hope and enthusiasm. We then come across a group of Portuguese friends and discuss the contradictions in the situation. They are still tinged with the memory and fear of PIDE, afraid to take any action, to do anything. I want a spray gun to write on the walls, to challenge the Maoist monopoly.

We think up new slogans: "Portugal Livre," a new drink composed of Portuguese brandy (bagaço) and Coca-Cola. Coca-Cola has been banned in Portugal, allegedly because of its "harmful" contents but really—as everyone knew—because of a government minister's monopoly on the soft drink trade. We discuss the fact that none of the girls have kissed the soldiers like in France after the Second World War or in Spain during the Civil War. They have given flowers, sandwiches, food, their hearts—but no kisses. Forty-eight years of sexual repression is difficult to overthrow in a couple of days. We talk about the demonstrations. Why has there been no music, so natural to the Portuguese? Experience is lacking. There have been no legal political activities. In the dark hours, at a certain moment never publicised but known all the same, even to those in prison, people would gather quietly, a speech would be made. If the police came, it was all over. That has been the previous experience.

The slogans have moved on, hour by hour: "*O povo unido jamais será vencido*," "Down with the colonial war," "Death to PIDE," "Socialismo, Socialismo." The mystification implicit in the first slogan is still very widespread. (What crimes against the working class were soon to be perpetrated in the name of this spurious "unity"!)

Twenty-three trade unions have quickly met and issued a joint statement. Their demands amount to little more than what the Junta has already promised. The unions were institutionalised by the previous government, denied autonomy, denied the right to withdraw labour, or even to hold a public meeting. If there was dissatisfaction, the Ministry of Labour had to be informed. Discussions then took place and the grievances were "coped with" (i.e., talked to death) in this way. There had been strikes, of course: a thousand people suddenly reporting sick on the same day and staying at home. Many Lisbon workers live on the other side of the river. One day, the ferrymen had all been mysteriously stricken and there were no ferries: pandemonium resulted. The ever-increasing cost of living (housing, food, clothes) had provoked illegal strikes that had become more frequent during the past twelve months. Strikes had taken place in Robbialac (the paint factory), Sacor (the oil refinery), Electro Arco (civil engineering), Sorefame (machine tools), and in many other places, too. The electrical industry had been particularly hard-hit and the bank workers had been particularly militant.

Support begun pouring in from abroad. The new regime is recognised by the Middle East countries, which had put a petrol embargo on Portugal because of Caetano's support for the Americans during the Arab-Israeli War. Brazil, still fascist, follows suit. Finally the NATO countries grant recognition.

The situation is moving fast. It is obvious that the Spínola "solution" can only be temporary. Spínola is not the instigator of the revolt. He himself has acknowledged as much, saying that "this is a movement without leaders." We remember that he was put under "protective custody" by the Captains during the first stages of the coup, and that he only later jumped onto the bandwagon. We learn how the movement had started months before, in Mozambique, how it had snowballed through the ranks until it reached Spínola's doorstep. Spínola is known and prestigious, a father figure of rebellion against Caetano. People have many illusions in him. How long will they last?

Palma Inácio, the well-known advocate of direct action speaks at the Theatre of Maria Matos and gives an interview to *República*. He is tired but still retains his old panache, this "Scarlet Pimpernel" who has been captured and escaped so often. He was involved in the rebellion of 1947. In 1951, he hijacked a plane and dropped leaflets over Lisbon and Porto. LUAR, the organisation to which he belonged, had carried out bank robberies in a style that commanded admiration. Inácio had once been asked by a judge sentencing him if he wanted to say anything in his defence. He wished nothing, he said, except for a dark night and a storm. That very night, he escaped from one of Portugal's top security prisons.

Mário Soares, the general secretary of the illegal Socialist Party is to return tomorrow. His policies may sound more radical than those of CDE, or those of the Junta, but he is a professional politician and things are already moving beyond him.

We drink at João's. The talk is quieter and more guarded. These swings of mood will be with us over the next few days: intense optimism, depression. We're already worried about being carried away by events, about only judging things through a minority. Someone makes a vague remark about losing what has been gained by going too fast. Most of us reject this, but we are too tired to argue.

So many things have happened to restore our faith in life and revolution. We are amazed by the working class who have taken the situation into their own hands, putting their own interpretation on the Programme. How much they could achieve, given the right conditions! I become more convinced than ever of the specific identity of this class. I'm flabbergasted by the subconscious memory people retain of their own revolutionary past. Present events have shaken that memory. Dates never learned at school, songs never sung openly, are recalled in their totality. It's been another great day, a day I never expected, a day I'll never forget.

DAY 4: SUNDAY, APRIL 28

Mário Soares arrives and is greeted by thousands. The joy at the station is immense: "Long live liberty," "Free unions," "Power to the workers." Vast crowds await Southern Express No. 1002, due in from Paris. No one could have imagined it, just a few days earlier. The "freedom train," as it is now known, arrives at Santa Apolónia Station, carrying hundreds of returning exiles: Mário Soares and other PS leaders, the actresses Maria Barroso, and Maria Coelho, LUAR members from Paris, certain PCP officials. All are choking with emotion as they step onto the platform. Fernando Oneto, exiled for his part in the 1959 rebellion, has tears in his eyes.

"These are our finest sons and daughters," someone near me says, and somehow it doesn't sound corny. The feeling is nationalistic in the extreme. At this stage, only a few are aware of all the mystifications of this "unity," of this "antifascism." Later, a basis of criticism must develop, and people must begin thinking in terms of anticapitalist forces, of working-class forces.

We march away towards Infante Santo, taking up the entire street. Car horns of stopped traffic blare at us in a crazy, sensual, liberated joy. Maybe a hundred thousand people are on the streets . . . who knows? Reporters and the TV are there and the crowd gives them the victory sign. They feel stronger than ever. Although we don't know it, thousands are marching in Porto, in Aveiro, in Beja, in Castelo Branco, in every tiny Alentejo village.

We are tired, tired from the emotion, from the lack of sleep, from endless marching. We go to M's house to eat something. I phone the school to see if I must turn up tomorrow. I have completely forgotten the usual banalities of life, such as having to get up for work in the mornings. We part after three days of bliss and total togetherness. I suddenly realise that I know absolutely nothing personal about her, that we haven't discussed anything at that level, we been so completely taken up with events. Yet, I feel that I know most of what there is to know.

DAY 5: MONDAY, APRIL 29

In its impotence, the school is another world. I talk to some right-wing teachers, who realise the importance of what is happening. They compare it to Cuba, to Uruguay. I enjoy their fear without sharing their illusions as to the "revolutionary" nature of these regimes. Those at the extremes of the political spectrum are the first to see the situation most clearly; instinctively, they have the best analysis.

I finish at 3 p.m. The banks are still closed. Between 2 and 5 p.m. they only pay out salaries on production of a note from one's employers. Since the Caldas da Rainha revolt, on March 16, a lot of money has been moved overseas. The superrich have panicked, lining their Swiss accounts in anticipation. I realise how unprepared we have been, how little we have known about the economy, about the shadowy meetings that must have taken place.

It is a day of preparation, discussion, and organisation. Work, everywhere, has come to a standstill. Meetings and argument have taken place instead. This word "normal" is so bandied about that it's lost all meaning. Yesterday, *República* carried the headline "Normalidade em todo o pais" (Normality everywhere). If this was normal, I'd hardly noticed it! It is the voice of the *burguesia*, trying to assert that the country still functions, that it is still theirs. "Normality" is stressed by all the political parties, showing how trapped they are in the old conceptions, values, mentality. It is ridiculous. People make jokes about it: "I won't pay for my coffee, that's normal," someone told a waiter in a café.

4 p.m. We learn that the Junta has declared a national holiday. "May Day will be a test for the new regime," write the foreign newspapers, echoed forthwith in the Portuguese press.

I go to Rossio and stand in amazement at the size of the crowds. I feel the adrenaline returning. The Hotel Workers' Union marches by, their voices raised in hope and expectation. Are they sweating out the grease of all those tourist kitchens where for so long they've worked in silence? They march twice round the square, gathering momentum and support, and then up the Avenida da Liberdade. I go up with them. Everywhere, small groups are discussing, fiercely.

It is a night of manifestos on radio and TV. Unions of every kind are organising, demanding. It is unbelievable. I have read such manifestos as historical pieces, from 1871, 1917, 1936. Now the radio is broadcasting them. Students from Lisbon, Coimbra, and Porto are making speeches. Songs of Frelimo (the Mozambique "liberation movement") are heard again and again, played perhaps for the first time over public radio. The act is subversive, whatever one thinks of these regimes. Then an official declaration: "The Junta informs the National Republican Guard and the Police that it welcomes the demonstrations of joy planned for the First of May by the workers, and asks them not to intervene."

Amid a propaganda barrage, the Maoists have occupied some empty houses in Boavista and moved people in. Boavista is the "Indian quarter," a shanty town of dilapidated *barracas*. *A Capital*, the evening paper, gets stories from some of the squatters:

> I've lived here, in a shanty, for fifteen years. I'm married with five kids. I did like everyone else and occupied an empty house. There were some young people, students, who told us to smash down the doors and take over. No one was caught during this action. I've been down for a house for about a year now. (Mariette Barbara)
>
> I've lived in this shanty since it was first started, thirty-four years ago. It was after a cyclone that we had to move into it. Seven months ago my husband threw me out. Since then I've been living with neighbours, dragging the kids from one crowded place to another. I'd really no choice. People started occupying houses and, well, I just did the same. (Lucinda Lima)

Later that night, the police and army arrive and stop further squatting. Those already in refuse to move; they are allowed to stay. The many other empty houses in the area are guarded by troops.

I am scared, as everyone else is, at what might happen on May Day. The Army has already fired shots into the air during a demonstration, because of what a major described as a "dangerous situation." He has warned that "We won't hesitate to use force if the population doesn't cooperate. They may demonstrate peacefully, but not provocatively." The tone is ominous, a reminder that the military are in charge. They are still very popular, however, and people immediately obey their orders. But contradictions are already coming to light.

The PIDE offices had not been immediately attacked and this gave them an opportunity to destroy certain files, in particular those relating to agents and informers. Later, their headquarters are opened to the press. Great caches of guns, grenades, and other light weapons are discovered, as well as files on every militant or suspected militant in Portugal. Left-wing banners and posters are displayed in a special room. Also, under glass cases, pamphlets and leaflets dating back to the 1930s. The PIDE have the best revolutionary library in Portugal: a complete collection of Marxist and anarchist writers. On the wall of the library, in large letters, a poem by Salazar, written when he was eighteen. Next to the torture chamber (a long bare room with lights and a stage) is a little Catholic chapel. It contained many Portuguese art treasures and was dominated by a statue of the Blessed Virgin. The PIDE had already created a museum. All that was needed now was for them to become the prime exhibit.

We learn that demonstrations in Angola and Mozambique have called for complete independence. In Angola, there has also been a demonstration calling for continued alliance with Portugal.

Africa will be a major problem for the government. The "liberation movements" in these countries must be the sole arbiters of their own destiny, whether that destiny be state capitalism or not. The new government must immediately grant them the complete right to self-determination, but the Junta hesitates. Spínola wants "federation," although the local people have already gone way beyond that idea. Angola, with the largest white population, will be the most difficult to "decolonise." A new political party has been organised there, among the whites.

The PCP has distributed a leaflet. They ask for things which have already been promised by the Junta. There is not a vestige of a class approach in all this. The PCP is tail-ending the MFA, and the MFA is the mouthpiece of the liberal bourgeoisie.

DAY 6: TUESDAY, APRIL 30

A changed political situation has such an impact on one's friends! People don't move at the same pace. What could be shared in opposition to fascism suddenly becomes irrelevant. A new situation is created.

I phone E and we plan the evening. During the afternoon, I clear up outstanding work, knowing that over the next few days I'm not going to have much time.

I read the news. Students and workers have occupied the main offices of the old regime. A former Minister has been arrested, withdrawing 80 million escudos from a bank. The flight of the fascists, and their hunt by the people, continue.

All sorts of political groups, including the PS, have now published manifestos. I find this both beautiful and horrifying. It is beautiful because only a few days earlier, many of these groups had not existed in the public eye. It is hard for anyone who hasn't lived in a fascist county to realise what the absence of a free press really means. Workers come out on strike, someone is killed in a demonstration, twenty people are arrested as "terrorists," and there is maybe a small derogatory note at the bottom of an inside page. An ignored and harassed "underground press" is allowed to function in most nonfascist capitalist countries. Here, there hadn't even been that. Suddenly, all voices make headlines and those whose voice had been strangled for decades begin to realise they can talk.

But it's horrifying, too, because the demands are so conservative. Every established party has been overtaken by events and is incapable of facing the new situation. The demands of the Socialist and Communist parties are already inscribed in the programme of the Junta. There's a chance to move through centuries, and these people only want to crawl forward an inch. There's a chance to blow the lid off completely, and they only want to peep inside. The workers, miles ahead of them, are calling for a minimum wage and for a whole list of other "practical" demands.

The PS manifesto is aggressive, though still reformist. Under the title "Coming out of Clandestinity," it outlines its main objectives:

1. An end to the colonial wars. Immediate cease-fire. Negotiations with the government of Guinea-Bissau and with the liberation movements in Angola and Mozambique.
2. Immediate amnesty for all deserters and draft-dodgers.
3. Liberation of all political prisoners in the colonies.
4. The right to vote at eighteen.
5. Immediate elections by universal suffrage to a democratic Parliament.
6. The removal of all those directly involved in the previous government.
7. A struggle against monopolies and the dismantling of corporations.
8. The establishment of diplomatic relations with all countries.

This is the most "radical" position so far advocated by any of the bourgeois politicians. Compared to the PCP, the PS's programme seems more sincere, more aware, and less manipulatory, in fact less party-political. The manifesto is unsigned, the result of long meetings over the Sunday.

The Communists are already campaigning for votes, trying simultaneously to please all sections of the population. They need to be more radical. The PS, however opportunistically, has at least made some demands relevant to working-class life. But people have lots of reservations about Mário Soares. He is the bourgeois politician par excellence, a member of the "Second International," a friend of Harold Wilson and Mitterrand, of Brandt and Mrs. Ghandi, those pseudosocialists who at every opportunity seek to make use of the oppression of others to build up their own self-image. Meanwhile, the Communist Party leader, Álvaro Cunhal, seeks to impose the party line by every conceivable means. Soares bends with every wind, makes friends, uses them, and uses anything that will help. Álvaro Cunhal had arrived at the airport to a well-deserved hero's welcome. The PCP, formed in 1921 in support of the Bolsheviks, had been smashed in 1941 by the political police of the time, called "Vigilance and Defence of the Nation." The Party was slowly rebuilt during the following years. Cunhal was arrested in 1949 and had been tortured. In 1951, he escaped with others from the high-security prison in Peniche and ended up in Russia, where he settled. Thousands had been exiled. Many are returning. Soares and Cunhal are only the tip of a vast iceberg.

On the way to town I pass E's house but get caught in a traffic jam: such things continue, revolution or not. I read the papers. The CDL have taken over the headquarters of the "Moçidade Portuguêsa," the old youth movement known as the "green shirts." The Junta have decreed new laws relating to the export of money and metal. But on the whole they seem afraid. They warn against provocateurs: "The present situation is delicate. It still hasn't been possible to control certain elements that will use it to provoke disturbances. We call for the greatest possible calm during the celebrations of May 1st, anything else would endanger the revolution."

The Junta can't possibly keep tabs on everyone and everything. Many prisoners have been released but no one knows how many. The authorities urge "all ex-political prisoners not yet definitely identified to go to the Archives of Identification to receive identity cards." A large meeting of university students has decided to pull down the statue erected by the fascist regime to the glory of Portuguese women and to erect, in its place, a tribute to Catarina Eufémia, the peasant girl killed by the National Guard in 1954. The statue is torn down and a simple placard put in its place.

We are still worried about tomorrow, May Day. I pass a supermarket and seek to buy some spray paint. There isn't any. I eventually find some in an art shop. The instruments of culture, revolutionary or otherwise, remain in the hands of the middle-class.

I meet M, extremely depressed by her colleagues. We burst into discussion and talk about our feelings since we last met. We mention group actions, people we'd spoken to. We go to an old tasca which had been a Marxist-Leninist student haunt. It's past midnight, but no one is where they should be. We hope they're out doing things, preparing banners, working with groups. We feel helpless. It seems ridiculous for two foreigners to try anything on their own. We get slightly drunk. Our depression becomes impatience and anger and we go out and write on the walls ourselves. We decide on the standard slogan "Down with the Colonial War" but finally add some graffiti, made up on the spur of the moment. We do it for ourselves, because of our own helplessness, because of our desire to be a part of the great movement already underway. And we feel good. People pass and give us the clenched fist salute. But we are also afraid. I am writing a large slogan. Halfway through, I panic and shout at M, "How do you spell 'revolution' in Portuguese?" M laughs loudly, her joy very real.

DAY 7: WEDNESDAY, MAY 1

We have never seen anything like it before. The whole of Lisbon is out, the emotion intense. All morning the radio has been calling for "calm and dignity." The authorities are supposedly afraid of the Right, a real enough fear since there are still some twenty thousand PIDE agents at large. But we feel they are very much afraid of the Left, too. We stand at the corner of Alameda and try to absorb it all: the noise, the spirit, the joy surging out in floods, after half a century of being bottled up. We meet some friends, as arranged.

This is the day of the workers and all Lisbon is here. There are lorries, obviously borrowed for the day, packed with people coming in from surrounding towns and suburbs. "No one paid us to demonstrate," a banner says, clearly referring to the practices of the previous regime. I am so moved I could cry. Others are weeping already. All day we march, lost in different parts of a crowd half a million strong. Flowers, carnations everywhere. Along the way, people are offering water to demonstrators, from their windows.

We make for the newly renamed "Stadium of the First of May." There are tens of thousands of people inside, more thousands outside, trying to get in. At the rostrum, the predictable politicians: Cunhal, Soares, the trade union leaders. The speeches begin. The hammers and sickles fly high as Cunhal speaks. Soares gets a warm reception. The speeches are depressing, reformist, opportunist. The real argument is taking place in the streets, outside. Workers explain to one another what *autogestão* (self-management) means or could mean.

We leave and head towards Rossio. The metro is the only means of transport. There are only two carriages per train. More can't be added because certain stations had only been built to that length and that as late as 1973. We squash in like Portuguese sardines. We arrive in the square, to scenes defying description.

The sailors' band is there, somehow caught up with the Maoist and Trotskyist demonstrations. Here is the so-called far-left. But it's like anywhere else in the city. There just isn't room, literally space, for sectarianism.

Young workers are dancing to the music. Police cars go by, with demonstrators on top of them. A bus passes, the driver tooting his horn in rhythm with other noises. There's no telling where that vehicle will end up: it's going in the opposite direction to the destination written on the front. The emergency exits of all buses are open, flags protruding from every window. A group of youths pass, "The Gringos of Samba," according to their banner. Their Latin American music is very catching. More people begin to dance. A group of students pass shouting "*O povo armado jamais será vencido*" (An armed people will never be defeated). People laugh at this subversive variation of the "official" slogan. The whole thing is confusing, chaotic. People are cheering anything and everything. Someone shouts "*Viva Spínola, viva o comunismo.*"

We go to the house of certain young singers whose songs had been banned. Their records, censored, were rarely played on the radio. Everyone is drinking. A singing session ensues, which after an hour moves back to Rossio. We stay there, sitting on the ground, until 3 a.m., singing, watching people jump into the icy cold fountain. Finally, exhausted, I decide to go home.

I shall never forget that First of May. The noise, the noise, the noise is still ringing in my ears. The horns tooting in joy, the shouting, the slogans, the singing and dancing. The doors of revolution seem open again, after forty-eight years of repression. In a day, everything is put into perspective. Nothing is god-given, all is manmade. People could see their misery and their problems in a historical setting. How can words describe six hundred thousand people demonstrating in a city of a million? Or the effect of carnations everywhere, in the barrels of rifles, on every tank and every ear, in the hands of troops and demonstrators alike? It is the climax of a week of hectic, fast-moving events. Working people have left an indelible mark on the situation. The call is for socialism and masses of ordinary people have been involved in making it. What started as a military coup is assuming new dimensions. The Junta is still in power, but it is the people, the working class in particular, who have called the tune. A week has passed, although it already feels like many months. Every hour has been lived to the fullest. It is already difficult to remember what the papers looked like before, or what people had then said. Hasn't there always been a revolution?

II THE FIRST THREE MONTHS

SIZING THINGS UP

There was double-talk everywhere. On May 1, the Junta announced that "the nation was supporting the workers." Now they claimed that "the workers are supporting the liberation of the nation." A middle-class group around the newspaper *Expresso* organised a Liberal Party (Centre-Left, they called it). Mário Soares, already behaving as Foreign Minister, went off to London to discuss things with Harold Wilson and the Labour Party. The papers were atrocious. *República* headlines: "The people are no longer in fear." This was nonsense, as nothing changed except the politicians. Those afraid of being without money or food still had these fears.

But the previously unimaginable was now on one's doorstep, a harbinger of things to come. A Women's Group organised a demonstration outside the headquarters of the Junta. *Capital* reported their demands: "After April 25 certain fascist buildings were reallocated to political groups. Since us women constitute over 52 percent of the population it might be thought that our groups would also be given a place. We are the main victims of fascist ideology which sought to relegate us to the traditional toils of women, completely alienated from the rest of society. It is known that the de-politisation of women and their tendency to vote right-wing is directly related to the complete absence of movements and organisations acting in their interests. Despite this, the Junta is not considering the Women's Movement as worthy of attention or interest. Why? Is it, yet again, to be discrimination against women?"

On May 28, *Diário de Lisboa* carried a manifesto by the prostitutes of Lisbon (who work mainly in the dock area). After pointing out that they "had to practice, illegally, what was the most ancient profession in the world" and that although their lives were generally considered "easy," this was far from being the case, the manifesto went on to demand the creation of a union where "free from all Puritan pressures, they could discuss the problems of their class." Their main concerns were their exploitation by pimps, the need to protect minors, the determination of a scale of charges, the promotion of a "free pavement" aimed at "developing tourism" and opposition to "the scandalous activities of conservative colleagues who only practice in expensive nightclubs." They offered their support to the MFA. It ended by offering that "for a period of a year, all ranks below that of lieutenant would only be charged half price."

Some three weeks earlier, *Diário de Lisboa* carried a manifesto of the "Movement of Revolutionary Homosexuals (Gays)." They were severely persecuted during the old regime, their bars and clubs being repeatedly raided and closed down.

In Paris, the offices of the Portuguese consul were stormed and passports handed out to draft-dodgers, to deserters, and to many émigré workers. The government was forced to grant a partial amnesty: those returning must join up. In all the working-class bars, there was intense discussion and argument. Football was nearly forgotten. Feelings were very mixed: tremendous strength and hope, but also an awareness of the crisis. Nothing was certain.

Perhaps the most beautiful thing was the sense of confidence, growing daily. There was nothing but goodwill for the working class throughout the world. People discussed the situation in France, England, Argentina, and Brazil as if they'd been professors of politics all their lives. My neighbour changed beyond recognition, as she wondered ecstatically if the workers can win. She said she "doesn't understand much about politics," but after months of silence, forced respectability, and fear, her open happiness and excitement were unbelievably refreshing.

Name-changing was the thing of the day: Stadium Tomás (the old president) became Liberty Stadium; Salazar Bridge became the Bridge of April 25th or Red Bridge. Strange to believe, the value of the escudo rose on the world market. Agostinho Neto, the leader of the Angolan Liberation Front (MPLA) sent a declaration to the Portuguese people. "This is a common victory for the Portuguese people and for the colonised countries because it was obvious that the Portuguese could not win their colonial wars."

On May 6, the fishermen of Matosinhos refused to go fishing for their company. The dispute lasted for four days. In the tourist complex in Troia, on May 9, some 4,000 workers stopped working. Timex, the watch factory near Lisbon, was occupied by its 1,800 workers who called for wage increases and for the purging of six PIDEs. On May 13, the 1,600 workers in the mines of Panasqueira (400 of them are Cape Verdeans) demanded a minimum wage of 6,000 escudos and stayed away to enforce their demand.

In Porto, thousands demonstrated in the poorer districts of the city asking for decent housing. Firestone workers in Lisbon, Alcochete, Porto, and Coimbra occupied their factories and called for the purging of their foreign managers. On May 15, 8,400 Lisnave shipbuilding workers went on strike and occupied the premises, while in the North, some 500 miners at Borralha joined the other striking miners.

As the First Provisional Government was being formed, University canteen workers joined the growing movement on May 16. Textile workers in Covilhá, Mira d'Aire, Castanheira de Pera were also involved. In Lisbon, many workers were on strike, from Sacor (oil refineries) to Messa (typewriters).

While the left papers were getting themselves organised or reorganised, the fishermen of Nazaré and the workers of Bayer (pharmaceuticals) came out on strike. On May 21, some 20,000 metal workers marched through Lisbon demanding higher wages. The first issue of *Luta Popular*, the Maoist daily, discussed a wide variety of disputes including the strike of the Lisbon taxi drivers. On the same day, the workers of the partly state-owned oil tanker company, Soponata, also became involved. The 600 workers on land occupy the offices, while the 1,400 merchant seamen radioed in their support from the high seas.

It was hard to imagine the extent of the protest, as they seemed to appear everywhere. On May 27, 5,000 workers of Carris (transport) refused to take out their buses. The unions pointed to the example of Chile (likening the Carris dispute to the transport owners' strike there). They were attempting to defuse the strike movement. But their efforts were only partly successful, as all the pent-up demands of the workers burst their previous bonds.

Spínola spoke to hundreds of thousands in Porto. This was the first time he went North. "The twenty-fifth gave the people freedom," he said. "We must preserve this liberty . . . And now that we have passed this first month of enthusiasm, of euphoria, we must begin to think in a mature way, for the future. We must defend our liberty from reactionary forces, from forces who wish to diminish this freedom. It is not by anarchy, not by economic chaos, by disorder, by unemployment that we can build the Portugal of the future. This is the way of reactionaries, of counterrevolutionaries. The Armed Forces and the people must unite against this road of destruction."

The armed forces, and the Junta in particular, were in power. What influence had the Movement of the Captains? No one knew. Officers were sent to various parts of the country to "organise and consolidate." But to consolidate what? Bourgeois democracy? Bonapartist power? The drive towards state capitalism? No one was quite sure. Few people asked themselves questions of this kind. One thing was certain: the army was a bourgeois army, both in terms of the class society it defended and of its own hierarchical structures.

M went back to France for a week; she was unsure about whether to stay. I said okay, see her whenever. I stayed in her apartment while she was gone, I had a key. The sun was so bright in her bedroom and I liked the way she had decorated the room.

The first government of Palma Carlos, which some journalist described as "more of a bee-hive than a proper government," tried to administer things. It decided matters of banking, minimum wages, and questions of "national interest." But it had to consult with Spínola, who made the final decisions.

The Left dominated the situation after April 25. They were everywhere: in control of the established institutions, of many of the papers, of TV. They organised massively on the industrial scene. Their optimism was high and not without reason: the economic struggles, the victories won, the size of their demonstrations, the universal critique of capitalism gave a tremendous boost to their morale. It would be wrong to imagine, however, that their communiqués, discussions, and demonstrations reflected the sum total of the fears or hopes that faced working people during those days.

There was hardly space for further mural graffiti. No one, not even the blindest tourist, could miss them. They covered every vacant wall, monument and public building, every corner that people can see, and other places too, which the lost stranger is unlikely to discover. PCP posters were ubiquitous. The newspapers treated all left-wing documents with respect and gave them full coverage. Communiqués from MES, LUAR, the PS, the PCP, and even the few surviving anarchists, some of them Spanish (organised around *A Balalha* and somewhat traditional in their views) were given full-page headlines in the evening editions.[1] *Diário de Notícias* was

---

1   A big exception here was Emídio Santana (1906-88), whom I met and liked and who was quite open to new ideas. He was quite active after April 25, although he retained his anarchist values above all else. The anarchist history in Portugal was very important and had played a huge role in earlier workers' struggles. After the right-wing May 1926

felt to be lagging behind in this respect. It was occupied by its typesetters and changed almost overnight from a right-wing paper to a more liberal-left-leaning one. One of the main grievances of the workers was that the paper "had not been working in the spirit of the 25th." Small groups of left-wing intellectuals could have virtually anything published. An odd group called MARP (Movement for Revolutionary Self-Management of the Proletariat) was granted whole columns for their manifestos and articles. The Communists and Socialists were also given whole pages.

The great families still dominated the economic scene and were not disposed towards any "liberalisation" that might jeopardise their privileges. Although the papers concentrated on political and decolonisation issues, some discussion of the economic and class structure of Portugal still got through.

In all of this, a certain image of Portuguese capitalism emerged. In 1973, there were some 42,000 companies, 36 percent of them employing fewer than ten workers, which showed how little industrialisation there was. But a mere 0.5 percent of them owned over half the total capital of the country, which showed the degree of the concentration of capital at the top. Some 150 companies (most of them related to foreign capital) dominated the entire Portuguese economy. An analysis of the twenty main firms showed the same family names constantly recurring: Guedes de Sousa, de Melo, Pinto Bastos, Mendes Almeida, Figueiredo, de Brito. Most of the directors in control before April 25 were still in place, though their power was increasingly challenged by the Committees. There was no doubt about the political sympathies of these families.

Various diplomatic and economic ties were established with state capitalist countries. As one newspaper put it, Soares was "up to his ears in diplomacy" with the Eastern bloc. Poland was allowed to participate in the International Industrial Fair in Lisbon, the first time a country from

---

coup, the labour movement suffered great repression and the anarchist CGT (General Confederation of Labour) was dismantled. In 1927, it attempted a general strike against the government, which failed and led to one hundred deaths, the deportation of some six hundred individuals involved in the conflicts to overseas territories, and the banning of their newspaper *A Batalha*. A general strike by the CGT and other organisations including the PCP, called for on January 18, 1934 also failed. The illegal activities by the CGT were then limited to Lisbon and the Algarve. In 1937, Emídio Santana, then secretary-general, took part in a failed assassination attempt on Salazar and fled to the UK, which returned him to Portugal to spend sixteen years in prison. The ensuing repression killed off the CGT completely. His autobiography was later published as *Memories of a Militant Anarcho-Syndicalist* in 1985.

behind the "Iron Curtain" had been allowed to promote trade in Portugal. A delegation of Russian "businessmen" also arrived in Lisbon.

The programme of the MFA called for "diplomatic relations with all countries." Since "all countries" presumably included Chile, Greece, and Spain, pressures developed on the government to clarify the situation.[2] The PS and the Trotskyist LCI held a demonstration at the Chilean Embassy where, in irony, they hoisted a Swastika.

Some things were obvious despite what the International press reported and had reported so poorly at this time. I think that the journalists who arrived had no conception of the language and culture, and were on a catch up mission, so that they reported back whatever they were told by the Foreign Press Department and didn't even do that very well. What they reported was either rubbish or farfetched. The *Guardian* and the *New York Times* were particularly inept there; *Time* magazine, for some reason, reported more accurately.

The First Provisional Government was not a Popular Front government in the strict sense. It was appointed from above by the Junta as "representing" the various classes and groups within society. Within the government, the PCP and PS walked a tightrope. As the Right started to block various decrees and to defend its own interests, the Socialists and Communists became increasingly uneasy about the coalition.

Every factory of any size was reorganised. The workers made demands that, in most cases, included a minimum wage and the *saneamento* (purging) of all former managers. No group had yet called for workers' control, but workers had virtually seized control themselves. There were Committees in many public companies. Sometimes, workers managed the enterprise completely; things were different in the private sector.[3]

TIMEX, SOGANTAL, MABOR, CTT

The Timex (the U.S. watch factory) story is instructive. The workers presented a list of demands which were rejected outright. They then occupied the factory, continued making watches and sold them. They ran the

---

2   Then right-wing states.

3   Later, I will discuss the growth of the Committees, their composition and functions, their relations with the unions, and some of their practical difficulties. At this point, I wish merely to describe some of the early disputes which marred the "honeymoon" period of the new regime. They show clearly that no amount of talk about the unity between the MFA and the people (the so-called MFA-POVO Alliance) could bridge the realities of the class struggle.

factory without the management. Representatives of the armed forces were present during the abortive discussions with the representatives of American capital. The workers remained in occupation for a whole month, during which time the demand to be paid for the days of the strike was added to the list of other demands. The Committee produced a "Proclamation to the Nation," which was published in all the dailies. It organised links with other factories and asked for financial support, which it got. The Jewellers' Union also gave help. The Timex workers did not align themselves behind any political party, though a small group set up a "Committee to help the struggle at Timex." The workers rejected all attempts by the Maoists to take over their struggle. The Proclamation, well worth examining in detail, stated:

> 1. The Timex workers have been on strike since June 3, in the course of a struggle which started in November 1973, developed in February and reached massive proportions since the beginning of May.
>
> The Timex factory is part of a great and brutal system of exploitation and domination, carried on in many parts of the world by imperialist American capital. They aren't choosy about the methods used to achieve their objectives which are to extract the maximum profit and work from the working class, by inhuman methods of exploitation. They know nothing about good human relations, good working conditions, economic needs. They only know one thing; PROFIT. It is against these conditions that we are rising. In particular we want a 40 hour week instead of 45. Most of our workers are young, between 15 and 19. They work 9 hours a day. They sit on wooden chairs under fluorescent light, using often poorly adjusted magnifying glasses and microscopes, working in conditioned air of low humidity and under a constant tension which may lead to nervous collapse and frequent fainting. The workloads aren't constant and are often arbitrarily increased, which tends to exhaust these young workers. After 5 years their health is often already ruined. Their working lives are shortened, for when they can no longer achieve the production required, they are sacked, carrying away with them all the wear and tear and injuries sustained, with all the ensuing problems of finding work.
>
> We are calling for the abolition of bonuses. This system always increases the speed of work and results in greater exploitation of the workers; to make more profit for the bosses . . . We also want

to abolish the bonus system in order to avoid divisions between workers.

We want a say in the running of the Personnel Department, if only to control the activities of management, to preserve more human working conditions and to avoid a return to the situation as it was before.

We are also calling for a fair wage.

The management has made no reasonable offers in response to our demands. They have intrigued to divide us and to block the progress of negotiations.

That is why we are waging a total strike, until our demands are met. . . .

2. The country is facing a period of bitterly fought struggles between the exploiters and the exploited. The bourgeoisie continue to dominate the people, trying to cheat them and to manoeuvre against them. Capital still believes it owns and runs our destinies. Against this we have to struggle. Ever since society has been divided into classes, a class struggle has existed. The ruling classes have everything: capital, schools, factories, the press. The people have nothing except their labour power. It is against that that the people fight. They will wage the class struggle to its ultimate conclusion, to the conquest of real liberty which will only be possible when there are no longer either exploiters or exploited.

3. The class which can really bring this struggle to an end is the working class. We have nothing to lose but our chains. Freedom can only be established by this class which, together with all exploited people, will overthrow the bourgeoisie and build a genuine democracy.

4. We appeal for support from the whole of this class, from country people, too . . . and from all truly progressive people.

Comrades, at Timex as in other places just now, a further step is being taken in this great advance of the exploited people of our country. We call your attention to this situation. And we appeal for

A DAY'S WAGES FOR THE WORKERS ON STRIKE

Through this we can show that we know what solidarity means, and how to defend the just struggle of the exploited, in deeds and not just in words.

A coordinating committee will wage the campaign. It will be based at the Timex factory and will consist of members of the Timex Workers' Committee. It will be supported by the Union of Jewellers, Watchmakers and Related Trades in Lisbon.

Certified collecting sheets will be handed out. To overcome the great difficulties of the moment these will bear the white seal of the Jewellers' Union. They can be got from our factory or at the address of the Union (Travessa da Glória no. 18, 30, Lisbon) between 9 a.m. and 6 p.m.

Note: This campaign, although organised by the workers of Timex, is not only to support the Timex workers. It is to support all workers who might find themselves in a similar situation.

Timex workers, May 27, 1974.

The Sogantal story was different. The firm made gloves and textiles. The French-owned factory in Montijo was occupied by its forty-eight workers demanding increased wages, shorter hours, and paid holidays. The management refused. They also refused to pay for time lost through the strike. The workers' answer was to carry on working and to sell the clothes themselves. A committee of five was elected to consult with the Costumers' Union in Lisbon. A worker described the strike:

> In the office there was a French director and a Mr. Guilherme who is a Portuguese. But this Portuguese director was not with us. He was on the boss's side. The factory told the papers that they had made 400,000 escudos profit. Really it was about 5 times that amount, because they always have these false accounts which nobody knows about. In the factory there was a great deal of stock. If we could sell some of it we could easily pay all the debts of the factory. But then the factory would have to close, as French capital was threatening to withdraw from Portugal. We didn't want that. We felt capable of running the factory ourselves. We didn't need the management. All we needed were people with more knowledge than us, but who would be on our side. We had ideas about exporting suits and clothes. In Portugal it would have been impossible to sell them all, since we made 800 per day. For all of us this was our first strike.

There were many similar cases in the private sector. One of the greatest deficiencies was the lack of a national organisation capable of coordinating these struggles, something which the workers of Timex were striving to achieve. The unions, divided among themselves, were in turmoil because the workers began to bypass them.

As in the private companies, in part private and part state-owned companies such as the Portuguese Airlines Company (TAP) and the transport organisation (Carris), ad hoc Committees were set up and called for the expulsion of the previous managers. Administrative Councils, composed of members of management and workers, took over the running of some enterprises. Members of the armed forces took part in some of these Councils. Totally public enterprises included the hospitals and Post Office, where a member of the armed forces, often a major or high-ranking officer, usually took over the management.

It was about this time that I joined a group of like-minded people, in the Barrio Alto district of Lisbon, to collaborate on a left-wing bookshop, composed of some former Maoists, now libertarian and revolutionary. We came from very different political and class backgrounds, with many Portuguese who had returned from Paris, (except for myself, a wayward Irishman). They were already publishing *Combate*, a nonideological newspaper, to report on occupations and experiences of self-management. Many of the occupied factories at this time were producing their own bulletins and broadsheets and relating their stories and discussing the issues that were at stake inside the factories. We based our articles on these bulletins, and reproduced many of them in their entirety, warts and all, (not just quoting certain sections, as other newspapers were doing in keeping with their own ideologies).

There was a steady flow of criticism from the Maoists who savagely and continuously attacked the Provisional Government (and in particular the PCP members who were taking part in it). Their daily, *Luta Popular*, carried an article in which the director of the paper, Saldanha Sanches, called on soldiers to disobey their officers if asked to do something repressive. On June 7, he was arrested and imprisoned. Saldanha Sanches had spent eight years of his life in prison and was serving a ten-year sentence at the time of his liberation on April 26. He was taken to the military prison in Elvas.

A demonstration against his imprisonment was organised by the MRPP and supported by all the Left groups. The communiqué spoke of the increasing repression, not only against Saldanha Sanches but also of "ideological repression and sabotage of strikes, a sabotage of the workers" struggle which was every day getting worse. Antistrike laws were being prepared. There was daily censorship of information in the papers, on the radio, and on TV. And above all there was the criminal continuation of the colonial war.

This demonstration was supported by some ten thousand people. The following week Saldanha Sanches was let out of prison for a day, to attend the funeral of a comrade killed in a road accident. Most people thought this decision of the MFA very fair. Few questioned the original imprisonment.

Álvaro Cunhal, leader of the PCP, was saying that "the great reforms would only appear after the elections." Meanwhile, the Maoists were giving out leaflets calling on the workers to pay attention to what they called his "revisionism." But the Maoist phenomenon was a lot of noise and had no real support among the working class. Most Maoists were seen as the sons of wealthy middle-class families, able to go to university. They were generally considered not "serious," and seriousness was taken as one of the most important working-class virtues. Cunhal concentrated on projecting his image as the "serious" leader of the workers and had the experience to warrant it, even though he was being so cautious. The message was simple: "The standard of living in Portugal was the worst in Europe. A great percentage of our people live in conditions which are truly miserable. We defend the right to strike. But we are against striking for the sake of striking. We are against the strike as the first and immediate form of struggle, against strikes undertaken not in the interests of the workers, but just to create difficulties for the Provisional Government."[4]

The PCP gave no support whatsoever to various strikes like Timex or Sogantal, or to the bitterly fought dispute at the Mabor tyre factory. In fact, it denounced them as harmful. Apart from one or two places, the Maoists had little implantation in industry, but they were a considerable force on the streets. The Provisional Government was not allowed to forget them.

On June 14, the prisons burst into activity. A group of prisoners at Limoeiro (where about 1,300 inmates were awaiting the decision of the government to grant them an amnesty) decided to go on hunger strike. The terms of the amnesty had already been decided, but the legal machinery to implement it had not yet been created. The amnesty granted all prisoners who had completed more than half their sentence the right to leave prison, and halved all other sentences. About 4,000 prisoners (253 of them women) were affected. These prisoners had been waiting since April 25 and were understandably anxious.

---

4   *A Capital*, June 2, 1974.

As the Limoeiro prisoners started their hunger strike, various sit-down protests took place in the yards. Two other prisons, Custoias and Matosinhos, also had disturbances. Some prisoners appeared on the roof with banners proclaiming "We too are victims of fascism. Down with fascism." The government decided to speed up the whole procedure.

A change of mood was increasingly noticeable in the government. The newspapers were tightening up and the radio and television were no longer as open as they had been. *Limite*, one of the best radio programmes, was banned. The bosses were also tightening the screws, and beginning to speak up. Building companies were complaining about the freezing of rents. Various capitalist parties were saying that the country was heading for economic ruin. While the first preoccupation of the authorities had been to maintain discipline and the proper chains of command within the armed forces, the second was to "stabilise" the situation in industry. For this, they had to deal with the more militant sections of the working class, who still wanted a minimum monthly wage of 6,000 escudos. The MFA accepted the inevitable confrontation and the Post Office workers, who could not seriously disrupt industrial production, were taken on as the scapegoat.

On June 17, twenty-five thousand postal workers (CTT) went on strike, paralysing almost all postal and telephone services throughout the country except those to hospitals and fire stations. Wages were the main issue, but there were other grievances: the structure of the service, understaffing, taxes. The government offered 4,300 escudos and said it was the maximum it would concede. The Strike Committee appealed to the public: "We are on strike because we want to better the lives of postal workers, and to better the service. Indirectly the strike will help you, the users. We ask for your understanding and Solidarity. The greater your support, the shorter the strike will be."

During the postal strike the bakers (mainly small shopkeepers) also decided to call a strike. They were seeking permission to raise the price of bread. The strike, very unpopular, was called a boss's strike. Its effect was to create some uneasiness about the strike weapon itself, which the authorities ruthlessly exploited.

The Communist Party attacked the postal workers' strike as "irresponsible." Intersindical refused to have anything to do with it. The demands were "impossible" — the postal workers were "attempting to become a privileged group at the expense of the mass of the population." The strike, the PCP said, was being undertaken for the sake of striking and did not have the support of the people. This last point was partly true. One of the reasons the postal workers gave for ending their action was that certain of their members had experienced physical threats from other workers.

The postal strike was the first large-scale confrontation between the government and an organised group of workers. It was supported by all the revolutionary groups, although not always wholeheartedly. *Diário de Lisboa* published on its front page the declaration and advice given by MES. "While talk of 'privileged workers' and 'impossible demands' was nonsense," they said, "we consider that the form of the strike, given the nature of the company, was not the most appropriate. To continue providing a service, but without charge, would not only have built up tremendous pressures against the company but would also have broken the isolation of the CTT workers and ensured popular support. MES nevertheless support this strike because the decision to wage it was taken by the workers themselves."

The point made by MES was important. People, not just the PCP, disliked the CTT strike just as they disliked the strike of the bakers. "We have freedom now," they said "but we have no bread and we can't post a letter." During the strike, the Army had made preparations to take over the Post Office. Marvão and Anjos, two Army cadets, had refused to obey an order, which they considered of a strikebreaking nature. They were immediately imprisoned. Various left-wing groups called a demonstration on July 9 in their support. The Army first advised people not to attend, and then surrounded the area where the meeting was due to take place. No one was allowed near the great roundabout of the Marqués de Pombal. The demonstration had to be abandoned.

The Army had also been used in June to break up the strike at Timex and to ensure that the property and stock were kept in the factory. There was little doubt, by the end of the month, that the Junta would countenance no action which seriously challenged the rights of property. The writing was on the wall. Only the politically myopic could fail to read it.

THE CULTURAL NONREVOLUTION

June 10, Portugal's national day, was a repeat performance of May 1. Hundreds of thousands demonstrated in support of the armed forces, wearing *cravos* (red carnations). The Junta showed its hand a little more. The Democratic Plastic Artists organised a festival in their newly taken-over Museum of Folk Art. The group had been opposed to the old regime and had performed a "happening" soon after April 25, wrapping up the statue of Salazar in black plastic coating. Their festival was to give rise to a significant military intervention.

The RTP (national TV network) had decided to broadcast the entire proceedings. It was to be one of the greatest experiments in live Portuguese television ever. Forty-eight artists, one for each year of fascism, contributed to a so-called "collective" painting. (Unfortunately it turned out to be no more than forty-eight separate paintings, on the same canvas. Only one of the artists was intelligent enough to allow some children present to do her painting for her. The others—perhaps with an eye on their reputation—carefully signed their efforts. During the festival, various cultural and musical groups put on live entertainment. The themes were obviously political. Some contributions were not particularly original. For instance, some Communist Party supporters marched through the hall in front of the cameras shouting "PCP, PCP!" One group, carrying the coffin of fascism draped in a swastika, marched towards the Tagus which ran alongside the Museum and dropped the coffin into the river.

The theatre group, Comuna, which had frequently been harassed by PIDE, put on a piece about the Catholic Cardinal Cerejeira, who had been closely implicated with Salazar and Tomás. The message was plainly anti-Catholic as well as anti-fascist. A few minutes before midnight, an order was given "by higher authority" to immediately cease the broadcast. Viewers immediately realised what was happening when an American film suddenly interrupted the show. The late news said: "Honourable spectators, the programme which we were transmitting directly from the Spring Fair was suspended because of higher orders. The TV workers who are certainly not provocateurs cannot agree with this decision. We consider it to be against the programme of the MFA. As a protest, we are resuming live broadcasting from the Spring Fair, for a token five seconds."

The decision to shut down the live broadcast had been taken by a major and by the ex-director of *República*, who between them were responsible for the Ministry for Social Communications. TV workers promptly occupied the broadcasting station. At a mass meeting, they resolved to remain firm in their mission to inform and create public opinion in the spirit of the programme of the MFA. A high-ranking officer later called the whole episode a tempest in a teacup, but it was obvious that creative criticism by groups like Comuna, cutting too near the bone, would not be tolerated.

When the forty-eight painters were doing their collective painting at the Mercado do Povo (at the time the live TV broadcast was closed down) an incident occurred which showed the ambiguity of popular attitudes to culture. A French friend from Paris, a little tipsy from a litre of wine at dinner, walked up to an unfinished canvas and proceeded to paint on one of them, the children's one. "Art is dead," he wrote in French: "L'art est mort." Pandemonium ensued. "CIA," "Fascist," the artists screamed, and attacked him so vigorously that he had to take to his heels. Stones rained down on him. "You've never been in Caxias," they shouted, irrelevantly. We barely rescued him from the angry painters.

The statement, in a sense, was too bold, too difficult to understand by those present. "Artistic" freedom, like so many other freedoms, had never been known in Portugal. Artists whose pictures from Angola and Mozambique had been shown had had their exhibitions closed down by the PIDE. Although "freedom" was the touchstone of everything, the various ideological freedoms were hardly touched upon. When some four hundred people (cinema workers, usherettes, etc.) demonstrated for higher pay in June 1974, one of their demands was "an end to a culture of nonsense." They didn't explain precisely what they meant by this. Possibly a wish for an end to obscurantism.

The MFA were caught up in this contradiction. They had abolished the censorship boards. Pornography flooded the marketplace, competing for space on the newsstands alongside the political newspapers. Porn and politics were everywhere.

The Cultural Revolution, however, never went very deep. There is a story that Gulbenkian, the oil millionaire, liked to live in Portugal because the workers always raised their hats to him as he passed in his car. A personal friend of Salazar, he gave millions to set up an international foundation devoted to the arts, with headquarters in Lisbon. Many avant-garde artists held exhibitions there. Among the chief patrons were people like Jorge de Brito, owner of the Portuguese International Bank.

The Gulbenkian was occupied by its workers in July 1974. They called for a *saneamento* (purging). A Committee of Struggle was set up, comprising a number of MES militants. The management refused to alter anything, claiming that real decisions in relation to the foundation had to be made in London and that the Gulbenkian was not a public company, and so on. The place was occupied. Hundreds of young militants poured into the building and organised a "weekend party." Despite large banners proclaiming "Art in the Service of the People" there was little attempt to discuss art or culture and there was little creativity on the site itself. Even the posters (constantly reminding one not to put out cigarette butts on

the plush carpets) lacked imagination. There were security pickets everywhere. The MES committee even laid a wreath on the grave of old man
Gulbenkian (whose death-anniversary coincided with the occupation).

COLLAPSE OF THE FIRST PROVISIONAL GOVERNMENT
I first met Teresa, a young Portuguese woman, around this time. By now,
M had returned definitively to Paris and was no longer in touch. Teresa
had wandered into our bookshop, Contra a Corrente, in Bairro Alto and,
like magic, we looked at each other and fell in love at first sight. She asked
a lot of questions—What do you mean by Revolution? What do you mean
by that?—so I had to explain a lot of things. She was receptive to my ideas,
and I learned a lot from her as well.

There was no doubt as to which class the Prime Minister of the time,
Palma Carlos, represented. The same went for Sá Carneiro (Minister without
Portfolio) and Vieira de Almeida (Minister for Economic Coordination).
Both had been important officials of the old regime. Vieira de Almeida
had also been a managing director of Sonap, the Petrol Company, and
Vice President of a large Luso-French bank. Both Sá Carneiro and Palma
Carlos were well known in the business world through their practices as
lawyers. The present Minister of the Interior, himself an ex-member of
the previous government, had been the director of OGE, an organisation
set up by Caetano to advise big business. The ruling class had reshuffled
its cards a little more.

The Confederation of Portuguese Industry (CIP), which represented
about 70 percent of businesses, published a communiqué warning that
the working-class onslaught was "dangerous to the national economy."
They supported the programme of the MFA and called for a Western-type
democracy as the fundamental guarantee of individual liberties. They
stressed the following points:

- Immediate measures had to be taken to overcome the crisis.
- Portuguese industry had a weak image abroad, which didn't
  promote investment.
- Companies represented three balanced forces: consumers, inves-
  tors, and workers.
- The loss of this equilibrium would lead to economic ruin.
- The first task confronting the CIP was to tackle the economic
  underdevelopment of the country.
- Private enterprise must be maintained.

Cunhal correctly accused the monopolies of organising against the new regime. "The reaction continues to organise politically and socially, but above all economically," he said. "Although some fascists were in prison, many others were still in their old positions." Meanwhile, the struggle of the workers continued relentlessly. The government's response was to introduce a whole new series of measures aimed at building up a strong capitalist base in the country. The wave of strikes had threatened the position of many small companies. The Minister for Economic Affairs introduced a bill giving 500 million escudos to small and middle-sized companies. Companies employing many workers were given more, so they could pay the minimum wages and meet some of the demands of "their" workers. Construction and transport companies were the main beneficiaries. The measures received support from all sides of the government and from many redundant workers. The latter organised a large demonstration in Porto and another in Braga, in the North, to protest against closures and sackings.

The coalition was subjected to tremendous strains, especially on the industrial front. The country was much more to the Left than its rulers, which explains why the PCP (up to its eyebrows in government) seemed so conservative and reactionary at the time. Serious offensives were mounted from the political Right and from the business circles it represented. The double pressures on Soares and Cunhal were enormous. It was a kind of balancing act. Let it go to revolution, or safeguard democracy? Which would you choose?

Divisions within the Provisional Government began to appear over issues such as the monopolies and over the question of the colonies. Jorge Campinos, a member of the Portuguese delegation to the peace talks with the PAIGC in Algeria, said that the Socialists would resign if the peace talks broke down. There were simultaneous threats of right-wing resignations if the "right to strike" was not qualified. The Junta, rather naively, criticised members of the government for acting like politicians. Party considerations should give way to national ones, said Spínola, or the coalition would collapse. But party considerations were "coming first" because the interests of "the nation" were not one, as Spínola and others would have had people believe. People applauded Spínola's speeches calling for a "great nation"—and then quietly proceeded to work in their own interest.

The question of the control of TV provoked one of the longest sessions in the parliamentary history of Portugal. The position of the Junta was, of course, finally adopted, but in these critical times, the Junta was reluctant to take decisions in isolation. It needed the support of the politicians just as much as the politicians needed the Junta. Admiral Rosa Coutinho, a member of the Junta, put the key issue in classical state capitalist terms: "Television is the most important means of communication in terms of its impact; it enters every home and is seen simultaneously by millions of people. Therefore it must be state-run, giving out information which belongs to the nation. As it is a state body it must obey the rules of the state, decided by the constitutional powers."[5]

The Socialists disagreed with the decision, judging it arbitrary and hasty. They said that they would fight against all forms of censorship, offering their solidarity to the TV workers. The PCP maintained silence, though Cunhal said in Porto that the Catholic population "had to be respected." The PPD defended the decision to set up a military body which would decide the policy and orientation of the TV network.

Early in July, news broke of a serious crisis within the government. At first it was thought that the Socialists and Communists were resigning, but it slowly became clear that it was the right wing that was planning to leave unless certain of their demands were met. The Prime Minister, four other Ministers, and two Secretaries of State were demanding: a) that the powers of the Prime Minister be expanded; b) that the date of the elections (March 1975) be brought forward; and c) that a referendum about a new constitution be held before the end of October. If these three demands were not met the Prime Minister would resign and the others would do likewise in solidarity.

The Junta considered a partial acceptance of the first point. After meetings with various political groups and with certain representatives of the armed forces, it became clear that a head-on collision was imminent. The Left countered with an attack on Palma Carlos. It warned of a plot to replace him with an even more right-wing Prime Minister. For four days the country was without an active government. Palma Carlos, interviewed as to why he was resigning, told the interviewer to "go and ask Russia"—a remark that was a political analysis in itself. Once the conflict of interests was shown to be insoluble, the selection of a new Prime Minister became the main task. The PPD said that they would continue to work within a coalition, thereby leaving Palma Carlos out on a limb. Spínola met with various members of the "Movement of the Captains."

---

5   Rosa Coutinho (1926–2010) became known as the "Red Admiral" because of his left-wing views and his political proximity to the Portuguese Communist Party.

Analysing the events, *Expresso* said that July 9 (the day the crisis became public) was the result of April 26. By this, it meant that the fierce class struggle unleashed by the coup had eventually overtaken the government installed by the Junta. The crisis also revealed certain things that had not been clear in the previous three months: the "Movement of the Captains" still existed, still played an important political role, and was still pressing for "democratisation."

Who, therefore, was in power? Obviously the owners and managers of the firms and factories were in control in any real terms. But they were subjected to enormous pressures from the workers, who had suddenly burst into political awareness, and were studying and discussing hawkishly their every move. At the level of politics this struggle led to heated arguments concerning the interpretation of the Programme of the MFA. The programme had been drafted so as to mean all things to anyone. But the class struggle allowed no such ambiguities. The definition of words became a political struggle—and led to an impasse. As Dr. Quaresmo Neto, Personnel Manager of the Seguros Tagus Insurance Company, an English language student of mine, very aptly put it: "We have a government that can't govern, a management that can't manage, and workers who won't work."

Three months after the coup, the situation in Portugal was fluid in the extreme. In many respects, it had not changed at all. The vast majority of the population continued as they had always done. Men went out to work in the morning and gathered in the tascas in the evening. Women stayed at home doing what they always did. Working conditions and social habits appeared to have altered but little.

But such an estimate would not do justice to the new feelings and emotions which had invaded people's lives. No matter the final outcome, the climate of political awareness had been changed. The men in the tascas discussed politics daily. The women, hanging their washing from their verandas, were forming political opinions of their own. Little discussion and action groups were organising everywhere. For many there had already been a pay increase. This was of real value as prices were still frozen.

Some were much worse off. Bourgeois elements were making less profit. They were less secure than before and were subject to the *saneamento* launched against them by various workers' groups. But many workers were also worse off. The minimum wage was only applicable to businesses employing six or more persons. To get round this, many employers had resorted to sackings, thereby reducing the number on their books to below that figure. For the great majority, however, the situation had improved.

What had happened had certainly been a political revolution. A new section of the ruling class had assumed power, and saw its interests better served by modern bourgeois democracy than by old-style fascism. The new rulers dreamt of changing the basis of power structure from a dictatorship of the aristocracy (linked to a weak bourgeoisie) to the type of dictatorship exercised by modern industrial states. In the upheaval, the working class sought to seize what it could. In July 1974, two main questions confronted the powers that be: how much the workers would ask for, and how little could they be given.

The peculiarity of the Portuguese situation was the disaffection from the old regime of large sections of the armed forces. Caetano's attempts at "liberalisation" had been ineffectual and had come too late. By extending the colonial war, he had aggravated the situation. He had lost the respect of his own troops. They had rebelled and by so doing had thrown Portuguese society into deep turmoil.

Here, indeed, was the essence of the whole scenario. By definition, no coup or putsch could be democratic. Neither, of course, could any coup bring about a social revolution. The whole concept of the revolutionary role of the MFA (peddled by almost all the left groups after September 1974) was profoundly mystifying. At best, the MFA might prepare the conditions for bourgeois democracy. But in doing so, it would have to unleash other forces, for years repressed. The working class, however, was numerically weak and had not yet gained the confidence or capacity to carry other classes with it.

The MFA had two choices. It could withdraw and allow the bourgeoisie to resume the reins of power, after ensuring that it understood the need to continue to reorganise and modernise itself. Alternately, the MFA could remain in power itself, taking over large areas of government and social organisation and seeking to cope with the problems involved (which were those of a class-divided society confronted with the tasks of industrialisation). But this would mean a role very different from the classical "Bonaparte" role attributed to armies in times of social stress. The armed forces would need to create a whole network of new economic and political institutions and could thereby become the embryo of a new state capitalism.

In neither case could the MFA remain neutral, as hoped for by the political parties. The whole notion of a "neutral" MFA, above the class struggle, was either demagogy or illusion. Given the international context, a socialist revolution would prove difficult without tremendous internal and external opposition. Spain was next door. But a viable bourgeois democracy was not in the cards, at least for the present. The armed forces remained in power, policing the contradictions they had unleashed and leaving the question of social revolution (which is the business of classes) unanswered.

III THE FIRST SIX MONTHS

THE RETURN TO REALITY

In the summer of '74, I travelled to New York and then Dublin. My good friend, D, picked me up from JFK in a big American car she'd borrowed for the day, a gesture that felt heavenly and extravagant at once. I had left revolutionary Portugal, a country in turmoil, and everything in America felt plain and "normal." People listened to me, trying to understand my enthusiasm and fervour and nodded their heads. My mother in Dublin feared for my sanity. It was like awakening from a dream. Even in Portugal, there was a kind of return to reality.

With the advent of the Second Provisional Government the previous wave of euphoria began to subside and reality began to reassert itself. Society was divided into classes and they had mutually antagonistic interests. The employers sought initially to limit the offensive by legal means but, when this failed, sections of the ruling class showed themselves quite prepared to envisage a return to an authoritarian regime.

The new Portuguese Prime Minister, Vasco Gonçalves, was a colonel who had been an activist on April 25. The Second Provisional Government comprised of seven military and eight civilian members. Both Cunhal and Soares retained their positions. Little was known, at this time, of the political leanings of its various military members but it was generally felt that this government was more "left" than the first, although also more heavily weighted with military personnel. The short life of this government (July–September 1974) was dominated by three important events:

- The confrontation with the government by workers in large enterprises like TAP and Lisnave
- The bitter struggle over the new antistrike law
- An increasing tendency for right-wing forces to organise outside of the government, and even outside of the MFA

These closely interrelated events, described in detail below, all contributed to an attempted right-wing coup on September 28 and to Spínola's exit from Portuguese politics. They also demonstrated the irrelevance of trying to attribute various degrees of leftness to governments of the bourgeoisie.

TAP, LISNAVE, AND OTHER BIG DISPUTES

During the summer of 1974, some four hundred companies registered disturbances of various kinds. Among these were some of the largest enterprises in Portugal: Mabor (tyre manufacture), Sacor (oil), Efacec-Inel (electrical components), Lisnave (shipyards), CTT (postal services), Timex (watches), TAP (airlines), and so on. Sacor was the biggest oil company in the Iberian peninsula, Lisnave one of the largest ship-building enterprises anywhere in the world (in Europe, second only to Harland and Wolff, of Belfast). Some of these strikes proved eye-opening for many workers.

TAP was a semistate company, run on a marginal budget. It competed with British Airways for a lucrative European and African trade, but had neither the capital nor the privileged position of London from which to operate. The issues that led to the strike were basic enough: the workers were demanding better wages and decreased working hours.[1] These demands could probably have been met by granting TAP better guarantees in relation to African flights.

The TAP workers had a history of militancy. Organised struggles had begun as far back as 1970, when workers all turned in sick together in pursuance of a pay claim. In July 1973, workers in the maintenance shops had called a strike which had been violently broken up by the National Republican Guard. The police had forced the men back into a hangar with submachine guns. The office staff had thrown paperweights and even adding machines at the cops. Three workers panicked and started to run. The police opened fire and all three were killed. Within the company there were still hundreds of ex-PIDE informers. Two PCP cells had operated at TAP since the late 1960s, cells of MES and PRP since 1974.

On May 2, 1974, a plenário had unanimously called for the *saneamento* (purging) of all fascists in the company and in particular of those responsible for having called in the police the year before. The union also made certain demands, including the election of three "worker"

---

1 See Françoise Avila, Carvalho Ferreira, Bertrand Lory, Claude Orsoni, and Charles Reeve, *Portugal, l'autre combat: classes et conflits dans la société* (Paris: Spartacus, 1975) for an excellent description of this struggle.

representatives to an Administration Council. The proposed lists were not challenged and three union officials were duly elected in a hall in Lisbon on May 5 (two were, in fact, in middle management). When the workers discovered that two of their "representatives" had raised their own salaries from 7,000 to 52,000 escudos and were being driven around by chauffeurs, they naturally lost confidence in the Administrative Council. Election to the Council was seen as just a sort of personal promotion. The union also came under a lot of criticism.

On July 21, a plenário of the maintenance men decided to break away from the rest of the workers. They wanted their working week reduced to forty hours. They again called for saneamento and for the freezing of all salaries above 16,000 escudos. These demands were unacceptable to the Flight Personnel (whose salaries reached up to 52,000 escudos per month). These differences of attitude, flowing from very real differences in material conditions of life, were to be repeatedly used by the government, the unions and the PCP to denounce the struggle of the maintenance men as "unrepresentative," "undemocratic," and "disruptive of unity." Disruptive they certainly were—of the false unity between groups of completely different social composition. On August 13, a plenary of maintenance men decided to take direct action to reduce the working week from forty-four to forty hours. In fact, they imposed a forty-hour week by only working forty hours. The Administrative Council issued a statement threatening sackings and attacking "those who are struggling for the destruction of the company." It stressed "the urgent need to increase productivity" and bemoaned the fact that its appeals were "systematically being ignored." "We continue to see work abandoned under any pretext. Indiscipline reigns and there is a total lack of respect towards authority. The whole thing leads to anarchy and it is impossible to discover who is guilty or responsible." The workers retorted that it was "quite natural for the Administrative Council to seek to increase the time during which surplus value is extracted from us. That's what might be expected from the interests which the Council defends. But that the unions should take the same attitude, by refusing to support us, only shows their reformist role."

The agitation at TAP began to have wide international repercussions. The banks (both national and international) as well as the Boeing Company refused to deal with the enterprise or to supply it with spare parts other than on a strict cash basis. The Portuguese company was bound up with international capitalism and could not itself supply spare parts for its own aircraft. It was very vulnerable to external pressures of this kind.

On August 19, another plenário, held without union officials, drew up a list of demands which included

a) The purging of all those whom the workers themselves judged to have shown anti-working class attitudes, such purging to be repeated as often as necessary;
b) All wage increases to be inversely proportional to current earnings;
c) An enquiry into the responsibilities for the July 1973 shootings and punishment of those guilty;
d) Equal share outs, each year, of part of the company's profits;
e) The right to reconsider collective contracts, whenever the workers chose.

The management was given a week to consider the proposals. After that, the maintenance men would stop work altogether. It is interesting to note how the "antifascist" demand for saneamento had become a class demand concerning those with whom the workers would work.

On August 25, the PCP cell in TAP issued a leaflet warning workers against the "manoeuvres of radical petty-bourgeois groups." It wanted discussions and agreement "amongst all the personnel" showing thereby a typically bourgeois attitude: equal decisional authority for people who were not equal in reality. On the following day, a further plenário decided on an unlimited general strike. A Strike Committee was elected and various commissions immediately appointed. Pickets were posted that same night. The PCP Minister of Labour arrived at the airport at 3 a.m. with a deputation of trade union and ministerial officials, and asked the Strike Committee to postpone the strike. The Minister was instructed in some basic working-class principles: namely, that only a plenário can rescind such a decision. He made threats that the airport is already encircled by the Army. A further plenário on August 27, held in the presence of the Minister of Labour, voted to continue the strike. As if to make it unequivocally clear who the "unrepresentative minorities" are, the administrative staff decides to join the strike by a substantial majority.

Many of the airport workers were particularly sensitive to the demands of the maintenance men. Together, they now halted all international flights, other than a flight carrying a delegation of Chilean trade union leaders and planes carrying troops returning from Guinea-Bissau. The maintenance workers, who had initiated the strike, remained absolutely firm.

The dispute was now a direct challenge to the government and the unions. At 1 a.m. on August 28, the Minister of Information announced that given the "intransigence" of the strikers, the airport would be militarised. The PCP cell at TAP issued a further communiqué: the strike was a "provocation" directed against "the interests of the Portuguese people in general." A confrontation with the MFA 'which might threaten their alliance with the working people' had to be avoided at all costs. The "adventurists" had to be "unmasked" for a climate of "security and discipline" to return to the airport. The strikers were even holding up the process of decolonisation . . . by slowing down the return of troops from Guinea-Bissau. It was in this atmosphere that the famous plenário of August 28 was held. It was attended by over four thousand workers. The meeting was due to be broadcast live on radio but so flagrant was the anticipated defiance of authority that, at the last moment, the arrangements were cancelled on instructions from the Junta. The plenário brought massive support from all other sections of TAP and offers of solidarity from many workers' groups throughout the country—in total defiance of the new antistrike law, just passed by the government.

A group of MFA officers then entered the meeting hall, applauded by the workers. The officers started reading: "We are soldiers. You are about to be placed under military discipline. Here are the relevant passages of the military regulations." The silence was total. Amid mounting tension, the plenário voted for the continuation of the strike. It also voted for the dissolution of the trade union committee. The MFA officers left. Almost furtively, someone presented an unsigned motion suggesting the strike be called off. The Chairman asked the proposer to come and move it. An old PCP militant, torn and ashamed, argued half-heartedly. There was violent opposition. Throughout, there was little reference to the MFA. Illusions persisted. At 5 p.m. an important MFA member arrived and asked to be informed of the decision of the plenário. Hearing it, he threatened, "You have half an hour to start work again or COPCON will intervene." For a while, pandemonium ensued. Then, after a sober analysis of the relation of forces, the decision to resume work was made—but a decision to "work to rule" and to establish, as a matter of urgency, close contacts with other factories who had offered support. A bitter communiqué was issued reporting the suspension of the plenário under threat of military force ("armoured cars outside, parachutists issued with submachine guns, munitions, knives, and the usual friendly police dogs"). The communiqué also referred to the workers' decision to revoke the entire trade union committee, and expressed its "deepest contempt" for the repression to which they were subjected.

From August 28 onward, the Army occupied all parts of the airport. The maintenance men pursued their work-to-rule. The Strike Committee, which included some MES members, was arrested, as were many workers who refused to obey military orders. The other TAP staff, remembering the CTT postal strike in June and not wishing to risk open confrontation with the Army, returned to work under extreme duress. The "democratic guns" won out against the "irresponsible adventurers."

COPCON remained in occupation of the airport during the next few weeks. The work-to-rule continued under the surveillance of G3-carrying soldiers, who were forbidden to speak to the workers. The workers were constantly threatened: "No one leaves the premises unless so many planes have taken off by such and such a time." Some maintenance men had to work fifteen or sixteen hours a day. The regime, meanwhile, boasted that everything was normal at TAP.

On September 17, the unions (supported by the PCP) called a plenário of all TAP staff with a view to "normalising the situation." Hundreds of maintenance men attended, voted out the Chairman, and took over the meeting. They decided to add to their other demands the demand that all troops be withdrawn. They also decided that the new trade union commission should be elected on the basis of direct shop representation, thereby ensuring a genuine workers' majority. The unions vehemently denounced these decisions as "divisive."[2] On September 23, the Army arrested several workers after "questioning" them. A big demonstration took place outside the barracks where they were held, and the workers were eventually released. On September 25, two hundred workers were sacked for "infringements to Article 6 of the Code of Military Discipline." Two days later, several thousands TAP and other workers put down tools and took part in street demonstrations demanding the reinstatement of all the sacked men. The government responded with: "Yes, all but thirty." The unions concurred. The men refused and the strike spread. A critique of the role of the MFA began to take shape. A joint demonstration (TAP, Lisnave, Efacec-Inel, CTT) was called for September 28. By a quirk of history, these demonstrators, demanding a saneamento of all workplaces, were the only ones on the streets with such demands when the right attempted their putsch.

---

2   *O Século*, September 29, 1974.

Following the attempted right-wing coup of September 28, the decree militarising the airport was rescinded, and the work-to-rule called off. The forty-hour week was gradually introduced. Most, but not all, of the sacked workers were reinstated, contingent on individual applications. They were told they would only be reinstated "on condition they took no further part in political activity."

Plenários of TAP workers continued. The demands were for renewed saneamento (the full list of ex-PIDE agents had not been released). A whole series of local issues (relating to cleaners, porters, engineers, etc.) were also discussed. Demands ranged from reduction of the wage differentials to nationalisation of the company under workers' control. In many respects the TAP experience showed both the capacities and limitations of the whole Portuguese revolutionary movement.

Another important dispute at the time was at the *Jornal do Comércio*. Its workers went on strike on August 25, 1974, occupying the premises and calling for an end to the "internal censorship." They also wanted the saneamento of their Director, Carlos Machado. An initially small demonstration outside the building grew as passers-by joined in. The workers attempted to produce their own version of the paper. Again, COPCON troops moved into the building, confiscating copies already produced, and forbidding the printing of any more. On September 4, all the other papers in Lisbon, with the exception of the PCP controlled *O Século* decided to stop production for a day, in support of the struggle at *Jornal do Comércio*.

Incensed, workers from all the other papers gathered in front of the *O Século* premises to stop its distribution. The government sent troops to disperse the demonstrators. The workers at *O Século* finally decided that—although they had already printed the issue—it would be wiser not to distribute it "in order to avoid a confrontation between the Armed Forces and the adventurists." PCP journalists condemned the action of *Jornal do Comércio*, talking of "strikes which could be used by Reaction and by the big monopolies" and hinting darkly at "forces that were objectively on the side of the enemies of the workers." Blissfully unaware of the impression it created, this same issue of *O Século* carried, in the next column, an interview with Antoine Pinay, a reactionary French ex-Prime Minister, who said he was "appreciative of the climate of tranquillity to be found in Portugal."

Of even greater significance, perhaps because of the numbers involved, was another major confrontation between the government and the workers of the Lisnave shipyards. The Lisnave workers were among the most class conscious in Portugal and their communiqués represent one of the high points of autonomous working-class struggle. The ship-yard workers had decided at one of their plenários that on September 12, they would march en masse to the Ministry of Labour. They wanted the saneamento of their previous director, but their main purpose was to draw attention and initiate opposition to the recently passed antistrike law. As far back as July, they had pointed out links between various members of their management and certain ex-PIDE agents, and had asked the MFA to dismiss the people involved. The request was ignored. In a communiqué, the Lisnave workers condemned the equivocations of the management, the hiding of injustices, and the anti-working class nature of the new legislation. They were particularly incensed by the use of terms like "economic wreckers" which the PCP constantly used against them whenever they proposed passing from words to action.

The proposed Lisnave demonstration was banned by the MFA. A communiqué forbidding the march was repeatedly read over the radio. A tenseness gripped Lisbon as people waited to see what would happen. On September 12, more than six thousand Lisnave workers, in their boiler suits and helmets, marched from the yard in rows fifteen abreast, tightly organised and carrying banners: "The workers of Lisnave want the fascists out," "Death to PIDE. Death to fascism. Down with capitalism." "The right to strike, yes. Lockout, no." "We support all comrades on strike." "Democracy for the workers, repression for the reactionaries." "Long live the working class."

It was a marvellous sight—the Lisbon proletariat in working clothes, in a forbidden demonstration, openly handing out their leaflets to the people of the city. The march was applauded all the way. It was joined by thousands of other workers, in particular Post Office workers. Otelo Saraiva de Carvalho, commander of COPCON, personally ordered a cordon to be thrown around the Ministry of Labour. "Either you stop us by killing some of us," one of the Workers' Committees told him "or you let us go. Either way, we'll continue the march." Faced with such a display of determination, Otelo didn't dare intervene and the COPCON troops eventually withdrew.

The Lisnave yards had had strikes before April 25, and the PCP had been very active in them. But now, the factory cell was issuing communiqués denouncing "adventurism." The demonstration, the PCP claimed, "represents hostility against the government and disrespect for the democratic order. The consequence will only be to provoke the reaction." The reaction, as will shortly be shown, needed no provoking.

THE ANTISTRIKE LAW AND THE RESURGENCE OF THE RIGHT

The Confederation of Portuguese Industry (CIP) was working along two lines. The first, overtly political, was to support right-wing parties and argue for a type of capitalist expansion in which they would participate. This required a limitation of the right to strike. The other was no less political, though less openly so. It implied the financing and support of fascist groups.

Fragments of fascist institutions and mentality certainly persisted. But on the whole the fascists could not act on their own, and looked for support to various right-wing parties. Many of the old fascist leaders had become liberals, "in the spirit of April 25." Some, momentarily imprisoned, had already been released. The National Republican Guard and PSP retained considerable power. On August 16, 1974, for instance, a radical group, the "Friends of Mozambique," had organised a demonstration in Parque Eduardo VII. They were prohibited from continuing with their meeting (the order being given by one of Spínola's associates). They marched down the Avenida da Liberdade and on to Rossio, in the centre of Lisbon, where they were met by police and asked to disperse. Before this could be done, the police opened fire. Four people were wounded and one killed: Vitor Barnardes, a worker and CDE activist.

The shock of the murder, typical of police actions before April 25, brought home the stark realities of the new "democracy." From the Left, the condemnation was unanimous. So, too, was the realisation that fascist-minded forces still existed, very much entrenched in positions of authority. The government refused to disarm them.

At about this time, the active role of the CIA was also revealed. Under the guise of a totally fictitious "Operation and Transport Company," it seemed to have two main activities in Portugal: photographing activists and having dinner with sundry Air Force officers. There were stories (hundreds of stories and rumours) that the remains of the old "Legion" were organising—indeed had already organised—under the banners of the "Liberal" and "Federalist" parties.[3] Another story, reputedly started by the PS and PCP, alleged that the FPL (Front for Freedom in Portugal), an exile group in Paris which provided sound left-wing analyses of the political situation, was made up entirely of ex-PIDE spies. Old habits and

---

3   The legion was a paramilitary force, set up in 1936. It was modeled on Mussolini's Blackshirts. Some six thousand of its members (known as Viriatos) were killed fighting for Franco during the Spanish Civil War. Heavily armed and still in their characteristic blue shirts, they numbered some eighty thousand members on April 25, 1974.

fears die hard: it was impossible to say what was true or not. Rumours were rampant on the streets and tascas. A riot by some two hundred PIDE agents in a Lisbon prison on August 12, 1974, helped to clear the situation somewhat: it brought thousands of demonstrators into the streets, denouncing their demands.

The antistrike law introduced on August 27 was typical of the balance of forces at the time. It was the culmination of much preparation and its sponsors considered its timing particularly important, but this was not left in their hands: the law was introduced at the height of the TAP dispute, at the worst possible time. It was to be immediately, very visibly flouted on a large scale—a highly complex piece of legislation that prohibited both lockouts and certain types of strike. The preamble declared: "The Political Constitution of 1933 prohibited strikes and lockouts. Breaking with this system, the April 25th Movement allowed and recognised trade unions and managerial associations, provided they were in the spirit of the Programme of the MFA." But it was the small print that mattered. There were thirty-one articles in all. Specifically forbidden were:

a) Strikes among the armed forces, judiciary, firemen, etc.
b) Political strikes, and strikes in solidarity with unrelated trades and industries.
c) Strikes leading to the occupation of factories.
d) Strikes not preceded by a period of thirty days' discussion with the management.
e) Strikes not voted for by a majority of the labour force involved.

Lockouts by management were specifically permitted when a strike occurred that did not comply with the above conditions or when the management considered that machinery was at risk. The main thrust of the legislation aimed at preventing solidarity actions and at breaking the wave of occupations that threatened the employers' right to manage.

Far from condemning such anti–working class legislation, the PCP and PS had actually helped to formulate it. All the left groups condemned the new law outright. Cunhal's savage attacks on them at this time demonstrated the extent of his collusion with capital. Indeed, the PCP, through Intersindical, had organised a demonstration in Lisbon (on June 1) against the wave of strikes. Avelino Gonçalves (PCP Minister of Labour and ex-union leader of the Northern Bank Employees) said that they were "against adventurism, opportunism and unrealistic demands which caused chaos and a division in the democratic forces."

It was difficult to know what the PCP meant by "democratic forces." There were none in the government, which was a hive of intrigue. Spínola was meeting with members of the "Liberal Party" and of the "Democratic Labour Party," in which many ex-PIDEs were organising. (The ex-PIDEs were also planning actions of a more direct kind.) Spínola had succeeded in getting Galvão de Melo appointed head of the organisation entrusted with bringing charges against PIDE. He had also succeeded in getting his right-hand man, Sanches Osório, appointed Minister for Social Communications. Firmino Miguel, a firm Spínolist, was Minister of Defence.

The new commanders of the National Republican Guard and Police were also approved by Spínola. The General and those around him were doing everything in their power to reduce the influence of the MFA. Spínola had asked his close friend, Champalimaud, to draw up a plan for economic reconstruction. Palma Carlos had already spoken of the need of the right-wing parties to unite. This began in September under Spínola's personal influence.

Some of the fiercest arguments were taking place on the subject of the colonies. MES and the Maoist groups were particularly critical here, never allowing people to forget whom Spínola served. Early in August, a Censorship Board had been set up with Spínola's man, Sanches Osório, in charge. The Board had power to levy fines on publications or to suspend them altogether. Two evening papers had been prosecuted for carrying allegedly inopportune material about the colonies. By mid-August, the Maoist *Luta Popular* was suspended for "concrete ideological aggression" against the government. He was released shortly after, following a joint demonstration of PRP, URML, LUAR, MES, GAPS, and the MRPP.

One of the results of the struggles in the colonies and of the proposed decolonisation was a plan to extend the area of nationalisation in Portuguese banking. The Banco Nacional Ultramarino was one of the decisive controllers of the Mozambique economy and it was clear that no radical decolonisation could take place while it remained even partially in private hands. The Banco de Portugal and the Banco de Angola had major stakes overseas. The capital in all three banks was to be centralised in the hands of the state. Minority foreign capital was to be compensated.

During the summer, T and I travelled through the North of the country on a camping trip. Everywhere, we found people discussing the same sort of things: nationalisation, self-management, communism, the class struggle. In a mountain campsite near Leixões, the guard, who had not left the site for five years, questioned me at length about April 25. In Figueira da Foz, a French tourist's trumpet blew out the notes of "Grandola, Vila Morena" only to have them echoed by a trumpet-playing fisherman from a window. A crowd gathered, ecstatic. Workers just outside Porto told stories of local PIDE agents who had not yet been arrested. Initially, they were suspicious of a foreigner. We'd ritualistically buy one another glasses of wine, and after a couple of rounds, they'd begin to say things I'd never dreamt of hearing: "The problem is capitalism. There are still fascists in the government. There are still PIDE agents living near here." The North, supposed to be the bastion of reaction, was in fact more polarised than the South.

SEPTEMBER 28

In an interview given after the events of September 28, Otelo Saraiva de Carvalho (Commander of COPCON) revealed that the Major General of the armed forces had known about gunrunning from Spain and Angola as early as September 8. A week later, his services had discovered that a plane had been hired at the Tires aerodrome in the name of the armed forces. It was to drop leaflets over Lisbon, announcing a demonstration to be held on September 28 in favour of General Spínola.

Spínola's speech of September 10, a speech in which he had spoken of a "silent majority who had to awaken and defend themselves from extremist totalitarianism" had been planned as the starting point of a campaign which would lead to a new coup. The movement was backed by various elements in the business world and in the armed forces and by certain shadowy groupings of the extreme Right. A few days after the speech, large posters began to appear in the streets of Lisbon, calling for a demonstration to reaffirm support for General Spínola. "No to extremism. Yes to firmness and loyalty to the programme of the MFA." On September 19, a plane duly showered leaflets over Lisbon and Coimbra.

A week earlier, right-wing parties like the Liberal Party, the Party of Progress, CDS, PDC, PPD, and several other smaller groups had all applauded Spínola's speech. The PPD, in *Diário de Lisboa*, said on September 13 that "his words constituted solemn advice and a grave warning for Portugal." The Christian Democrats extolled his "lucid considerations." The Liberal Party stressed that lack of confidence in the economy was at the root of the crisis, and bemoaned the fact that the antistrike law had been "defiantly and openly" broken.

The PCP and left groups warned that a massive operation was being planned against the working class. The first real evidence came when it was discovered that a massive bulk purchase of tickets had been made for the bullfight that night. The tickets had been paid for by Champalimaud and de Melo and distributed free . . . to those they'd persuaded that the country was heading for economic ruin.[4]

The Praça de Touros is not a place frequented by working people. The cheapest tickets cost thirty escudos and prices rise steeply for the boxes. Workers tend to see the bullfights on television. When Vasco Gonçalves, the Prime Minister, entered the ring, the crowd cheered, thinking it was Spínola. When they discovered it wasn't, the cheering stopped. Later, Vasco was actually booed. At the end of the evening, the crowd applauded a bullfighter (the son of a Count who had been imprisoned for selling arms to Biafra) as he rode around the ring holding high a poster advertising the proposed demonstration.

Left-wing groups massed outside the Praça. MES, PRP-BR, and the Maoists handed out leaflets saying that the "silent majority" demonstration was a signal for a coup. The National Republican Guard arrived and, using their horses, pushed them back. The Communist Party issued a statement warning the government of "reactionary forces." The MDP and PS also issued statements condemning the proposed demonstration. The PRP-BR had already asked some important questions: "When Marcelo and Tomás can go to Brazil, when Casal Ribeiro, Moreira Baptista, and Silva Cunha (the ex-leaders of ANP) are freed, when reactionaries are protected, when workers in struggle are suppressed, when wages are fixed at starvation level and prices allowed to rise, who benefits: the workers or the reaction?"

Fighting broke out as the Spínolists left the bullring. Poles and fists were used as hundreds rushed in. This was the first mass violence between civilians since the onset of the revolution. It became particularly vicious when the second wave of Spínolists attempted to leave the ring.

The next day, a Friday, demands grew louder that the demonstration be banned. The MDP issued a call for vigilante groups to block all roads into Lisbon. They issued pictures showing the "silent majority" poster for what it was: an only feebly disguised clarion call to a fascist rally. Student organisations, Maoists, MES, all denounced the proposed demonstration. Members of PRP-BR pasted up handbills in the main stations of Porto calling on coach drivers not to take paid demonstrators to Lisbon. Most

---

4   An official report later established that the Espírito Santo Bank had financed the posters and tickets to the tune of 12 million escudos.

of the drivers agreed not to. Only Galvão de Melo, a general who had recently compared April 25 to the Brazilian right-wing coup of 1964 spoke on behalf of the government, publicly supporting the rally.

Everyone waited for the march to be banned. But the expected announcement never came. Instead Major Sanches Osário, a staunch Spínolist, spoke for the MFA. He said the demonstration would take place. At about 7 p.m. troops started to move towards the radio stations. Several battalions of National Republican Guard were seen heading towards the park of Monsanto. People began to assemble near the main entrances to the city. Spontaneously, barricades were erected. Large red banners appeared with the slogan "Stop the Reaction." Rádio Renascença, the once-Catholic radio station now under workers' control, reported all this, encouraging thousands more to mass in the streets.

At 9 p.m. the national radio went blank, followed some time later by Rádio Clube Portugués and the TV. We later learned that they had been taken over by the National Republican Guard. Emissora Nacional was the only station to continue functioning, but did so sporadically. Rumours and information spread like wildfire over what had been known (during the fascist days) as the "Arabic telephone."

PCP officials appeared on the barricades with red armbands. So did PS members. Leaflets were handed out calling for vigilance. People were saying that both Otelo and Gonçalves were being held at Belém.

In a later interview Otelo said that Spínola had denounced him as responsible for the barricades. "The rumour that I had been arrested caused 'loyal' MFA units to head towards Belém to rescue me. On the telephone I asked them not to be alarmed. They didn't believe me." Other stories had it that the extreme right-wing generals Luis Sá Cunha and Kaulza de Arriaga were organising a coup. Confusion was rampant. Civil war seemed on the cards.

Workers outside Lisbon took out what arms they had in store and set up barricades on the roads into the city. Anyone heading in the direction of the capital was searched. At the Tagus Bridge, a Mercedes was fired on by troops for failing to stop. To the North, a hearse with a coffin full of guns was discovered. Two lorries were stopped at Vila Franca de Xira and found to contain arms and explosives.

The night was cold, but no one left the barricades. Friends brought coffee and bagaço for the vigilantes. Troops were on the move. No one knew where they were going, though it turned out that many were arrest-ing known supporters of the proposed demonstration. Hotels like the

Hilton were searched and right-wingers rounded up and taken to Caxias. At 3 a.m. Major Osário read a communiqué, again permitting the demonstration. He asked that the barricades be taken down. Meanwhile, other troops were moving to the barricades, helping civilians maintain them.

At 8:40 a.m. on Saturday, September 28, Emissora Nacional came on the air again, this time to the strains of "Grandola, Vila Morena," the Zeca Afonso tune that had signalled the April 25 uprising: "We have just witnessed a whole series of activities by reactionary forces. These forces have not understood the historical necessity of April 25. They have sought to create panic among the people by trafficking in arms and by economic sabotage . . . To ensure that the road to a new society is safeguarded a few dozen people were detained in the early hours of this morning."

Thousands immediately thronged into the streets and further reinforced the barricades, waiting all morning. At 1 p.m., a communiqué banning the demonstration was read by Spínola himself: "Given the changed circumstances witnessed this morning, and for the sake of avoiding possible confrontations, His Excellency the President does not deem it advisable to proceed with the announced demonstration in Praça do Império."

Another communiqué, read several times, asked the people to have confidence in the forces of COPCON, to help the MFA, and to withdraw their pickets "because the situation no longer justified them." Troops moved into strategic areas. The crowds, still friendly, discussed the situation with them in small groups. Traffic began to flow again. There was a deep awareness that the Right had suffered a decisive setback.

By 2 p.m. thousands of workers massed in Belém for a counterdemonstration called by several Workers' Committees and by Intersindical. It turned into a vast "victory" parade. At 3 p.m. the Left demonstrated in the nearby working-class suburb of Alcantara. Forty thousand people turned up and marched through the streets, shouting the slogans of the previous night. The joy was more political than on May Day. People shouted more fiercely, and with more determination and conviction. This second demonstration was mainly sponsored by MES, though all the revolutionary groups (with the exception of the Maoist MRPP) supported it. All along the route, people showed solidarity by raising their fists or by applauding from their balconies.

Sunday was quiet. People tried to figure out the full implications of what had happened while waiting for further broadcasts. That night Vasco Gonçalves spoke to the nation.

There had been no papers on the Saturday and Sunday and both the radio and TV had been silent for long periods. Leaflets took over and wall-sheets appeared everywhere. The MDP-CDE sheet claimed that weapons had been found in the Sheraton Hotel. During the crisis, the role of these unofficial channels of communication had been tremendous. Little pieces of information seeped through in each leaflet, preventing chaos and fear.

That night, a full list of those arrested was read out over the radio. Those arrested included all the better-known and most active fascists of the old regime, as well as the two biggest capitalists in the country: Espírito Santo and Champalimaud. Warnings were issued that further arrests were imminent.

On Monday, September 30, workers returned to the factories—not to work, but to discuss the events of the weekend. The first national papers appeared. News was now pouring in from all over the country. A plot to assassinate Vasco Gonçalves had been unearthed: a rifle with a long-range telescope had been found in a house opposite his residence. The offices of the *Partido do Progresso* had been searched and an arsenal found, including submachine guns. The premises of the Liberal Party had been stormed and although the police had intervened the windows had been shattered by PS and MDP militants.

Later that day a haggard-looking Spínola appeared on TV and spoke to the nation, resigning as President. He could "no longer face the climate of anarchy where everyone made their own laws and where it was impossible to create an authentic democracy for peace and progress." People laughed as he finished. Victory was being consolidated. The possibility of revolution seemed just a little closer.

General Costa Gomes was named as the new President. He had impeccable conservative credentials: one-time Commander of the National Republican Guard, ex-commander of the armed forces in Mozambique (in 1961), General Chief of Staff since 1972. He sported just a tinge of "anti-fascism": in March 1974, he had been dismissed by Caetano for failing to give the oath of allegiance.

The political parties all issued statements on the events. The PCP called for continued vigilance by the people and armed forces. Both the PS and PPD applauded the MFA and called for acceleration of the democratic processes. The PS urged support for the voluntary day of work set for October 6. A MES statement claimed that "the last five months had shown that it was not possible for the MFA to stand aside and allow the bourgeois forces to strangle the workers. Recent struggles by the working-class vanguard (the workers of TAP, of Lisnave, and all those who since April 25 had been repressed and lied to) showed clearly that the working-class support for the MFA must go hand in hand with support by the MFA for the working class."

LUAR, in a communiqué, spoke of the dismissal of Spínola. "Spínola resigned," it said, "because he wanted to be the sole interpreter of the programme of the MFA and because of his support for the interests of an expansionist capitalism and international high finance. He wanted to use the programme (of the MFA) to suppress the legitimate interests of the working classes and the majority of the Portuguese people." No comments were made on the fact that the "programme" was so ambiguous that it could be legitimately used for such a purpose.

A large demonstration was called by the PCP and Intersindical for the Monday night outside the presidential palace at Belém. Everyone now noticed how all the major PCP demonstrations were being called outside the seat of government, whereas other groups were demonstrating either in districts such as Alcantara, or in the centre of the city. The demonstration was nevertheless a very joyful one. Thousands of non-party members turned up. "Vitória! Vitória!" the PCP shouted. Other slogans, perhaps more sincere and more proletarian, also appeared: "Soldado amigo, o povo está contigo" (Soldier, friend, the people are with you), or—again—"We came of our own free will, nobody paid us."

The following Sunday was October 6, the day after the anniversary of the proclamation of the First Republic. Despite the large working-class forces that had rallied to its side, the government was still talking of the "national interest," an utterly mystifying concept. That night, there was a gathering outside the Hilton Hotel. Galvão de Melo had gone there to have dinner with certain elements reputed to be CIA agents. Some three thousand people congregated outside, waiting. COPCON forces arrived, but did not intervene. Civilians stood in groups discussing the situation. Finally Galvão de Melo came out without a carnation. The crowd surged forward shouting "Death to the CIA," "Death to Fascism." The general barely escaped in a government Mercedes.

THE THIRD PROVISIONAL GOVERNMENT

Shortly after September 28, a new administration was established that lasted until the next right-wing coup in March 1975.

The composition of the Third Government differed little from its predecessors. Three members of the Junta were dismissed along with

Spínola. Six members of the previous government lost their positions. Five new military appointments were made and the job of Minister of Social Communications was taken over by Vasco Gonçalves himself. Colonel Pinho Freire and Lieutenant-Colonel Mendes Dias, both professional military men, took over the Air Force, replacing Diogo Neto. Vítor Crespo and Rosa Coutinho took over from Silvino Ribeiro and Firmino Miguel as chiefs of the Navy. Galvão de Melo was, at last, dismissed. No startling new legislation was announced. The preparation of evidence against the ex-PIDEs was temporarily taken over by COPCON and the dismantling of some of the fascist organisations (such as the Legion) completed. The process of decolonisation was accelerated.

These changes represented a victory for the Coordinating Committee of the MFA. Spínola's insistence on a "Spínolist" reading of the programme had been promoted by his direct connections with high finance (in the persons of de Melo and Champalimaud). It became known that Spínola had attempted to put a halt to the process of decolonisation in Angola through a deal between the leader of the FNLA, the president of Zambia (who was the latter's step-brother) and the Americans (who had wanted to protect their substantial interests in Cabinda). Spínola had also supported the rebellious PIDEs in Mozambique in early September.

Following Spínola's flight, the MFA restructured itself. At the apex of the giant pyramid was the Supreme Council of the Movement, known as the Council of 20. It comprised the President, the six remaining members of the Junta, the five military ministers (the Prime Minister, two Ministers without Portfolio, and the Ministers of the Interior and of Labour), the commander of COPCON, and seven members from the Coordinating Committee of the MFA. The MFA Assembly comprised 200 officers drawn from the three branches of the armed forces (115 were from the Army). The General Assembly was based on various Councils in the three branches of the Services, in turn related to various regional councils and assemblies.

The MFA was now represented at all levels of government and civil administration, but its politics were no longer unanimous. A certain polarisation was beginning to take place. Their fortnightly Bulletin spoke loudly of "democracy," "decolonisation," and "dynamisation," but gave no clue as to what they meant by it.

Vasco Gonçalves appealed for a day's work on Sunday, October 6. His aim was to show that the MFA still enjoyed the support of a large section of the Portuguese people, and that Spínola's talk of "anarchy" was unfounded. Tens of thousands of workers turned up for work. Others spent the day cleaning the streets and walls of Lisbon. The walls of the capital, over the five months since April, had accumulated so many slogans and graffiti that it was difficult to find space for more. People who wrote new slogans often had to encircle them if they wanted passers-by to notice. Students went to the shanty towns to help families there; others went to hospitals. Certain groups were critical of the project. The workers of Efacec asked: "We live in a capitalist society, where the largest slice of the riches produced goes into the pockets of the bosses. In our case, any extra wealth created will go abroad, only increasing the bank accounts of our employers and allowing them one more trip to Bermuda or yet another car. Because there are more important things to do than work for the boss we propose that each section turns up and decides for itself what to do on Sunday."

CTT and other workers likewise proclaimed their right to decide where the extra work should be done. The whole question of "the good of the state" and of "the authorities knowing best" was being challenged by these actions. The class nature of the new state had already been exposed— and quite clearly—by the workers of Lisnave, TAP, Efacec, Timex, Sogantal, Charneca, CTT, and many others. Despite the sycophantic position of the PCP (in relation to both MFA and government) large sections of the working class were moving towards a revolutionary critique of Portuguese society.

International firms began to show renewed concern for their interests in Portugal. A company without books, trading under the name Cindusta, was discovered in Madeira. One of its offices was aboard the yacht *Apollo*, moored just off the island. The twelve Americans who lived on the yacht were seen photographing demonstrators. Enquiries showed that Cindusta was a subsidiary of "Operation and Transport Company," previously shown to be a CIA front. The CDE of Madeira—supported by PS, UPM (Popular Unity in Madeira), and FPDM (Front for Democracy in Madeira)—called a demonstration against their presence. A fight between demonstrators and members of the crew sent the latter scurrying off to unknown waters.

In the wake of the "September days," many left groups began getting a say in the papers again. Between July and September, these groups had only received marginal coverage. In a sense, these groups were themselves marginal, as events organised by working-class forces within the factories (and by bourgeois forces outside them) were more important.

IV THE UPSURGE

THE COMMITTEES

The political repercussions of September 28 only became apparent later in the year. The Party of Progress was banned, most of its leaders arrested and its offices closed. Other right-wing parties likewise ceased activity or at least pretended to. The strike movement, meanwhile, gathered momentum. During October, some four hundred factories and companies registered "disturbances." These ranged from workers presenting a list of demands to routing the entire management.

The relationship between the Workers' Committees and the trade unions is worth examining in some detail. The unions had been inherited from the fascist regime in which they had been affiliated to the old ENT created by Salazar in 1934. In most cases, they were completely discredited. There were now some four thousand unions across the county, organised by trade. In some instances, they would not "represent" more than half a dozen workers. In Lisnave, there were thirteen unions; in Mabor (the tyre plant), twenty-three; in TAP, fifteen. The situation was similar in other large enterprises. Small union federations existed in name only, sometimes bringing together strange bedfellows: one of the unions in TAP was the Union of Air Navigators and Seamen. The only large, "strong" unions were the Union of Bank Employees (which had attempted a demonstration in Lisbon on May 1, 1973) and the Union of Agricultural Workers. Together, they were to constitute the hard core of Intersindical, the federation led and run by the PCP. Some unions were still fronts for the ex-PIDE. What Anton Pannekoek and the German Spartacus League had said about the unions in Germany in 1919 was particularly true in Portugal: they were instruments to control the workers.

The immediate response of the workers to the need for autonomous organisation was the General Assembly or plenário. All those employed in a given enterprise would get together to discuss their situation. The plenário would usually elect a Workers' Committee or ad-hoc Commission, which would be entrusted with the task of drawing up a list of demands. In the organisational vacuum that had followed April 25, the Committees had been thrown up as the natural organisation to defend the workers' interests. They pressed for economic demands and, at times, for a restructuring of industrial life. Many called for an end to exploitation: profits should no longer be left in the hands of private individuals. Although the Committees were not revolutionary organisations (very few of them called for the abolition of wage labour or for an end to the capitalist mode of production), they showed an extreme distrust of the unions and, in many cases, of the new institutions created by the MFA. This is not to say that the MFA was unpopular. Workers simply wanted things to move faster. By the end of October 1974, some two thousand such Committees existed throughout Portugal.

The Committees were usually elected for one year and were liable to recall. In some cases, this power had already been exercised. Their aims and concerns were wide, and at times in head-on conflict with the state. The Lisnave Committee, for instance, called the demonstration of September 12, 1974, against the "antistrike" law despite their proposed march being banned by the government and attacked both by the unions and by the PCP cell within the shipyard. Similarly, the plenário of TAP workers had been the one to call the strike in July that led to the "militarisation" of the airports. The Committees often ran parallel with both unions and with the official management.

Plenários and Committees confronted a wide and challenging variety of problems. Some were apparently trivial, but on closer inspection proved to be important; others were clearly significant to all. A few were purely local, but many had a much more general relevance. Some related to managerial attitudes and others to attitudes deeply engrained within the working class itself. Difficulties were created by seeking to adapt to a contemporary reality which was still capitalist, but difficulties also arose through conscious attempts to prefigure the communist future. It is worth devoting a few pages to these matters. The main problems were:

A. *Finding a place to meet, accessible to the majority of workers.* In most factories, this would be the canteen. But sometimes there wasn't a canteen, or the canteen wasn't centrally situated. Such accidents of geography made it easier for some workers to attend plenários than for others. In many cases, there was nowhere central to meet. Even big enterprises, like TAP, had this problem. Therefore, meetings had to be held off the firm's premises. Certain companies, moreover, had very divided labour forces. The company, taken as a whole, was spread over many regions (office staff in Lisbon, factory staff in Setúbal, with branches scattered throughout the country). In these cases, meaningful representation proved quite a problem.

B. *Coping with the political tendencies.* Various political parties operated within the plenários. Their preoccupations often appeared sectarian to many attending the assemblies. Union members sought to find a base by getting elected onto Committees. Various left groups used the Committees for purposes of propaganda and recruitment, raising extraneous issues (talking for instance about "the traitor Vilar," leader of the PCP-ml, or about "the traitor Cunhal"). Factional disputes on the macromolecular level, which had little to do with the real (and serious) problems at hand, obstructed attempts to see the company in the general context of the economy, detracted from the discussion of real issues, wasted working-class time and effort, and created mystification. The plenários were often interrupted by heated arguments, only some of which were relevant to the workers' real concerns.

This was seen most clearly in the plenários of Setenave, a big ship-repair firm in Setúbal, forty kilometres from Lisbon. In May, a strike had been called, which lasted twelve days. The Committee was recalled for "fraternising" with management and a new one was elected that grouped all sections, including engineers, electricians, welders, and so on. This is what one of the workers thought about one of the plenários: "The last General Assembly of Setenave had no interest for me. It just discussed a load of matters which had nothing to do with the problems at hand. Parties attacked parties . . . you're MRPP, you're PRP, and so on. Everyone was more interested in this than in discussing the real issues. It shouldn't be as a member of a political party that one attacks the Committee, but as a worker. I agree with some of the attacks on the Committee. With others I don't."[1]

A second participant stressed that the workers should be strict in insisting that the plenários deal only with problems relating to the company or perhaps also with more general problems of workers, unemployment, and so on. A third worker said: "the criticism was directed more against parties than against the real work of the Committee. Criticism is okay if it's constructive . . . If April 25th didn't take the money from the capitalists, how on earth was the Committee supposed to do it?" Yet another worker spotlighted a key issue: "in the base groups, we really know each other. We often don't know the people on the Workers'

---

1   *Combate* 10, November 8, 1974.

Committee. More members of the base groups are to go onto the Workers' Committee. I agree with this. Everyone should know someone on the Workers' Committee."[2]

Sometimes, a much greater unity prevailed, however, and this was seen where workers had understood the need to meet often and to involve themselves to the maximum in the struggles at hand. In the Lisbon electrical engineering company of Efacec-Inel, for instance, the mere election of a Committee was considered insufficient. A plenário on May 21 presented a list of demands. Another, on June 1, discussed what to do when the management refused the demands. On July 8, a third plenário voted for a strike and occupation. A Defence Committee was set up on the very first day. Later, a Cultural Committee, an Information Committee, and a committee to coordinate pickets were also set up. A paper was published, which was sent out to other occupied factories. Films such as *Battleship Potemkin* and documentaries about other struggles were shown. Discussions on the nature of the political crisis were organised. Over 90 percent of the one thousand workers participated.

C. *Deciding their own terms of reference.* In the plenários, differences of opinion often formed concerning the demands to be formulated. Sometimes, these reflected differences in the composition of the workforce in a given firm. At other times, differing policies would be dictated by obviously differing managerial attitudes, or by varying relationships between the management and the MFA.

Propam, an industrial bakery employing some 150 workers was in many ways typical of the smaller companies. After April 25, a committee had been set up and the MFA invited to visit. Later, some office workers and two members of the Committee were sacked (the management claiming that they couldn't pay the minimum wage). The MFA arrived in the form of two young captains, who accused the management of "incompetence and lack of lucidity." A report was sent to the government. The government replied that it had no powers to interfere with private property. The MFA insisted. Finally, three workers and three managers set up an Administrative Committee. Things went well for two weeks, the bosses accepting the will of the workers. But the bosses began to question the "legality" of MFA interventions in such matters. One of the workers on the Administrative Committee was fired and the other two could do nothing. Sackings began in the offices. The management took advantage

2   *Combate* 13, December 12, 1974.

of the August closure for holidays to dismiss a large number of workers. A plenário on August 28 decided that a strike was the only solution:

> Our demands were the sacking of the management for incompetence, and the right to work . . . The government approached us and asked us nicely not to release our decisions to the press, to avoid "shocks." The Ministry of Finance issued a document on our economic viability as a company. The boss has recently begun writing things on the walls, and also writing lying letters to the government. He has also written to the parents of the younger employees, saying what bad company they were keeping . . . Most of the (new) sackings have taken place in the offices, because they supported the MFA officers and refused to obey the management. Also because the boss never comes here (in the factory itself) and it would be hard for him to find a good excuse. Also because we, on the factory floor, are specialised workers and it would be difficult to recruit other qualified staff. There is only one other factory like this in the whole country . . . The boss is an extremely authoritarian person and the simple fact that he cannot now give an order to a worker has become unbearable to him . . . He stopped thinking of the interests of his company and began thinking about his own survival and not the survival of 150 workers.
>
> Propam owns three factories, a yeast plant, a flourmill and a "treating plant." Besides this there is a whole sales and distribution network. There are 1,850 shareholders in this company, but a group of eight people really run it. The shareholders (who own 95 percent of the capital) don't run anything here . . .
>
> Here we have twenty unions for 150 workers. But they are not organised. We elected a new Committee and presented our demands. There had to be a saneamento. The office workers at first agreed with the Committee but later set up a Committee of their own. We had meetings which continued late into the night and sometimes into the morning. No decisions were taken without a plenário. But there were differences with the office workers, who were mainly in Lisbon. They were more afraid. We were asked not to say what happened at the meetings between us, so that it wouldn't get to the management, who were also in Lisbon.[3]

---

3   *Combate* 10, November 8, 1974.

More drastic methods were sometimes used, not always unsuccessfully. At Mueller Miquinas Lda, the workers had kidnapped the two American managers and kept them prisoners until a ransom of 100,000 escudos was produced. The parent company paid up and lodged a formal protest with the government. The Ministry of Labour replied that in view of recent wage increases the amount was due in back pay anyway. The managers fled. Among the problems discussed was whether or not workers should take part in the management of companies which still remained in private hands: in a nutshell whether or not they should help employers increase their profits. This was generally and increasingly rejected. Attitudes were more varied in relation to firms which the workers had taken over and where the employers had fled. At stake were issues central to the whole discussion about self-management, about its recuperation under capitalism, and about its central role in the institutional framework of a socialist society.

D. *Problems within the class.* The real problems within the class were considerable. They reflected differences of "status," age, sex, and between employed and unemployed workers. Calls to narrow the range of wage scales produced considerable opposition from the better-paid workers. Generally, as in TAP, this was got round by raising the lower scales and freezing the top ones. But in the case of specialised categories (like pilots, who threatened to sell their labour power to another company), these questions were not easily dealt with. There was also a definite tendency for the better-paid workers, who were often more articulate, to dominate and sometimes even to manipulate the plenários to such an extent that other workers walked out.

The workers sought to tackle certain aspects of the relations of production, the relations they experienced in their daily lives, and in many cases succeeded in doing so. They discussed what type of organisation of work they wanted. This had the effect of lessening the separation of the workers from their means of livelihood, allowing them to situate themselves more consciously within the total process of production. Different functional groups (cleaners, welders, electricians) discussed many issues relating to those functions. As long as capitalism remained, all this was little more than the self-management of their own exploitation: it did not abolish the exchange of labour power for wages. But the insights achieved could be of lasting value to the building of socialism.

Young workers were the most militant. Occasionally, scathing leaflets would be handed out in the plenários, many of them very witty and containing real criticisms of the Committees and of the type of discussion taking place there. A leaflet circulated in an electronics factory in Setúbal spoke of how the Committee "was actually worse than the old management." Another said, "We have passed from a situation of hunger to a situation where we can say we are hungry." Those behind the leaflets were often wrongly called Maoists. Their leaflets tended to be one-offs. The older workers (and in the last analysis, the revolution would have to mobilise their support) tended to be more conservative. They had the most to lose. They often warned against "adventures." "Who would pay the wages if the firm was taken over?" they asked again and again. There were often no funds to start with. There was no security. To lose one's job was to jeopardise one's survival. They knew about wage labour. Organisation was paramount, they rightly stressed.

The committees also had to face up to the macho attitudes of some workers. In Abel Alves (at Santo Tirso, near Porto) a textiles factory employed six hundred workers, mainly women. The men earned more than the women, who only earned eighty-eight escudos per day. The women wanted to work at night, but neither the boss (nor their husbands) would let them. Contradictions of all kinds abounded. After April 25, the firm of Parceria A.M. Pereira, for example, began publishing editions of Marx, Engels, and Lenin. On February 17, 1975, it was occupied by its workers, who may or may not have read the texts, but who had certainly received no pay since September.

The problem of scab labour cropped up repeatedly. The workers of the building firm of Soares da Costa had gone on strike on August 20, 1974, for pay increases. Scab labour had been sent to the site. The scabs were beaten off, but four workers had to be taken to hospital. The strike lasted six weeks. The number of unemployed workers only made matters worse. In the middle of July, some five thousand workers had marched (in a demonstration in Setúbal organised by employers in the building trade) shouting, "No to anarchy, the building industry bosses are sons of the people."

The workers of Soares da Costa reacted with imagination and sensitivity to this threat: "We, the workers on strike, understand the situation of many workers who come from other sites and find themselves without money to buy food, or without lodgings. We are putting our resources at the disposal of these brothers to give them food and somewhere to sleep. Comrades, our struggle is just and we are determined to win." The workers collected funds and gave out money to unemployed workers, but the task was an impossible one, given the number of unemployed and the men's own hardships.

E. *Problems of self-management.* In many cases (Timex, Sogantal, Charminha, Sousabreu, and others) the management had fled or been routed and the Committees were left to run the factory.

At Nefil (a furniture factory in Guimarães, near Porto) the old management had been completely routed. The 237 workers sold the goods produced at the gates and to street distributors. But how was the money to be shared? As one worker put it: "The question is very difficult. It has really been a headache, this workers' control. People want to adopt a more united, more socialist attitude, those earning more giving some to those who earn less. But this raises a lot of problems. One proposal was to pay out according to the type of work. Another was to pay according to need. Yet another was to pay everyone the same. People realised that everyone couldn't be paid equally. If this happened it would cause disunity among the workers. We still haven't reached agreement over this. The proposal to cut some wages and increase others (where there is real need) is the most popular."[4]

There were problems with this type of sales. At Luso-Vale, on December 16, a thousand pairs of rubber boots proved difficult to get rid of, as the means of distribution were still in the hands of international capital. It was perhaps the workers in multinationals who were hardest hit by all this, as the Workers' Committees were impotent against the might of international capital.

The questions of common ownership and of judicial and effective power over the means of production were rarely raised explicitly (though they were always in the background). Many groups called for nationalisation as a means of achieving such control. Only a few could see beyond this reinforcement of state power, and envision a genuinely communist society. Problems of immediate survival inevitably surged to the forefront. The workers in occupation needed raw materials, machinery, money. In the absence of any other source of help, they were forced to call on the government or on the MFA. This happened even at Muller, Maquinas Lda, as described above.

In many firms under self-management, the workers continued to produce the same type of goods and encountered major problems of distribution. Many of the bigger firms had so scattered their production units that many of their plants only turned out components of the ultimate product. There was no question of being able to sell or distribute

---

4   *Combate* 17, February 14, 1975.

such components within the country without a structured distribution network and without an awareness of overall demand. Moreover, many of the components were exported. Applied Magnetics, for example, was a branch of an American company. It produced parts for computers, which were then sent to Puerto Rico for assembly. From there, the finished products were shipped to the United States. When the workers went on strike and occupied the factory, the company simply folded: 650 people, mainly women, found themselves out of work. A workers' communiqué said: "The reason can only be political. The management are familiar with the political situation in Portugal. Such a move can only be part of a global plan on the part of capitalism."

The clothes factory of Camoda, in Odivelas (in the industrial belt of Lisbon) was a modern building, set up with German capital in 1972. The raw materials were bought in Portugal and the finished clothes sent to Germany, where the profits remained. After April 25, the manager had said that there was no money for wages and the thirty-two workers began to work a four-day week while the supervisory staff, continued to work full time). The CT went to the Ministry. The employers promised to resume full production within two months. In December, the manager fired a member of the CT and called two others into her office. The workers replied by calling her to a shop-floor meeting. She then fired the other two members of the CT, calling them wasters and revolutionaries. "Why do you call me a revolutionary?" one of the girls asked. "Is it because, when you come down here and say that there are no wages, we answer that we can't go home without money?"

The firm was occupied and the workers continued to work. The problem, as usual, was markets. The Minister of Labour promised help. People began to realise that the real issues went much deeper. Employers were using sackings and closures as a means of disciplining workers. In reality, this was a fundamental question of restructuring the whole economy in terms of communist production, of production for use. The task could only be tinkered with on a local basis.

The workers also had to cope with reactionary propaganda against self-management. In the tourist complex and holding company Grão Pará they had to deal with pressure from the bosses, who had fled to Spain. The 1,300 workers had taken over the whole complex which included hotels and buildings, run companies such as Matur, Grão Pará, Interhotel, Somote Orplano, Autodril, EDEC, Comportur, and Rota do Atlantico. They were supported widely by other workers. In a communiqué on

Christmas day they said: "Through the strength of its workers Matur has achieved something unprecedented: the conditions to guarantee its own survival. We have frustrated the plans of the management (who are abroad) by achieving an index of 90 percent bookings . . . We denounce the management for threatening our positions through the spreading of rumours."[5]

The management abroad were spreading stories to the effect that hotels were closed, that service was bad, and so on. The hotels were expensive and continued to be, even under workers' control. In a capitalist society, capitalist economics prevailed.

The unions also created problems for the CTs, often through luke-warm "support." At Famalicão, the workers of a textile company put out a communiqué:

> After being vigilant in the factory over the weekend, so that our right to work could be assured, we were surprised when, on Monday morning, the management and section chiefs didn't turn up. In view of this cowardly action we have decided to start working normally, on our own . . . Since the office staff like-wise didn't show up, some of our mates took over these tasks.
>
> Last Friday a group of reactionaries, criminals, well-paid lackeys who sold themselves to the boss, untuned various machines in the blanket finishing section. They took the fuses out of a combing machine, hiding them in one of the turbines.
>
> The union didn't show up either, as they'd been asked to. In a meeting with a union leader last Saturday the CT presented a minimum programme of 5 points, for collaboration. But they let us down . . . in the most difficult hours they preferred to be absent.[6]

F. *Problems of liaison.* Many small companies invited members of the CTs of larger companies to attend their plenários. Efacec-Inel, through their CDDT (Committee for the Defence of the Rights of the Workers) attended many, like at Fortis-Otis (elevator manufacturers) in Lisbon. These visits paved the way for the setting up of a federation of Workers' Committees. In their paper Efacec-Inel published news of many of these visits.

When small companies were part of large combines they faced difficulties which could not be solved by mere occupation. For instance

---

5   *Combate* 14, January 1975.
6   *Combate* 11, November 22, 1974.

the monopolistic group Miguel Quina controlled over sixty companies, including Mabor, *Jornal do Comércio*, Eurofil (plastics), and Icesa (dock-yards). In each company there existed separate CTs. An ad hoc Committee was set up, representing the combine as a whole.

Workers employed by CUF, the giant monopoly which comprised some 186 companies ranging from insurance through animal fodder to textiles also had problems of communication. A Federation of Workers' Committees was set up to establish and maintain contacts between those employed by the different companies.

G. *Saneamento*. One of the major problems confronting the CTs was that of saneamento, of purging managements of their former fascist sympathisers. This was often difficult to achieve on a local basis because those to be purged had very deep roots in the economic institutions of the country and because the real power of these institutions (banks, trusts, newspapers, political groups) had scarcely been dented. The struggle over saneamento was often a question of the balance of forces in a particular firm or community. On this background the CTs lost as often as they won.

The experience of Eurofil (a plastics factory) was interesting in this respect. The 1,600 workers had occupied their work place to stop the sacking of 300 of their comrades. The Navy intervened. The sailors (although called in by the management) mixed with the workers and took their side. An ad hoc Committee wrote, concerning this particular firm, "This group has always had close relations with the fascist regime. It continues to employ people gravely implicated in it. We know how some of these have acted in the past: Gonçalves Rapazote, ex-Minister of the Interior and active agent of repression. Guilherme Braz Medeiros, from Diáno Popular. Antonio Costa Félix, from the Borges Brothers Bank, who signed the note asking for permission to attend the demonstration of the 'silent majority.' José Miguel Maia Pereira from the same bank, a member of the Portuguese Legion and FAC.[7] José Costa Deitado, director of the newspaper of the Party of Progress and active member of this neo-Nazi party. Fernando Pina e Almeida, now in Caxias, who established the link between the PIDE and this company."[8]

The list is interesting in that it gives an idea of what was involved in saneamento. The CT sent a report on the firm to the MFA listing the

---

7 FAC: Anti-Communist Front, related to the Portuguese Legion.
8 *Combate* 17, February 14, 1975.

"irregularities" and asking for intervention. But this reliance on others (and in particular the MFA) was to prove the main stumbling block in most attempts at saneamento. As a worker in the textile company of Abel Alves de Figueiredo put it, in reply to a question concerning a delegation to the Ministry of Labour: "If it (the Ministry) has to be cleansed I think it can only be done by the working class itself. The working class has to put this particular house in order."

The workers were gradually becoming more aware of the global nature of capitalism. Attempts at solidarity became more frequent, the analyses of problems more coherent, the solutions proposed more radical and more political. In issue no. 8 of their *Strike Bulletin* (dated July 17, 1974) the workers of Efacec-Inel put it this way:

> Our struggles are just, and if we strike we shall be heard. This is why we must organise not only against this or that boss, in this or that factory, but against the capitalist system as a whole.
>
> Comrades often ask: "If there were no bosses, who would give us work?" We all know that to work we need a factory, machines and raw materials. We also know that the factory and the machines were made by other workers, just as it was other workers who sowed the cotton, worked the wool or dug up the iron ore. It therefore isn't the boss who gives us work, but the miner, the metalworker, the farmer. Where did the boss get the money to have his factory? Very easy, comrades! We gave it to him. It is the only way to make a fortune. Those who do the work only get what is necessary to survive. It is the workers who produce the surplus, which the boss uses to buy machines. Since it is workers like us who run the factory, why are bosses needed?

Here, in a nutshell, were all the problems of Capital spontaneously felt by the workers. The questions were profound, dealing with value, surplus value and wage labour. By December 1974, there were over a hundred of these "workers' control" situations; by March of the following year, there were over two hundred. In most instances there had merely been a change of management. The capitalist mode of production never altered. The new management were the committees. And although international capital was uncooperative in terms of sales, credits and raw materials (Marks and Spencer reduced their purchases from Portugal by 60 percent because they didn't want to trade with "workers' control"), enterprises continued to function.

It is difficult to draw up an overall balance sheet. Despite the number of meetings communication remained difficult. One of the main short-comings was the lack of any organisation controlled from below. The unions and parties fought for domination of the plenários. In many cases the Committees didn't represent the majority of the workers, despite the fact that the workers had democratically elected them. Although an editorial in a strike paper said "It is only ourselves, organised with other workers, who can change society. Our capacity for work, our sense of justice and social conscience will in the end create the kind of society that we workers want," the workers in many cases put the onus of strug-gle on the Committees and remained passive themselves, expecting the Committees to get on with it, alone. Power was a hot potato.

THE TRADE UNION QUESTION

There were three basic proposals concerning trade union structure: *plural-ismo*, *unidade*, and *unicidade* (pluralistic, united, and monolithic, or totally integrated). They had been proposed by the PPD, PS, and PCP respectively. The employers at this stage were weak and poorly organised and preferred to deal with a fragmented trade union structure. On October 4, the PPD voiced their viewpoint: "*Pluralismo* results from the free assembly of the workers, and not from any law limiting the right to unionise. It is *unicidade* which has existed since April 25. This pattern can be seen in all countries where there is a dictatorship, be it of the Right or of the Left."

The PS was more sophisticated. It called for *unidade* (trade union unity). But it opposed the setting up of a single trade union federation to which all workers would belong. It had little industrial base itself and was afraid of the power that would be wielded by the PCP if Intersindical were to become such a federation. Both the PPD and PS were fighting Intersindical though rarely mentioning it by name. The trouble was that Intersindical was giving them the weapons to fight with.

The PCP and its satellites called for unicidade. Their implantation in industry was such that they could readily control any general body that was set up. The unity they wanted was the unity of the spider with the midges caught in its web.

A demonstration was called by Intersindical for January 14. It was supported (because sponsored) by the PCP. The MDP-CDE (which had recently constituted itself a political party) gave immediate support, adding to existing fears that it was merely a front for the PCP. The idea was to have "one big union" for the whole of Portugal. The Council of Twenty issued a statement claiming that they unanimously supported *unicidade*.[9] Two days before the demonstration the spokesman for the CCP of MFA, Vasco Lourenço, read a statement on TV: "The MFA knows full well the problems which face the country and has the necessary cohesion to deal with them. It is clear that the vast majority of workers have opted for uni- cidade. However certain people would like to see a split in the MFA or in its Superior Council. They raise doubts about the positions of its members and make insinuations about some kind of compromise between the PCP and the MFA, saying that this compromise was against the PS and PPD."[10]

The question began to threaten the whole Coalition Government. At a meeting of the Council of State, both Sá Carneiro and Mário Soares threatened to resign if the law was implemented. Outside the govern- ment the question was discussed feverishly. Various groups published detailed positions. Over the radio stations support for *unidade* was read out in communiqués from unions, in discussion programmes and in pro- grammes dealing with working-class history. Rádio Clube Português and RTP were strong in their support. In fact, outside of the Maoists, almost every left-wing group supported the demonstration that was rapidly becoming more a demonstration of PCP influence (and of its ability to drag all sorts of so-called left and revolutionary organisations in its wake) than anything relating to the real interests of the working class. Except for small theoretical groups there was no opposition at all. Three hundred thousand workers from all over the country finally massed in Lisbon for the largest demonstration since May 1, 1974.[11]

Banners were varied: "Banks for the People, Now"; "Against Capitalist Unity of Unions"; "Struggle to Create Popular Power"; "Workers' Government, Yes—Bosses' Government, No." Banners of Workers' Committees and unions floated side by side in the breeze, epitomising the very different ideas prevailing within the class. Passing the PS headquarters the crowds shouted louder and louder "Out with the CIA, Out with NATO." From 7 p.m. onward, the demonstration wound slowly around Lisbon like a gigantic earthworm, pulling itself and its contingents along behind it,

---

9   In the summer of 1976, it came to light that the voting had only been twelve for and eight against. The MFA had claimed their vote was "unanimous" in order to hide their developing divisions. Among the dissenters were some future members of "The Group of Nine."

10   *A Capital*, January 12, 1975.

11   *Combate* and *A Batalha* were examples. The *Economist* said at the time that *unicidade* was the only capitalist solution since it allowed a firm control of the labour force, which would not exist if pluralism was adopted.

flexing its muscles outside hostile buildings, dragging itself along to the offices of the Ministry of Labour, where representatives of Intersindical and the Minister of a labour himself, José Costa Martins, started to speak. Costa Martins said it was "no longer a question of which type of unity, but rather whether the will of the majority was going to be respected or not."

The Socialist Party was not going to be pressurised by such a display of force. Their meeting on January 16 brought out fifteen thousand people to defend the idea of pluralismo. Mário Soares who, over the previous days, had been busy discussing Angola with the MPLA, FNLA, and UNITA in the Algarve had returned to Lisbon. He turned on the PCP. "If the PCP doesn't play the game of democracy this will be a tragedy for the Portuguese people." Second-in-command Salgado Zenha claimed that "this was a decisive moment, the future of democracy and socialism is at risk. The proposed law about the unions was not made by the unions. It was made at the Faculty of Law in Coimbra . . . The Provisional Government never knew its content . . . As socialists, we oppose the law. The Minister of Labour is in the hands of Intersindical. We also denounce the PCP, which is sabotaging democracy in Portugal."

Soares followed up this attack by saying that it was not merely a question of the unions. "The radio and TV were also being manipulated. To give an example: if there were really a million or so workers in favour of unicidade, why was our offer to debate the question on TV refused? Who is afraid of open discussion?"

But all this was demagogy. No one was talking about the real issues. The argument between the PPD, PS, and PCP was really about how best to control the workers, in the Portugal of the future. Everyone was showing his true colours. On January 21, 1975—a week after the giant Intersindical demonstration—the Third Provisional Government voted to pass the law. On paper, this tidied things up. In reality, things hardly changed. Relations between unions and Committees remained an open question.

Opposition to PCP domination of the trade unions was not confined to the PS and PPD. There was opposition at the base, too. While the politicians felt threatened by the power of Intersindical, the workers did too, but in a very different way. PCP control of the unions was an obstacle to the waging of the class struggle. As the class struggle could not be wished away it found other means of self-expression.

Most working-class demands, as has been shown, were formulated by the Committees, not by the unions. When it came to organising to get anything done the unions in general and Intersindical in particular, cautioned against striking, saying it would only help the fascists. At this stage a number of Committees—and even some of the unions—openly attacked PCP domination of the trade union apparatus. This took several forms:

The workers in the chemical industry had been holding plenários throughout the summer months and these decided to call for an increase in wages. The union—in which the Maoists had some influence—soon found itself in open conflict with Intersindical and attacked it—and its supporters in the media—for restricting free discussion on the question of strikes. At the end of October, the union leadership issued the following statement, which was published in several papers: "We must alert public opinion against the efforts of certain opportunistic forces that use all sorts of methods to control the existing unions and to carry out their treason of the working class. We know the methods of spreading rumours and of lying. But now we see the principal organs of communication openly collaborating in this process."

The union continued its battle against Intersindical and the Intersindical position on strikes, but later broke up. One part fully reintegrated itself into the Committees movement. Those for whom control of a union was more important set up a new group—the AOC—"to fight the revisionist PCP."

Other activities, although triggered by specific circumstances, led to even deeper insights. The dockworkers of the Port of Lisbon had marched into the town on November 11, calling for economic equality with other workers and denouncing the Dockers' Union as being an ex-PIDE organisation. (The President of the Dockers' Union had been a member of the ANP.) "A total remodelling is necessary," their communiqué said, "since the union is completely implicated in the old regime. We must continue the struggle outside the unions."[12]

THE EMERGENCE OF INTER-EMPRESAS

In January 1975 it was decided, on the initiative of Efacec-Inel, to set up a Federation of Workers' Committees under the name of Inter-Empresas. This linked twenty-four firms, among them the largest in Portugal, "to aid and support workers" struggles. Inter-Empresas formed a bloc on a par with Intersindical and in many ways soon became more popular. The companies represented were: Efacec-Inel, TLP, TAP, Lisnave, Setenave, ENI, Siderurgia, Cergal, Plessey, Timex, Fábrica Portugal, Rebel, Dyrup, Tecnividro, Sotécnica, Applied Magnetics, Acta, Bertrand, Nitratos de

---

12   *A Capital*, October 15, 1974.

Portugal, Messa, EIP, Pfizer, Xavier de Lima, and INE. The workers in many other companies gave support. Some of the firms involved were part of large combines and the workers proceeded to contact their mates in other companies within the combine. The Ministry of Labour didn't help at all, preferring to deal with Intersindical, of whose political support it was sure. The Minister of Labour and the leaders of Intersindical were, anyway, both in the orbit of the PCP.

Inter-Empresas had no political or judicial status either within or outside the production process. Yet the problem of political intervention did not happen by default. When NATO forces were scheduled to arrive in Lisbon on February 7, 1975, the government forbade all demonstrations, explaining that the visit was purely a routine one and had been organised a year earlier. Inter-Empresas was not convinced. Nor were thousands of other workers who saw it as an attempt to assert an authoritarian presence in Portugal.

Inter-Empresas called a demonstration. The government initially prohibited it, saying the moment was "inopportune." The PCP attacked the proposed demonstration viciously, comparing it to the activities of the "silent majority" on September 28. The PCP then organised a "carnival" for the same day, which was a traditional holiday. Inter-Empresas remained firm. It reiterated its call for people to demonstrate both against NATO and against the high level of redundancies. "We cannot separate redundancies from imperialism. The question of redundancies is not a question of bad management. It is the direct result of a system—the capitalist system—supported by imperialism. We cannot allow NATO, the shock troops of imperialism, quietly to land on our soil."

On February 6, the "Federation of Southern Unions" (one of the main sections of Intersindical) put out a statement denouncing the Inter-Empresas call as "yet another attempt to create confusion among the workers." But the demonstration went ahead as planned. Some forty thousand people took part. A huge banner, stretching from one pavement to the other led the way. It read: "Redundancies are the inevitable consequence of the capitalist system. The workers must destroy this system and build a new world."

The demonstrators made for the Ministry of Labour. Security police arrived in force, but retreated seeing the size of the crowd. COPCON then turned up, and followed the demonstration in jeeps.

As they passed the American Cultural Centre the demonstrators shouted loud and clear: "Out with NATO, out with CIA." The soldiers of

RAL-I (Light Artillery Regiment no. 1), instructed to guard the building, were bewildered. This was no right-wing demonstration. When the demonstrators shouted, "The soldiers are sons of the people," they echoed the slogan, raising their fists in solidarity. It was a sight to melt any proletarian heart. The demonstrators were in seventh heaven.

Outside the Ministry of Labour (deserted by its PCP incumbent) a worker from Efacec-Inel read out a manifesto. He called Intersindical an organisation for class collaboration and said, "The task of the working class is not to negotiate with the ruling class but to destroy it." Cheers from the audience. He then gave an accurate description of what was happening. "The demands in the factories are increasing and the workers are beginning to relegate their union organisations into second place. The Workers' Committees came into existence as the means chosen by the workers to further the class struggle. Reformist and revisionist organisations are attempting to take over the unions and to emasculate the Committees." Repeated attacks on the PCP were made, though the Party was never referred to by name.

The demonstration certainly had an impact. NATO troops in uniform were refused permission to land, most of them having to spend the week on their ships. February 7 had marked the entry of Inter-Empresas onto the political scene. Its demonstration had been supported by all the revolutionary groups. But Inter-Empresas didn't form a political organisation of its own. The Federation remained economic. Politics, for the moment, was left to the politicians, who were looking after their own interests. Major Melo Antunes's Economic Plan was approved by the government on the very next day.

The new Economic Plan included seventy short-term measures. Talking about the plan (*Diário Popular*, February 28, 1975) Melo Antunes elaborated on his vision of socialism. "It excludes the social-democratic control of the management of capitalism . . . but it does not exclude a pluralistic society . . . the class struggle now under way must take into account the alternative role which the middle classes can now play." Through CIP, forty-seven thousand companies announced their support for the new plan.

The demonstrators of February 7 had demanded the destruction of the system and the building of a new world. All the government could dish up was a mixture of small-scale nationalisation and a vague Third Worldism: a "revolutionary" recipe for maintaining capitalism.

V THE AGRARIAN STRUGGLES

THE RURAL STRUCTURE

The rural pattern differed strikingly between North and South. In the South, a few *latifundiários* (big ranchers) controlled some 1,103 latifundios of more than five hundred hectares, occupying 30 percent of all the land under cultivation in Portugal. But in the North there were only thirty-seven latifundios larger than five hundred hectares and over half the holdings were small plots of less than one hectare (a hectare is about the size of a football field) of usually arid and rocky land.[1] Here, whole families eked out a miserable living, growing vegetables or in some cases minding a few sheep or a cow or two. They subsisted on their own produce. Clearly the smallest plots were underdeveloped.

Many of the agrarian "capitalists" in the South never lived on the land themselves, only visiting it at certain times of the year. Eucalyptus and cork trees provided a way out for many, since they required few workers and little care. Other latifundios were only used as hunting grounds. One of the richest latifundiários, Manuel Vinhas, who was also one of the largest shareholders in SCC (beer), had installed a silver-plated urinal coated with velvet (surely an object of envy for reactionary Dadaists) in his mansion near Alcácer.

Agriculture was clearly in stagnation. It accounted for 30 percent of the national product in 1954, but fell to 18.8 percent by 1975. Cattle-rearing techniques were primitive and vegetable products accounted for over half the total agricultural produce. The situation for agricultural workers was even worse than these figures might suggest. Rural unemployment was widespread, partly masked by seasonal fluctuations. From November to March, there was hardly any work at all. The average yearly

---

1   In the North, 212,111 rented holdings together only covered 332,353 hectares. For anyone with a little imagination, this will spell out the size of most of the Northern holdings.

wage indicated an unbelievable, almost unimaginable poverty. People were peasants and treated as such.

Protective tariffs were the main custodians of social privilege. They had existed for agricultural products since the time of Salazar and the Estado Novo. Because of the assured home market very little development had taken place. The extraction of surplus labour and surplus value were assured by the National Republican Guard and the police. The average daily wage in 1968 was 59 escudos for men, 30 for women. When the great strike movement began in 1953, in the Alentejo, 109 peasants were machine-gunned for demanding a wage increase. A peasant leader, Catarina Eufémia, who had led a deputation from the fields to the house of the manager to ask for better conditions was ambushed by the National Republican Guard and killed. The protest was treated as a communist insurrection and brutally put down. Such are some of the memories of the agricultural workers of the Alentejo.

EARLY CONFRONTATIONS

April 25 created its own movement in the countryside. The Union of Agricultural workers in Beja (Alentejo) was one of the first to organise. In September 1974, it proposed a new contract for agricultural workers. Discussions took place with the Free Association of Farmers (ALA), the mouthpiece for large and medium-scale farmers, in the presence of the Minister of Labour and of representatives of the MFA. The new contract raised the minimum daily wage to 120 escudos. Its third clause allowed "lands which were either totally or partially undeveloped to be taken over by the number of workers considered necessary to ensure their cultiva-tion." It prepared the way for "agrarian reform" and was obviously open to very varying interpretations.

The PCP slogan was "the land to those who work it." The Party, which had wide support in the countryside because of its previous history of strug-gle, was seeking to gain the widest possible electoral support, from agricul-tural labourers to smallholders. It directed its critique at the owners of the fifty or so great latifundios, calling for the nationalisation of these estates.

A number of small unions had sprung up and a "League of Small and Medium Farmers" began to gain support. It had been set up by the PCP to divert support from ALA, most active in the southern Alentejo. Because they lacked organisation, workers were fired more easily on the large estates than in the factories. In early November 1974, three hundred workers were sacked from a farm in Serpa, Alentejo, the owners having refused to abide by the new contract. The union under the control of the PCP, whose nucleus had existed prior to April 25, organised a demonstration on November 4. It urged:

> We must take immediate measures against absenteeism and economic sabotage. This would get rid of the labour surplus and improve productivity in the countryside. The agricultural workers realise the crisis in the country, a crisis for which they are not responsible and which is due to fascist policies and colonial wars, fought in the interests of the large capitalists. We understand the complexity of the economic situation. We are willing to make sacrifices if necessary. We will not press for our immediate demands. But the bosses must make sacrifices too. They must agree to increase our miserable wages. They have extorted exorbitant rents. The workers cannot forget what the bosses have done during 48 years, however much the bosses might prefer to forget it.

But new forces were also being thrown up. The Red Committee of Alentejo was gaining support. It referred as follows to the new agreement worked out between the union and the government:

> The agricultural workers have a new contract for a year. But why doesn't the contract guarantee work, and all that work implies? Why, when it rains, does the boss only pay one hour's work? On these days don't we also eat? Why is it that the workers can be fired at two days' notice? Why do the bosses continue to live the high life, while the workers live in shameful poverty? The sowing time ends and the olives are picked. But after that, what happens? The tractor drivers and the rest of the workers are thrown into misery. How long will this go on?
>
> Why is there a distinction between full-time and casual employment? In the end we are all full-time workers. Haven't we all worked all our lives for the bosses? If we work one month for the boss, and then change bosses, are we any the less full-time?
>
> Who finally makes this distinction? It is clearly the bosses. The rich say we can't all be full-time because there isn't work all the year round. But whose fault is that?
>
> Who is it who keeps thousands of hectares in poor condition, just so they can go and hunt? Who puts fierce bulls to graze, where

wheat should be planted? The people don't want to know about bull-fights. They want bread for their children. Fierce bulls are put on land which the people need. They are fattened merely to be killed in the ring, while the people need meat.

And who is it who goes to pick olives, which thousands eat, from the olive trees? And who leaves the olives, lying to die on the olive branches?

Who pays for the guns of the "silent Majority," the guns that have crossed our frontiers? Who is guilty of refusing bread to the poor? Who is going abroad to buy arms to massacre the people?

No one should have illusions about all this. The crisis in the economy is going to increase. Having lost the profits of colonial exploitation the bourgeoisie have only one way to maintain their wealth: to increase exploitation in Portugal, causing more redundancies, increasing the work load, obliging the workers to pay with misery for the crisis which the bourgeoisie and they alone created. No one should have any illusions. While there are bosses there will be poverty.

It is not only in Alentejo that there is unemployment. All over the country the bourgeoisie are causing massive cutbacks. In some places it is said that the bosses are doing this to pit the workers against the government. But to whom are the workers to look, if the government passes laws which allow the employers to do this?

Comrades! Against the manoeuvres of the bourgeoisie the workers must answer with revolutionary action. The unity of the workers in town and countryside must be reinforced to overthrow, once and for all, the power of the ruling classes and create a popular democracy which will

- give the land to those who work it
- expropriate all the latifundiários
- give the factories to those who toil in them
- nationalise all the banks, so that the people can administer public money.

Red Committee of Alentejo, November 1974.

The Red Committee represented some thousand workers from the region of Castro Verde, in southern Alentejo. It was nonparty. One of its members was arrested for killing a *latifundiário* (a certain Columbano, who had been a PIDE agent and had caused the imprisonment of dozens of local activists). While the Committee advised against any further "individualistic acts," it nevertheless put what had happened in proper perspective:

> The action of our comrade José Diogo was an act of popular justice, a blow against reaction. It was the almost correct answer to the great estate owners. We say "almost correct" because it is not in this manner that we can overthrow the regime of bandits who have always robbed the people. The blow cannot come from the single hand of a single comrade, but from our united hands.
>
> José Diogo's reasons are our reasons too. We are the workers on one side of the barricades. On the other side are the robbers, the latifundiários. After April 25, the workers, without fear, asked for their rights. We were prepared to talk to the owners. But they weren't prepared to talk. They wanted open warfare. If this is what they want we shall give it to them. We, the workers, are not going back.
>
> The owners walk like wild beasts. They know that the workers want an end to private property. They know that we want the land for those who work it.
>
> Comrades, we are approaching the decisive battles here, in Alentejo. Our comrade Zé Diogo deserves our support. The boss says that this tractor driver murdered Columbano. The boss's truth is one truth; the truth of the workers is another. Our truth is this: a worker defended his right to work and struck a long-standing fascist. Columbano, an old friend of Salazar, was known to be a PIDE agent. Let us show that the arm of Zé Diogo is the arm of all workers.
>
> An end to misery.
>
> For the right to work.
>
> Solidarity with Zé Diogo.
>
> Popular justice, yes. Fascism, no.
>
> Long live the working class.[2]

Diogo was arrested by the PSP. He was released shortly after, only to be rearrested by the MFA. He eventually faced charges, but for the moment, the entire legal system was in chaos, oscillating between the old civil courts and the decisions of the MFA.

---

2   *Revolução*, December 6, 1974.

TAKING THE LAND

At the end of January 1975, *A Capital* featured an article with a photograph of a land occupation in Outeiro (near Beja, in the Alentejo) carried out by an armed group of workers. Other occupations quickly followed. COPCON often disarmed the groups involved but did not seek to evict them. The occupations took two distinct forms, depending on the area. Basically, these were the reappropriation of leased plots by evicted tenants, and collective occupations by agricultural labourers.

In Alcácer do Sal, in western Alentejo, some very large estates were to be found. The land was either leased out to tenants who then worked small plots, or it was used to grow olive and eucalyptus trees. Large areas on the estates were going to waste. Tenants who had worked the land for some forty years had recently been evicted. At first three or four of them reclaimed their holdings . . . by occupying them. Others, emboldened, followed suit. They then held a big meeting at which various suggestions were made. One was to work the land individually, each tenant being responsible for his former plot on the estate. Some unemployed workers present disagreed. They wanted a "solution" that would involve them too. Finally, it was decided to set up a cooperative and pool all the holdings. The National Republican Guard was instructed not to interfere and the local MDP–controlled Municipal Council promised support. One of the leaders, Maria, described events as follows:

> Before, because we could do nothing, we kept quiet. But after April
> 25th we talked about these lands which had once been owned by
> others. We gave a list of the previous tenants to the Câmara. Dona
> Laura Carraças (the owner) refused to attend a meeting. We decided
> to occupy the lands . . . The land was divided between 90 of us . . .
> We are thinking of creating a cooperative and of uniting with the
> other occupations to make an even bigger cooperative. We have
> begun to work the land and we hope to get a tractor.[3]

Near Santarém, north of Lisbon, the same was taking place. At Carrascal, in January 1975, some hundred agricultural workers and ex-tenants occupied a farm which had been bought in 1969 by Augusto Felix da Costa. (The latter had evicted all the tenants and many of the local population had been forced to emigrate.) The owner fled. A delegation was sent to the MFA who ratified the occupation. The second type of occupation was carried out solely by agricultural workers. The land of the Duke of Lafões,

---

3   *Revolução*, January 24, 1975.

for instance, had long been left underdeveloped. The workers of Alcoentre, in Ribatejo, had suffered much hardship as a result. They occupied the land, setting up the cooperatives of Torre Bela and Ameixoeira:

> When the nation needs food, it is a crime to allow the land to lie fallow, or to be overgrown by eucalyptus. What right have the capitalists to leave the land in such a state? the workers asked. Occupying the estate, they requested some old agricultural machinery belonging to a nearby penal colony. The agricultural workers demand that these machines, which are lying idle, be put at the service of the people. There are properties managed by the penal colony which are not being cultivated. These could be put at the disposal of the workers of Alcoentre, who are thinking of organising themselves in a cooperative. Collectivisation and socialisation of these lands is the only way of giving control to the producers.

In the face of these events, which it had initiated but was unable to control, the PCP denounced previous occupations as "anarchistic." It proposed that all future occupations be undertaken and managed by the unions (which they controlled).

The workers, however, didn't listen to this suggestion. Most of the occupations which were to follow were organised by workers recently made redundant. In Casebres (in Alentejo, near Alcácer) workers occupied land in the parish of Our Lady of Machede. The PCP, present at the original meeting, advised against the occupation. Captain Cardoso of the MFA said that "if the workers lifted a finger against these particular lands, they would all end up in prison." A PCP member informed the local garrison in Évora and troops were sent out to stop the action. A meeting was arranged between the workers and a group of small farmers in the area, who likewise advised against the occupation. The workers complained to COPCON, who offered support. The women walked out of the meeting, rounded up the men, and went ahead with the occupation. The land in question belonged to a Don João de Noronha, a *latifundiário*. Some 1,500 hectares were involved at this stage. Later, after March 11, all 4,000 hectares of the estate were occupied. As in many occupations, women took the initiative.

There were many other such cases (in Monte da Virgem, in Vendinha, and in Reguengos de Monsaraz, to mention but a few). After the occupations had been completed, the union would usually appear on the scene, seeking to give it an "objective," such as the forty-five-hour week or a minimum wage. At the demonstration at Beja, on February 2, 1975, the

Minister of Agriculture, Esteves Belo, had spelled out the government's line: "The country at present imports many agricultural products for national consumption. All land must be worked fully to create new wealth. The state will undertake the expropriation of land from large estate owners. These lands will be administered by the state. A certain cultural revolution will be made in these estates, which in the end will ensure maximum productivity. The owners will be obliged to cooperate. The state agrees with and supports all occupations of land not at present under cultivation."

But not all the great estates were to be taken over: "There are estate owners who are doing their job. They must receive our respect."

A pattern was beginning to emerge whereby every spontaneous struggle led to an intervention of the state, thereby widening and strengthening its area of social control. We shall return to this theme later. This state-capitalist programme was supported by all the political parties in the coalition. Occupations of uncultivated land continued. Some far-sighted landowners actually supported the movement, handing over selected parts of their estates to the workers.

Of greater importance were the moves taken by such autonomous groups as the Red Committee of Alentejo; after the PCP and MDP, they were the groups most to be reckoned with. The PCP and MDP were important, not because of their mass support, but because they had taken over the old rural apparatus: the Juntas, the Casas do Povo and the administrative centres. The Red Committee and others were important because they more closely expressed the aspirations of ordinary agricultural workers.

At this stage, there was no serious attempt to implement collectivisation of the land, or to abolish capitalist norms of distribution. These matters remained restricted to discussions among left-wing intellectuals. Both the PCP and MDP accepted collectivisation in theory, but made no attempt (either before March 11 or after) to implement it in practice.

In the North, the situation was very different. Here existed the majority of the smallholdings, and political ignorance and old fears died hard. The ex-ANP estate owners, in the rich, wine-growing districts of the Douro valley, were now members of the CDS or PPD. Workers were still left with their old insecurity. The Church in most cases was anticommunist, "communism" being depicted in terms of the PCP. Sermons and CDS leaflets spelled all this out in no uncertain terms. The evening papers from Porto or Lisbon rarely reached these regions and, when they did, were likely to be several days old. At least 35 percent of the people, possibly more, were illiterate.

Two forces sprung up to challenge this. The first was the MFA, who, since September 1974, had initiated what they called a campaign of "Cultural Dynamisation." Groups of MFA supporters entered villages, played revolutionary songs, and talked to the people about their problems. They explained what April 25 meant: that anyone could speak their mind, now that the PIDE agents had been imprisoned. In general, these visits were successful, though often only the "natural leader" of the village spoke out. In some cases, the meeting produced surprising results, at times broadcast over television. In one village, for example, the MFA arrived, sang songs, talked about April 25, and then asked the villagers to speak. An old man said that there were very few problems in the village. When the MFA insisted that some problems surely existed the old man replied that there were none. "There were one or two communists, but they weren't really a problem."

Another force in the countryside was the students. Making use of the demand for higher education, the government had decreed that before anyone could enter a university, a technical college, or a school of agronomy, he or she had to do a year of fieldwork. The idea was to send educated young people into the provinces, to teach the others to read, and to impart to them what skills they had. Some twenty-eight thousand students were involved. The plan was supported by the UEC, the PCP's student organisation.

This Serviço Cívico was criticised by most students from both right- and left-wing positions. It was also criticised by the Northern workers and farmers as "insulting." Right-wing students objected to the scheme because it jeopardised the social privileges of the middle and upper-class youth: the only way round the Serviço Cívico was to give up going to university altogether. Left-wing students criticised the scheme from a variety of positions. A MES teachers' group issued a statement which epitomised such attitudes to the plan. What the left-wing students objected to was not the principle of the Serviço Cívico, but its organisation and planning by a capitalist government.

Students of the "agricultural colleges" occupied their colleges, insisting:

a) That they would undertake no work which could be done by the agricultural workers who were being made redundant and
b) That they should have complete autonomy from the MFA and from party-politicians. They would only implement decisions taken by joint plenários of agricultural workers and students.

Thousands of students nevertheless went to the countryside, teaching and working on the farms. They constituted a miniarmy of militants, who "helped" in organising occupations and planning. Education in agricultural techniques, soil analysis, and "agitation" went hand in hand. Other problems, like distribution of food to the cities, were also discussed. Collectivisation of land remained, however, the prerequisite to any reorganisation of agriculture. While this did not theoretically prove too great a problem in the latifundios of the South, it was a very different matter in the North.

VI THE POLITICAL CHESSBOARD

THE RIGHT

The MFA was the real locus of decision-making during the period before the first elections (April 1975), a period which they designed as "pre-democratic." But neither the armed forces as a whole nor the MFA were homogeneous bodies. They represented various ideological and class positions. This, however, only became obvious later.

The political parties followed more clearly divergent ends and soon appeared to monopolise the struggle for power. These civilian groups fought for or against the elections articulated various alternative patterns of social reconstruction.

By July 1974, between seventy and eighty political parties existed. After September 28, certain right-wing groups ceased to exist or fused with others. With Tomás and Caetano gone, the old Right was in havoc and latent divergences within the Caetano camp came to a head. The old ANP had never been a cohesive body, and its former deputies now landed in many parties. The CDS, founded by Freitas do Amaral, ex-adviser to Caetano and professor of law at Lisbon University, was by far the most powerful and active. Other founding members included Pintado, Brandão, and Machado, all former deputies who had represented the mainstream of the old conservatism. The CDS was supported by the catholic Opus Dei and by certain priests, especially in the North. Backed by the CUF trust and the de Melo family, the CDS used all available modern techniques of political marketing: slick posters, advertising, films, and videos. They published their programme in *Diário de Notícias* on November 25, taking up two whole pages. They advocated state "support" for hospitals, education, etc. Their strategy was to begin in the provinces, where there was less political sophistication, and work towards holding a conference in Lisbon. Regional CDS publications spoke of "the communist takeover in Lisbon" and "our overseas territories, overrun by red terrorists."

The PDC (Christian Democratic Party) was also an offshoot of the former regime. Perhaps the real representative of the old fascist movement, it stood to the right even of the CDS. Salazar himself had founded it after the coup of 1926. Many of its supporters had been—and still were—members of the Portuguese Confederation of Industry (CIP). The party claimed thirty-seven thousand members in the North (in December 1974) though these figures were probably sheer fantasy. It supported a presidential system, with Spínola as President, and used the right-wing symbol of the Gaelic Cross (which had been used by the Crusaders). The PDC had extremely active graffiti writers: the walls of Lisbon were plastered with its initials. It openly espoused the Catholic Church as an ally. In many ways, the PDC represented the purest forms of Salazarist ideology.

Other groupuscules of the extreme Right were poorly organised but not totally irrelevant. They were splinters of the former repressive apparatus of the state. Small groups of ex-Legion members, ex-PIDEs, and small businessmen could still muster enough wealth (and weaponry) to constitute a source of trouble. The Liberal Party ("Communism is worse than Fascism"), the Party of Progress (ex-Federalist Party) and the Popular Portuguese Movement had all been active enough to be implicated in the September 28 disaster. They lay discredited behind their respective arsenals. Behind April 25, in their eyes, was the incompetence of Caetano whom they denounced as a liberal and blamed for the multiracialism that existed in the colonies. Other groups, like the Independent Social-Democratic Party (PSDI), represented the middle-business world. Led by ex-Prime Minister Palma Carlos, it had also attempted to "halt the left-wing tide." But these groups could not agree among themselves (except on September 28) and remained weak.

The youth section of the CDS attempted to meet on November 4, 1974 in a Lisbon theatre, just down the road from the old PIDE headquarters. The Maoist MRPP demonstrated outside the theatre, shouting, "The PIDE killed in this street," and "against fascism, popular unity." They linked arms across the narrow road, confronting the riot police who had arrived. The police opened fire, using tear gas. The Maoists replied with stones, whereupon the police shot into the crowd killing one and wounding sixteen. Among the wounded was Saldanha Sanches, director of the MRPP newspaper *Luta Popular*, who had been released from prison after September 28 as a result of left-wing pressure. At 9 p.m., incensed demonstrators marched off to the CDS headquarters, broke down the main door, and destroyed all the documents and files, helping themselves to duplicating machines and other equipment. The CDS claimed that they had sought the aid of COPCON, but that no response had been forthcoming. COPCON arrived and was cheered by the crowd. No arrests were made. The whole episode showed a considerable ambiguity over tactics on both sides. MES called the action "exhibitionist" and called for "struggles against concrete forms of capitalism and exploitation."

THE CENTRE

During the first six months, all political groups were treated equally by the predominantly left-wing press. A manifesto from PRP got as much space as one from the PPD or PS. The so-called revolutionary Left called demonstrations and controlled the streets in many ways, while the Centre parties (PPD, PS) and to a certain extent the leftish PCP controlled the government. The first PS congress, on December 13, 1974, was showered with fraternal greetings from all the parties of the Second International. Their guest of honour had been Santiago Carillo, who spoke on behalf of the Spanish Communist Party. This easy "internationalism" gave the PS a certain political muscle. But their congress also revealed the frail structure on which the party was built. Internal squabbles threatened to wreck the whole edifice on important issues such as the relationship of the party to the Church, or to the left-wing groups. Mário Soares had always been a member of the Lisbon upper crust. His family owned the Colégio Moderno, an exclusive private school where many of the current professional politicians had received their education. In gesture and speech he showed all the attributes of the middle class. He was an opportunist par excellence, always in touch with the base of the party, and a master at riding storms. GAPS (an independent group within the PS) contained members of Soares's own family. This tendency had supported the Maoists on certain demonstrations. Many CDE supporters had flocked to the PS after April 25 and were to the left of the leadership. In fact, soon after the first congress, a major split occurred in the PS, which took three thousand members out of the party. The new group (the FSP or Popular Socialist Front) said that what was at stake was not merely a question of leadership or personalities, it was the class struggle. Led by Manuel Serra, it called for solidarity with MES and LUAR. Outlining a programme in eleven points, it attacked "a cult of personality which defended, with nice Marxist phrases, the interests of the ruling class." Like most other groups the FSP defended the "Alliance of the MEA with the people."

Soares was the darling of international social-democracy. His party received financial help from all the major parties of the Second International, and especially from the British Labour Party and French Socialist Party. Edward Kennedy sent friendly telegrams and in February 1975 actually attended a round table discussion with the PS leaders.

The difference between the PCP and PS positions on the question of trade union organisation reflected the differences in the type of future each envisaged. The PCP saw the future in terms of state capitalism whereas the PS defended the so-called mixed economy. This difference was the main source of the PS's popularity among international capitalists. The PS was less sycophantic than the PCP and more attuned to the general mood. They could denounce the persecution of the Maoists (though in a back-handed way: "such groups are unimportant"). PS militants never indulged in the sort of deliberate antistrike campaigns spearheaded by the PCP. The PS had supported the CTT strike in July, while the PCP had violently denounced it. They appeared liberal compared to the ultraconservative "communists."

But the PS call for "pluralistic democracy" was merely just a call for liberal capitalism. Support was measured in those days by the ability to mobilise mass demonstrations. By these standards the PS was not as deeply rooted as the PCP, whatever may have been revealed later during the elections. By the same yardstick the PPD was also weak, its support being among the middle classes who, on the whole won't gladly take to the streets. During the first few months after April 25, the bourgeoisie and middle classes had no independent political voice whatsoever, other than through these parties.

The government coalition of parties was due more to an imposed necessity than to any willing cooperation. In fact it always threatened to break up, although none of its component parties could safely have resigned. Over issues like Intersindical and the Parish Juntas fierce squabbling persisted. If they were to get anywhere the PCP needed to remain close to the MFA. But they also needed to eliminate their political rivals, or at least (and for the time being) to keep one step ahead of them.

A week after the smashing of the CDS congress in Porto the PS had called for a demonstration in Lisbon to commemorate the abortive Porto uprising of 1895 by Republican forces. This demonstration might have proved very popular.

The PCP and its satellites reacted strongly. They spoke of a "new conspiracy" from the Right and called for the "reinforcement of democratic unity." They proposed their own demonstration, also for January 31, 1975.

The MDP–CDE, MES, and FSP of course supported the PCP. "A new silent majority is arising," claimed MES. FSP warned that "bourgeois organisations in the service of capitalism were spreading propaganda to the effect that the democratic rights conquered on April 25 were in danger. What exists is very different. There are conservative and reactionary forces who fear the advance of the democratic process and are trying to stop it, just as they tried to on September 28. The conspiracy of the bourgeoisie is being promoted by those who, on the 28th, affirmed (with little conviction) that they supported the programme of the MFA. We call for a large mobilisation on January 31, at 7:30 p.m. at Entrecampos, to support the MFA and to smash the provocateurs and conspirators."

Communiqués from MDP and MES, read over the radio, were in much the same vein. A confrontation between the PS and the PCP seemed unavoidable. If the Socialists backed down they would be politically disgraced. They stuck to their guns, attacking the PCP for not being democratic, and asserted that they would carry on with their planned demonstration. On January 30 the Maoist MRPP, not to be left out, called for a third demonstration in yet another part of Lisbon.

Mário Soares appeared on television. He said that as far as his party was concerned "the demonstrations called by the PCP and others were counterdemonstrations." He also asked people "to fight for the elections and against the reaction." Cunhal refused to take part in a televised discussion of these matters.

Tension mounted, fed by plenty of rumours but few facts. "NATO ships had been spotted off the northern coast of Portugal." The "news" seemed to give credence to the idea of some right-wing attempt on Portugal. It was even rumoured that Soares had asked for international aid.

After last minute meetings between Soares and Cunhal both demonstrations were eventually called off. The FSP and MDP duly endorsed the decision. Only MES decided to carry on. The MRPP said that nothing would stop their demonstration. MES said they would have a short meeting, no more. COPCON circled the Rossio where the MRPP demonstration was to be held. Half a dozen Maoists were arrested. The crisis had been postponed, not resolved.

THE LEFT

The left groups as a whole should have benefited most from the political vacuum left in the wake of April 25. But, fossilised in their orthodoxies, they had no internal dynamic which might have led to revolutionary forces gathering around them. Their constant claims to be vanguards (and the discussions round this theme) isolated them time and time again. No self-respecting workers were going to allow themselves to be led by a bunch of student radicals, for by and large that is what the groups were. Even when they attracted workers they never managed to rid themselves of their leadership complexes: the workers remained the mass whose function it was to confirm the correctness of duly worked out revolutionary theories. No amount of magic formulas about "the emancipation of the workers being the task of the workers themselves" could get round this.

The array of initials of the various groups was staggering. A glance at a paper at the time would have confronted one with an *embarras de richesses*, with a proliferation of "workers' organisations" to choose from. The Maoists alone provided CARP, CCRML, OCMLP, PC de P (2 factions), FEC-ml, URML, MRPP, etc., etc. For the aficionado of political esoterica the study of their ins and outs might be an interesting, if formidable, task. For someone who already had a headache—after eight or nine hours at work—it was really asking a lot!

A Maoist section had broken away from the PCP in 1964 and formed the FAP (Portuguese Armed Front). A whole series of divergences over tactics had followed, leading to more and more splits. The PCP believed that the break would come within the armed forces (in which they were to be proved correct) and concentrated their action there. Their armed section, known as ARA, although inactive since the 1950s, was nevertheless kept in nominal existence right up to April 25. Other groups launched frontal attacks against the regime and its institutions. In 1969 the Maoist PC de P was formed. Other splits followed, embracing Guevarist and Maoist ideas.

On November 22, 1974, the Maoist MRPP announced its intention of becoming a political party and entering the elections. An interview in *Expresso* on that day attacked the existing government. "The reaction is also within the government," it said. "The government has two tactics: with a smile and democratic pretences they try to fool the people—but when this is no longer possible they use repression and violence. As soon as the counterrevolution, organised and led by the government, is sufficiently strong they will allow it to win." The MRPP differentiated itself from most of the other left-wing groups in seeing the events that led up to April 25 as essentially an attempt by the ruling class to modernise itself. They decided frontally to attack the new regime. They had smashed bank windows on April 25, had openly attacked the police and led the violent offensive against the CDS youth congress in December.

Most of the other left groups held different views on April 25 and sought to "ally themselves to the progressive wing of the MFA" believing that this immoral embrace would bear political fruit. The PRP-BR for instance, which had been born of splits in the PCP in 1970, decided to organise within the general movement after April 25. Unlike the MRPP who wanted to create their "true," "real," "Leninist party of the working class," the PRP-BR oscillated ideologically between the idea of an autonomous movement of the workers and the need for a traditional Bolshevik type party. Combating the fascist and reformist unions they sought to set up "revolutionary unions" in the factories.

Another group who attempted to integrate themselves into the "general movement" was MES, the Movement of the Socialist Left. MES had arisen from a split in the PCP and CDE in 1973. It embraced many intellectuals and technicians and it had militants (or ex-militants) in the Second Provisional Government. In many respects MES was more open and honest than other left groups. It regarded itself as a "movement" rather than a party and claimed that "the conditions for forming a party were not yet right." In an interview with Lucio Magri (member of a breakaway group from the Italian Communist Party) MES spoke of the difficulties of organisation: "The PCP was the only party to emerge from an underground existence with a strong organisation. It is the only party able to mobilise the masses. However the PCP is far from being a vanguard in the Portuguese revolution. What worries us is that the revolutionary vanguards are tiny minorities, 'groupuscules,' while all proclaiming at the same time the need to create a mass party."[1]

Here, in essence, was the problem, though posed in ideological terms. Would all the vanguards become mass parties? Or would there be a falling-out of prophets. MES sensed the difficulty first and launched the slogan of popular power in January 1975. But "popular power" was for MES merely a different route to the same goal: a mass party which they would control.

PRP-BR at first held that "revolutionary unions" would be the base of the party. After fumbling for a while in this particular cul de sac they were eventually to launch their so-called revolutionary councils. But for the time being they were concentrating on building unions.

Thus for both MES and the PRP the problem was that of working-class organisation. While both advocated self-organisation, they both

---

1   *Esquerda Socialista* 8, December 4, 1974.

saw themselves as the hub of that self-organisation. They were blissfully unaware of any contradiction in this.

LUAR, in existence since 1967 as a direct action group, was different. LUAR militants saw themselves as an army of militants who would help the workers whenever called. Concentrating on local issues, they became a "service group" for occupations of houses or other buildings. They rarely if ever sought to manipulate struggles. Both the charisma of Palma Inácio and this type of activity made LUAR popular with the workers.

Politically LUAR comprised tendencies from Luxemburgist to council communism. Their man slogan was "socialism from below." While MES saw the nationalisation of the key industries as the road to socialism (adding that it should be carried out "under workers' control") LUAR criticised this position:

> Nationalisation of the key sectors of the economy is not enough. It is impossible to decree socialism, and then force people to submit to control and decisions by the state. Above all there must be no demobilisation of the autonomous activity of the base, under the pretext that is demanded by "responsible representatives" of the working class . . . The only guarantee for the workers is if power is exercised by the workers themselves, where they live and work. If socialism is not to be a kind of rationalisation, which subordinates and uses the workers with a view to increasing productivity; if socialism is, on the contrary, the subordination of the work process to the interests of those who perform it and their emancipation from capitalist domination, then socialism cannot mean a government for the workers led by a party, group, class or caste. It must mean government by the workers, for the workers . . . Support for the MFA should therefore be conditional, support for its progressive measures which, paradoxically, lead to a diminution of state power as a power above the workers, allowing them to create the embryos of alternative forms of social organisation.[2]

It will be seen that even those whose vision of socialism was most libertarian still had many residual illusions about the role of the MFA and of the state, while those who had few such illusions (such as the MRPP) had a vision of socialism which made of it a nightmare and alienated all potential

---

2   *Fronteira* 6.

support. The MRPP understood power and wanted it for themselves. If they were the wave of the future, no wonder people were seeking dry land.

MES, PRP, MRPP, and the smaller Maoist groups were all active in the factories, usually entering struggles after they had started and seeking to "help" them. In most cases they played a negative role, creating divisions and bringing with them problems which had not been there before.

It was of course impossible for all these vanguard groups to get along with one another since they often clashed in the competition for proletarian clientele. After a while few new people joined such groups. When one party won militants it meant that another had lost them and this probably explained why the various groups attacked one another more fiercely than they ever attacked the Right.

When MES had called for "nationalisation of the banks and insurance companies under workers' control" in their Congress in early 1975 they were attacked as follows by PRP-BR:

> MES held a congress behind locked doors. Intellectuals in the service of the workers, let us look at their practice. Before April 25 MES was engaged in semilegal activities. It was April 25 which created the conditions for MES to grow. A legal party, it was through legal processes that it grew. "Every government needs an opposition" Lenin once said, and this is precisely the role of MES. As an opposition it is "well behaved," "stable," and "just." They are outside the coalition and therefore call for the "dictatorship of the proletariat." But tomorrow they could very well walk the corridors of power. This can be seen in the invitation extended to the PCP to attend their congress. MES, so hard, so antireformist, claims that the PCP is not reformist because it is implanted within the working class. By that logic they should ally themselves with the British Labour Party.[3]

Occasionally there were alliances too, over specific issues and because the groups were too weak to continue squabbling. Despite their individual peculiarities the groups shared—at an almost instinctive level—Lenin's contemptuous and deeply bourgeois belief that the masses left to themselves could only develop a trade union consciousness. In this the groups were Leninist in the deepest sense of the word. For all their talk of socialism, their aim was to set up state capitalism in Portugal, with themselves

---

3   *Revolução 25.*

in the seats of power. They differed from the PCP only in that they were weaker, and verbally more radical.

All the left groups had access to the press though the non-Maoist groups were given more space. Their communiqués and programmes were published and received wide publicity insofar as the papers themselves were distributed (this was much more common in the South than in the North). Within the newspapers themselves (i.e., as journalists, etc.) they had a firm implantation.

THE POLARISATION

While the parties of the Centre were making propaganda for "democracy" and "against fascism" the CDS continued to be attacked by the Left as a "reorganised fascist party." The first major CDS congress, on January 25, 1975, had to be abandoned altogether.

Delegates had been assembling from early morning in the Crystal Palace Hall, in Porto. By noon the gathering had broken up into working groups to discuss specific issues. At 3 p.m. they held a press conference saying that the CDS had opened the door to a noncommunist and genuinely democratic Europe. The large banner behind the Central Committee read, "For Progress in a more Prosperous Society." Mr. Geoffrey Rippon, the British (Conservative) Shadow Foreign Secretary spoke of the friendship between both parties. In the same vein the Vice President of the German Federal Republic claimed that the congress represented "the hopes of free Europe."

Elsewhere in the city the forces of the far-left were gathering. Under the aegis of an umbrella organisation (GAAF), members of LUAR, PRP-BR, LCI, MES, and JS (Young Socialists) had called a demonstration for that evening. Shouting "Against Popular Fascists" and "Death to the CDS and whoever supports them," they marched off in the direction of the Crystal Palace. They stopped outside a barracks and asked that the congress be called off. "The congress will not continue because the people won't let it," they shouted. Towards 8 p.m. they arrived at the hall, their numbers now swollen to about five thousand.

Inside, the speakers began to panic as they realised they were surrounded. Discussions in the hall became tenser when it was learned that the armed forces had taken over certain positions from the Riot Police (PSP). Finally, just after 9 p.m., Freitas do Amaral advised the congress to take precautions. Barricades were set up, using old mattresses and chairs. At 9:30 p.m. the congress adjourned *sine die*.

Darkness fell. The arrival of the National Guard (National Republican Guard) with dogs and machine guns to defend the delegates incensed the demonstrators who started shouting, "Catarina Eufémia will be avenged" (referring to the peasant girl murdered by the National Republican Guard in 1954). Stones were thrown. The police answered with tear gas. The demonstrators moved towards the main gate of the hall, forcing it open. The first shots from the police were heard. Hand to hand fighting broke out between leftists and CDS delegates who had formed a defence guard. Molotov cocktails were hurled at the CDS cars outside. A Mercedes and a Jaguar were burnt to ashes. A corner of Porto had become a battlefield.

People in nearby houses passed lemons to the demonstrators, to help them avoid the worst effects of the gas. Cheers broke out when an Alfa Romeo burst into flames. The cry went out: "Burn the CDS." Twelve wounded were taken to hospital.

Finally COPCON arrived. Some of the soldiers were embraced by the demonstrators. The PSP retired and violent incidents stopped there and then. A lieutenant asked everyone to withdraw, giving assurances that the congress would be suspended. No one moved. An appeal over the radio fell on deaf ears. COPCON asked that the CDS flag be removed from the hall. Still the demonstrators refused to move, their ranks now swollen by many young workers. The situation remained deadlocked: the CDS delegates inside the hall, the forces of the Left surrounding them.

Towards 11:30 p.m. a detachment of National Republican Guard on horse-back was brought up. Barricades were built as soon as they were spotted. But COPCON forces took up a position between the two sides, firing shots over the heads of the National Republican Guard. The National Republican Guard retreated. Well into the night the demonstrators stood firm outside the hall discussing the situation. By 5 a.m. only about a hundred were left.

Paratroopers were flown in from Lisbon. It was feared that the situation would flare up again in the morning and that a confrontation between the military and the National Guard might ensue. By 8 a.m. a force of army vehicles set up a blockade, surrounding the entire area. Some 180 cars raced out of the pavilion grounds. The battle was over. It had left seventeen wounded (twelve civilians and five police).

Throughout the night, various political groups had taken positions on the events.

The CDS, in complete disarray, spoke of withdrawing from the elections. Organising and preparing for them would, they said, now have to be done in secret. In fact the CDS did hold a secret congress in Lisbon on February 22, 1975. No information was given out afterwards concerning the number of delegates attending, or where they came from.

From January 1975 onwards congresses and meetings of both CDS and PDC were repeatedly attacked. A meeting of the PDC in Braga was fired on by an unknown group. Between January 1975 and the April elections it was estimated that nearly half the political meetings organised by these two parties (and by the PPD) had been broken up or hampered in some way. The PDC was almost totally discredited. Only meetings addressed by Major Sanches Osário could attract a crowd. CDS, it seemed, was on the point of extinction. The next target for the Left would surely be the PPD.

On March 7, 1975, the PPD held a meeting in the Naval Club in Setúbal, a large industrial area forty kilometres from Lisbon. Some two thousand demonstrators from LUAR, MES, FEC-ml, FSP, UDP, PRP-BR gathered outside the club in Avenida Luísa Todi. About a hundred police also assembled to protect the meeting. The banner of the PPD was burnt amid shouts of "Out with the PPD and the Reaction." The police tried to stop the demonstrators from entering the club. They opened fire on the crowd, shooting low from the position of the bullet marks. One demonstrator was killed and fourteen wounded. The news was broadcast and forces from all over the area began to mobilise. Setúbal boasted many PCP supporters though they were by no means in control. As fighting continued troops from the Escola Prática de Infantaria were brought in to reinforce the paratroopers and soon took over from the Riot Police.

"This is the gravest incident since April 25th," said the PPD communiqué. "It endangers the whole revolution. The Maoists, inflamed by the death of their comrade, shouted "Setúbal is red" . . . "Down with the Reaction" . . . "Comunismo" . . . "Exterminate the Popular Democrats." They marched off to the headquarters of the PSP, demanding that those responsible for the shooting be arrested. The paratroopers watched the situation closely, but did not interfere.

The fifty men in the police station were besieged all night and the whole of the following day. The Colonel in charge of the paratroopers approached some of the demonstrators but got nowhere. Later that evening he spoke through a loudhailer and told the demonstrators that the police were being taken away. The troops were booed. "The soldiers are with the people," the colonel stressed. "Why, then, are the police being freed?" came the answer. The police vans (with the police inside, for a change) were beaten and generally roughed up as they sped off. Final toll: one dead, thirty injured.

It had been a revealing episode. The troops, afraid of losing support, had not interfered. If they had been ordered to, would they have attacked the demonstrators? Many of the soldiers were personally known by the local people. This was the crucial point, and the authorities knew it. They were wise enough not to put the matter to the test.

A small group of Maoists went off to the headquarters of the Escola Prática to protest about the incident, but the vast majority scorned any confrontation with the troops. A British *Guardian* reporter and a photographer with the American magazine *Time* were roughed up as they phoned their reports to Lisbon.

The reporters were "gone over" because of the unfavourable way they had reported the CDS meeting in Porto, and because of their hostile attitude to the entire political scene in Portugal. In general European and American newspapers tacitly supported CDS and PPD, by innuendo if not directly. Reporting street events they generally lumped the PCP together with all the left groups (which maddened the PCP). In their selection of newsworthy items they stressed the climate of fear without mentioning the joy. They constantly emphasised what the professional politicians said, rather than what people were doing. They trivialised instead of seeking to understand. They seemed to stay most of the time in their hotel rooms or in the international bars of Cascais, only to emerge when invited out by PPD or CDS politicians. Or was it policy decided in London and Paris which dictated the content of their reports? With one or two exceptions (*Financial Times*, *Le Monde*), Western reporting had been invariably negative. This was not only referred to by the Prime Minister (Vasco Gonçalves) and senior members of the MFA (like Rosa Coutinho) but also by Mário Soares and Álvaro Cunhal. Reporters are the worst kind of chameleons. They change colours with every political wind and it would be utopian to expect anything else of them. They cater for the moment, and the moment is capitalism.

VII THE MFA

BEGINNINGS

The Portuguese armed forces have a long political past. They have been the springboard for both the republican revolution in 1910, and the successful putsch of 1926. Between 1926 and the Second World War Portugal witnessed a staggering number of attempted coups. Unlike similar groups which achieved power in Europe in the 1920s and 1930s the Portuguese fascist movement drew its strength from the military. There had been no mass movement for fascism, as in Italy or Germany. Fascist power in Portugal was vested in the hands of a series of paramilitary formations. The Lisbon Military Academy, an elite school of officers, was widely regarded as the backbone of the Salazar regime. The Ministry for Security was subordinate to the Chief of the Armed Forces. So was the chief of the National Republican Guard (Republican National Guard). Civilian duties were undertaken by specially designed paramilitary groups like the Legião Portuguêsa and the Guarda.

The officers of the armed forces had enjoyed some elbowroom within this apparatus. They had sought to use this freedom during the abortive coups of 1930, 1931, 1954, and 1962. No such freedom however existed for the ranks. It was not until the unsuccessful coup led by ex-General Humberto Delgado that the PIDE began to infiltrate the armed forces. But even then their action was limited and they could not act autonomously. It was usually the National Republican Guard who were mobilised against rebellious units of the armed forces, on specific orders from the military elite.

The structure of the Portuguese armed forces had been in flux since the Second World War. The class composition of these forces had also begun to change. During the 1950s the military profession fell into disrepute among the top families in the country. The aristocracy and the upper-middle class stopped sending their sons to the "prestigious" Military Academies, driving them instead towards university or professional qualifications. By the early 1970s all higher ranks in the army still carried the names of elite families. But as one descended the ladder these names disappeared. With the opening of three colonial wars admissions to the Military Academies were halved. By 1972–73 they had fallen to a quarter of what they had been in 1958.

Because of conscription many officers had to be appointed direct from universities or colleges, rushed through a minimum period of military training, and shipped off to Africa almost immediately. Many of those later involved in the coup of April 25 had been students during the early 1960s, at a time of great discussion and upheaval.

Training schemes, during the 1960s, had allowed soldiers to attend university and technical colleges to study engineering and mechanics. Many soldiers of working–class and peasant origin had been promoted on the strength of the qualifications thus acquired. Through contact with students (and in particular with Maoist groups) little pockets of resistance had been set up. From 1971 on, small political nuclei such as RPA (Resistência Popular Antifascista) had been created within military and naval units. They handed out leaflets and carried out propaganda against the war and the colonial policies it stemmed from.

Pay was obviously a weak point within the whole system. Conscripts earned some 150 escudos a month, less than the price of a pair of boots. Remuneration rose rapidly for the officers. A conscripted man with a family was condemned to unimaginable hardship when shipped off to compulsory service in the colonies. The duration of conscription was two years in 1962. It had risen to four years by 1971, and usually involved anything from nine to twenty–four months of service overseas.

The intransigent position of the Salazarist and Caetanist regimes benefited only a handful. The profits reaped from Angola and from South African payments for workers from Mozambique (who crossed the frontier to work in South Africa) enriched Portugal's rulers. But the cost to the working class in repression and death was not shown on any national balance sheet. Thousands of young men deserted. Tens of thousands refused call–up and fled the country.

The armed forces were challenged frontally, too. Groups like LUAR, PRP–BR, and others attacked the policies by attacking military units: barracks were raided, ships blown up. It was against this background that the "Movement of the Captains" was born.

Like every other institution the armed forces had attracted PIDE infiltrators and spies. But the officers' ranks proved less amenable to penetration. The first contacts between officers took place in June 1973, as a reaction to a celebration by the right-wing "Association of War Veterans" who had called for "further concrete action against the red terror."

Many different groups were probably meeting at about the same time and only later joined forces. The government decrees of September 1973, allowing returning conscript officers to integrate into the old regular cadre, caused much unrest. So did the wage demands of the regular sergeants. According to the journalist Luis Carandell, who had been in contact with the movement from its inception, the first coming together of various currents of disaffection took place in Cascais, a middle-class Lisbon suburb. The two hundred officers present had all been professionals. Smaller meetings later took place regularly, to discuss the implications of the war and the political situation. A meeting in Óbidos, on December 1, 1973, took the decision to carry out a military coup, as soon as the opportunity arose.

Portugal's turn towards trade with the EEC countries was misinterpreted by right-wing generals as a policy of "liberalisation." They attempted a putsch in December 1973, under General Kaulza de Arriaga. Its failure was the result of opposition by the "Movement of the Captains" and only helped consolidate that movement further.

A manifesto generally believed to have circulated among the armed forces in February and early March 1974 clearly shows what was being discussed. An accompanying letter called for solidarity with comrades who had been arrested and were being held in prison at Trafaria. It urged all concerned to hold fast, and not to allow divisions to appear within the three branches of the armed forces.

Four days after this manifesto came the abortive revolt at Caldas da Rainha. Another manifesto from the "Movement of the Captains," dated March 18, spoke of four comrades having been arrested. It applauded the decision of Generals Spínola and Costa Gomes and of Admiral Bogalho not to take part in the demonstration of support for Caetano. It spoke of the troops at Caldas having been excessively hasty, but expressed total solidarity with what they had done. "Their cause is our cause," it said. The manifesto strongly condemned the forces of the PIDE/DGS, of the National Republican Guard and of the Portuguese Legion for their role in stopping the RI-5 (Fifth Infantry Regiment), who had left Caldas that night. It called for caution, and urged its supporters to be ready and to await the appropriate signal.

Brigadier Otelo Saraiva de Carvalho (then a major, and to whom—for reasons of brevity—we shall henceforth refer to as Otelo) spoke later of the difficulty of organising under the Caetano regime. (*Expresso*, January 4, 1975). He said that on March 12, 1974 he had gone to General Spínola's house to ask him if he knew what Caetano was shortly going to announce in the Assembly. Spínola revealed that he, Spínola, was to be dismissed as well as General Costa Gomes. Gomes had authorised the publication of Spínola's book *Portugal and the Future*, in which a call had been made for a political rather than a military solution to the war:

> We prepared a plan of action and Lieutenant Colonel Garcia dos Santos, Major Casanova, Major Monje, Major Azevedo and I collaborated in it. Five units were to be involved, among them RI-5, Escolas Praticas and a unit of paratroopers . . . On March 13 we met and decided the plan was impossible. The coup had been planned for that night. But as it was postponed the various units disarmed, all except light-infantry regiment RI-5. Major Casanova tried to calm them, telling them there would be a new plan. He asked them to wait until the following Monday. We had a meeting on the 15th, Major Monje, Captain Marqués Ramos, Major Casanova and I. It was reported that certain units were very impatient. We heard from Major Lamego that a unit was armed and ready to go onto the streets. A great enthusiasm spread through everyone, especially Major Monje. We separated at 9:30 p.m. and were not to meet again until April 25. I went off to carry out my assignments. The others went to Caldas. We had no means of contacting one another. I found out later that Major Monje spent the whole night phoning various units to see who would advance on Lisbon: no one would leave. In the end only the unit from Caldas left. Major Monje went to the house of Major Casanova, waking him up and asking him to accompany the Caldas troops and try to get them to return, as they were completely isolated. I went to Lisbon and passed the house of Major Monje: there were three cars of DGS agents in front of it. I went to Encarnação where Major Monje was supposed to be meeting the columns as they arrived. I saw nothing, only carloads of DGS and police. I remained there until 7 a.m. and saw the columns of BC-5 (Fifth Cavalry) and Seventh Cavalry arrive (to stop the coup). By that time it was useless. I returned to Lisbon and learned that Monje and Casanova had been arrested.

The March 16 coup failed. But the arrests and tortures which followed strengthened the resolve of the Movement. It was decided not to write any more communiqués. The Coordinating Committee met and agreed upon a programme. To prevent the growth of nuclei of disaffection, many of the officers thought to have been involved were posted to other units. This helped, as it allowed them to spread their ideas to areas not previously affected. Copies of the programme reached Spínola and Costa Gomes by the end of March. They made certain changes which in turn were further altered by the Coordinating Committee for the Programme (CCP). The signal came on the morning of April 25; it had been worked out in the fashionable "Drugstore 70" by Otelo and a disc jockey whom he trusted. "Grândola, Vila Morena" was played over Rádio Renascença and a current hit played over Emissores de Lisboa.

APRIL 25, 1974

Two distinct groups had been moving towards political intervention. First, the Movement of the Captains with, at its head, the Coordinating Committee which included Melo Antunes, Vasco Gonçalves, Vítor Alves, and sixteen others. Scattered throughout the country were small groups of officers and captains (some eight hundred men all told) who were to coordinate the various units.

The second group was smaller and was only used by the Movement to provide itself with a certain respectability and cover. It centred on Generals Spínola and Costa Gomes, and officers like Major Sanches Osório and Firmino Miguel. Contacts between the two groups were frequent and some officers belonging to the "Movement of the Captains" supported the group around Spínola.

The coup itself was carried out by the "Movement of the Captains" and Spínola himself did not know the exact details until military preparations had actually begun. Captain Maia, a Cavalry commander in Santarém, twenty-nine years old and with active service in Guinea-Bissau and Mozambique under Spínola, was one of the principal contacts between the two groups and one of the leaders of the assault on Lisbon: "I received the orders two days before the 25th and after that I was watched closely by agents of the DGS. I contacted all units and told them 'to be ready for what we were looking for.' Until the actual event very few officers knew the timing."

The Cavalry unit was the first to arrive in Lisbon. They passed a unit of National Republican Guard, who thought they were on manoeuvres. No resistance was met. If there had been trouble there was a plan to retreat to Santarém, and to hold out there. Contacts between the Coordinating

Committee and Spínola took place in the morning and Spínola agreed to join Captain Maia. Captain Maia had meantime surrounded the National Republican Guard Headquarters in Carmo, and gone to meet Caetano. "I know I no longer govern," Caetano had said. "I only hope to be treated with the dignity to which I am accustomed." He asked who the leaders were. Maia answered that he only knew them by the code name OSCAR, but that six generals were involved. Caetano refused to surrender to anyone of lesser rank than a general. Finally, after conversations between Álvaro Roquete (Minister of Tourism) and Spínola, the Prime Minister resigned.

The immediate result was the setting up of the "Junta for National Salvation." The group around Spínola predominated on this body, with five representatives as against two from the "Movement of the Captains." The Junta comprised the Chief and Vice Chief of the Armed Forces (Generals Spínola and Costa Gomes), the Chief of Transport (Brigadier Jaime Silvério Marques), Captain Pinheiro de Azevedo (Navy), Captain Rosa Coutinho (Navy), Colonel Galvão de Melo (Air Force), and General Diogo Neto (Air Force). Spínola, as president, appointed a government.

Thus, immediately after April 25, it was the group around Spínola who took the reins of power, although this power was anything but absolute. Strong influence was exerted by known public figures and by leaders of the political parties, as well as by the Coordinating Committee for the Programme. This body continued to exist, as a body distinct from the Junta. The "Movement of the Captains" became the Armed Forces Movement (MFA). Similarly, the Coordination Committees in each branch of the armed forces continued to meet, both together and separately. The sum total of these committees eventually became known as the General Assembly of the MFA.

With the collapse of the First Provisional Government of Palma Carlos, the Coordinating Committee became, with the Junta, the most important decision-making body in the country. Palma Carlos had wanted more power for the politicians and less dependence on the armed forces. To the CCP this was tantamount to renouncing the decisive role it had played on April 25. Members of the Committee saw it as putting their whole programme in jeopardy.

Here was one of the essential weaknesses (or perhaps strengths) of the whole movement. The so-called programme was ambiguous and open to a number of interpretations. It was a matter of political power what particular interpretation was to be given, at any particular time and by any particular group to such notions as "democracy," "assistance to the underprivileged classes," etc.

By August 1974, Spínola had himself taken over negotiations with the Angolan liberation movements. He was making more and more political statements without reference to the movement as a whole. The group of officers around him, and in particular individuals like Sanches Osório, were putting pressure on him to halt the swing to the Left within the country. The demonstration of the "silent majority" was, Spínola claimed, a clear call for a strong presidential system.

On the night of September 27, Otelo went to the presidential palace. He later described what happened:

> Instead of speaking with us, Spínola summoned a meeting of the Junta. Vasco Gonçalves went. It was a sad scene. An attempt was made to sack three members of the Junta. I was told that I was no longer in command of COPCON. I told them that Costa Gomes had always been in command and that I was merely his assistant. I phoned COPCON and told them that I would organise events from there . . . Spínola attempted to entice units to his side and to create a climate of doubt between these units and ourselves, the MFA. The Cavalry units, the parachutists and the commandos didn't know whether to stay with the General, or to trust our intentions.[1]

Melo Antunes attributed the crisis to complacency within the MFA:

> This complacency, this excessive tolerance resulted from a false idea of what the democratic process was, perhaps motivated by too much liberalism, by a jacobin tradition of democracy which still exists in Portugal.[2]

The Third Government had not altered the existing political structures. It had merely changed the leaders. The Superior Council of the Movement came into being. It was primarily technical and shared power with the General Assembly of the MFA, the latter body being made up of 240 offic-ers. The General Assembly consisted of officers in all three sections of the armed forces. The army was represented by 114 out of the 240 delegates.

The General Assembly was therefore what the MFA had become in the days that followed September 28. Their bulletin Movimento was published

---

1   *O Século Ilustrado*, October 19, 1974.
2   Ibid.

fortnightly. The October editorial said that "Spínola has fallen but the infrastructures which allowed Spínola are still intact."

SOLDIERS' AND SAILORS' COMMITTEES

The MFA General Assembly claimed that through the Councils of Arms direct links existed between themselves and the lower ranks. There was increasing pressure however from the lower ranks for more formal inclusion into the structure of the MFA. In many cases authority and orders had been questioned or disobeyed. On May 1, 1974, soldiers had been forbidden to demonstrate though this order had been openly flouted. On May 3, a soldiers' meeting in Tancos Barracks was stopped. In the first week of June, soldiers from Torres Novas had said they would refuse to go to the colonies. Demonstrations had been organised by the mothers of those involved.

In June 1974, two soldiers who had refused to break up the CTT strikes were arrested and sent to Trafaria, the military prison. On July 9, two more men were arrested for handing out Maoist literature in the barracks.

On October 6, soldiers in Lisbon refused to participate in the "Day of Work" organised by Vasco Gonçalves and were imprisoned. The newspaper *Comércio do Funchal* was fined for publishing an article about the matter. In November, some soldiers who had broken up a CDS rally in Lisbon were arrested. On November 28, eight soldiers were arrested for organising a meeting outside the barracks of Escola Prática, an infantry division in Mafra, near Lisbon. All four hundred cadets were transferred to the General Contingent, thus bringing them within tighter control by the Junta. Their manifesto is informative. It was triggered by the banning of a show in the barracks of Eisenstein's film *Battleship Potemkin*.

> The cadets have, from the outset, resisted all forms of education geared to fighting wars of aggression in the colonies. We are against the systematic denial of our right to hold meetings and to debate freely. We are against the invocation of rules totally alien to the new spirit, which the paper Movimento (magazine of the MFA) has encouraged. We are against the heart-to-heart talks of the command, who say such things as "the army is apolitical," clearly showing thereby that they are on the side of the reaction . . .
>
> The unjust imprisonment of our comrades compels us to act. We have refused to eat and we shall continue to refuse instruction. And we shall do this in the presence of a member of the Central Committee of the MFA, to show him what is happening here.

Irrespective of our political differences and without reference to political parties, the time actively to defend the programme of the MFA is now.

Inside the barracks fascism continues. Our struggle will not stop. Free the prisoners. Purge the fascists.

Signed by 400 cadets of the First Unit of Mafra
(published in *Combate, Revolucão, Esquerda Socialista*).

Solidarity groups were formed in other barracks, most notably by the cadets of RAL-1, in Lisbon. Arrests of these dissident soldiers were carried out by COPCON.

Maoist soldiers were particularly liable to arrest. In December, one of the men arrested during the smashing of the CDS congress in Lisbon in November, Etelvino de Jesus, went on hunger strike. This provoked a demonstration by Maoists in Lisbon. Maoist soldiers who attended meetings in uniform were subject to immediate arrest. LUAR, likewise, had attracted many soldiers who had attended demonstrations in uniform. Here too arrests had followed.

Despite the repression many barracks had set up committees bypassing their commanders, or at least threatening a dual power situation. Even members of COPCON had been known to act independently of orders from above. The allegiance of many troops could not be relied upon by their officers.

On January 8, 1975, an entire infantry battalion (Battalion 4911) refused to go to Angola and called for "support to the MPLA." The leaders were promptly arrested. Many units began to publish their own papers. RAL-1 in Lisbon published the magazine *Contestável* (to contest) in which they were not always in agreement with the MFA and its paper (*Movimento*). The Cavalry unit published the magazine *Chaimite*, the Air Force *O Elo*. Many of these journals openly called for the democratisation of the armed forces.

The troops of RAL-1 had openly supported the Inter-Empresas demonstration called on February 7, 1975, and there had been many other, less spectacular occasions where the troops sided with the workers. By doing so they often pushed the MFA further to the Left.

A special case was the "Campaign for Knowledge and Dynamisation", an "agit-prop" idea emanating from a unit of the Fifth Infantry Division and promptly recuperated by the PCP. It was hoped to transform normal military exercises into political exercises. Colonel Varela Gomes organised the campaign for the MFA, but had very little control over the content of the missions. Units went into the countryside, "explaining" the coup and why it had been necessary. They asked people to organise in their areas to discuss their problems.

WHAT POLITICAL ROLE?

The Council of Twenty was the effective political leadership of the MFA, though its decisions depended in many instances upon ratification by meetings of the 240 delegates comprising the General Assembly. The question of the future political role of the MFA was paramount.

On January 4, 1975, an MFA plenário discussed the problems of the new Constituent Assembly due to be elected in April. As early as November 1974, Vítor Alves, an important spokesman for the "moderate" role of the MFA, had envisaged three possible relationships between the military and this Assembly. The MFA could either elect delegates to it, or send observers, or claim a 10 percent or 20 percent representation. While promising civilian power by the end of 1975 Alves stated "What is happening in our country has nothing in common with Ethiopia or Peru. In Portugal the military appeal to civilians to rule and to guide the country." But the question of the precise political role of the MFA was open. In any case events were to help decide the issue.

It was the MFA Assembly which discussed the general economic and political problems facing the country. The Council of Twenty then took the decisions and drafted them into plans. These were then brought back to the Assembly to be voted upon.

Influence in the Assembly was of paramount interest to the political parties. It was their only lifeline to power. On February 8, 1975, *Expresso*, analysing the MFA Assembly, saw two possible solutions. The first, sponsored and supported by officers close to the PCP, was commonly known as the "Dominant Intervention Theory." It held that "the situation of exploitation only ends with the destruction of the capitalist system in Portugal and the substantial decline of foreign dependence. It is necessary immediately to define the phases and stages for socialising the means of production, to define the limits of private capital and the type of support which should be given to small and medium manufacturers." The second solution, PS-influenced, was known as the "Moderate Plan." It called for "the abandonment of all secret meetings, the publication of what the structures and powers of the MFA were, and for elections to the MFA Assembly by all rank-and-file units of the armed forces. It also called for the free discussion by the Assembly of its domains of power and of the MFA's relation to other bodies."

No conclusions were reached. *Expresso* saw the MFA as divided into three camps. The first, generally considered close to the PCP, centred around Vasco Gonçalves, Otelo and certain members of the Junta. The second group was known as the Spínolists. It represented those officers who had been on the General's side before April 25 and was considered right-wing. The third group, politically liberal although not very well defined, centred around Vítor Alves and Melo Antunes. It was thought to have wide support in the Air Force.

Elections to the Council of Arms, early in March 1975, revealed support for the second and third groups. Otelo and others were not reelected. The question of a future role for the armed forces was coming to a head.

MARCH 11, 1975

March 11 came as a complete surprise. It wasn't that a right-wing coup hadn't been expected. The real surprise was that it was launched so soon and so ineptly. The defeat of Otelo (as well as of other known MFA "leftists") in the election to the Council of Arms had certainly been a setback for them. But it hardly warranted the optimism felt on the right. It wasn't optimism, however, which drove the Right to attempt a coup, but fear.

Rumours had started circulating that COPCON was about to arrest all right-wing military leaders within the MFA (and that LUAR was about to attempt an 'Easter Massacre'). They allegedly had a list of 100 Spínolists whom they were on the point of assassinating. The stories were given credence by the circulation among right-wing officers of a document to the effect that their days were numbered.

If the two T6 planes and four helicopters used in the attempted coup of March 11 had waited another ten minutes a massacre would certainly have ensued. Troops of the "left-oriented" RAL-1 in Sacavém (near Lisbon airport) were about to sit down to lunch in their canteen when bombs began dropping on their barracks. A Volkswagen and its military driver, one Joaquim Carvalho Luís, were blown to pieces. Rocket fire blasted gaping holes in the walls of the canteen. With the first news of the attack thousands of civilians headed for Sacavém. An RTP (TV) team, stationed nearby, rushed to the scene.

A unit of paratroopers, commanded by Captain Sebastião Martins approached the RAL-1 headquarters. "I've orders to occupy your barracks," Martins told Captain Dinis de Almeida, the RAL-1 commander.

"I have orders to defend the barracks. What's on?" Almeida answered. Martins took a document from his pocket: "Surely you know about the orders?"

"What?" answered Almeida. "You're prepared to attack us just because of a piece of paper?"

"It is not just a piece of paper," Martins replied. "There are individuals in high places who aren't pleased with the way things are going. It is in the name of these people and in defence of the elections that we are acting."

"The MFA have guaranteed the elections," Almeida retorted. "In this country orders come from the President, don't they? If you don't agree, we'll have to fight it out. But remember the people are not with you."

Civilian crowds had appeared on the scene. They joined in: "The people are not with you! The people are not with you!"

Martins's paratroopers, seeing they had been fooled, agreed as a unit to go over to RAL-1. Men who might have been killing each other rushed forward and embraced. Civilians, likewise, were caught up in the joy and excitement. Everything was decided there and then. And (a sign of the times) the two units, without phoning for orders, decided on a joint action which was to influence the whole future course of events.

The repercussions were explosive. Thousands, remembering September 28th, put up barricades in the streets. In September, they had done so in desperation: the March barricades were barricades of exultation, of relief, of solidarity. Throughout the afternoon journalists and radio announcers called for popular vigilance. They were answered in all sorts of ways. The April 25th Bridge into Lisbon was blockaded. The road from Porto was also blocked. Armed civilians and leftists manned key points and cross-roads. Cars were searched as far away as Leiria, Coimbra, and Setúbal. Young workers with guns stood holding the streets. In Porto, frustration was vented on the CDS offices which were completely destroyed. Most of their files were burnt on a public bonfire. In Lisbon the CDS headquarters were also sacked. Spínola's house in Cascais was looted and yet more files burned. Otelo spoke on TV, promising that "if necessary, COPCON would arm the people to defend the revolution." Words came easily. It was already obvious that "the Revolution" wasn't going to be overthrown on March 11. By evening the right wing was crushed. Spínola and 18 officers fled to Spain. From there, they made for Brazil in the wake of Caetano and Tomás.

Spontaneous actions broke out everywhere. Bank workers closed the banks in the early afternoon and arrested their managers. Eight directors of the Espírito Santo Bank were about to sit down to a meeting when armed workers and soldiers burst into their office and lined them all up against a wall. Lisnave workers left their factories in Margueira and organised pickets on the streets, searching cars. Thousands of others did likewise.

For three days the Left and workers' group exercised total power. An article about Spínola in the Parisian paper Témoignage Chrétien (March 6) had said that U.S. ambassador Frank Carlucci (who had CIA connections) had given the go-ahead for a right-wing takeover in Portugal. Otelo's remark on March 11 that "Carlucci had better have plans to leave the country or face the consequences" was seen as related to the failed coup. Kissinger, according to a *Sunday Times* (London) report, had sanctioned the use of the CIA.

On March 11, the National Republican Guard and the paratroopers had been the only troops to have sided with the Right. General Freire Damião, commander of the National Republican Guard1 and General Rui Tavares Monteiro (of the Air Force) had planned the whole operation. They had expected support from liberal MFA members but never got it. Damião sought refuge in the German Embassy (who finally handed him over to COPCON). Monteiro ended up with Spínola, in Brazil.

The funeral of "soldier Luís" showed how far off target the Right had been. Hundreds of thousands of soldiers and workers turned out, to pay their respects. The RAL-1 Manifesto of March 11 illustrated the prevailing mood:

TO ALL SOLDIERS AND SAILORS, WORKERS AND PEASANTS
TO ALL ANTIFASCIST MILITARY AND DEMOCRATS
TO ALL THE PEOPLE . . .

The criminal fascist attempt this morning against the soldiers of RAL-1 goes to show that the purges and demoting of right-wing troops and of known reactionaries (who sell themselves to capitalists and imperialists) are not enough to stop them preparing the counterrevolution and throwing the entire popular movement into bloody conflict. Comrades, While the PIDE continue to be treated lightly (that is when they're not actually released), while the fascist parties continue to enjoy a legal existence, while the people are fired on in Setúbal (March 8), while soldiers and military personnel in struggle against fascist repression are held prisoners in their own barracks, while the bourgeois parties falsely defend the people by organising carnivals, while all this goes on the people continue to be brutally exploited and oppressed.

But, comrades, the soldiers are sons of the people. The soldiers and all the antifascist military know how to turn their guns against the bourgeoisie and against the fascist officers, and line up on the side of the people.

Comrades,

The soldiers and all the RAL-1 military (who have always struggled against fascism and those who seek to protect it) are against oppression. We demand the immediate execution of all the fascists and those who seek to hide them, whether they be military personnel or not, generals or not.

Death to fascism

Popular Justice

Imperialism out of Portugal

Immediate execution of all fascists

The soldiers are sons of the people.

> The soldiers and all military personnel in RAL-1,
> bombed by the fascists, Encarnacão, March 11, 1975.

These events resolved, for a while, the whole debate over the political future of the MFA. The Movement was "institutionalised." A "Superior Council of the Revolution," numbering twenty-eight people, was set up as a supreme policy-making body. It would remain in power for three years. All political parties planning to take part in the elections were asked to sign a pact endorsing this arrangement.

The first action of the new Council was to nationalise the nineteen commercial banks. Only three international banks were left in private hands. Between them the commercial banks had controlled the bulk of the Portuguese economy. Over 99 percent of loans granted had been to private individuals or firms. The insurance companies, mostly controlled by the same families, were also nationalised. Of the thirty-five national companies three held over 33 percent of the market and were owned by Champalimaud, de Brito, and the Espírito Santo family.

Steel, transport, electricity, and petrol were also nationalised. Prices were declared "frozen" until the end of 1975. An estimated 50 percent of the total industrial capital of the country passed into the hands of the state. The minimum monthly wage was raised to 3,600 escudos while a programme of agrarian reform was proposed. A sum of 5 million escudos was to be invested in cooperatives and agrarian associations. An Institute for the Reorganisation of Agriculture (IRA) was set up to overlook regional councils. The movement towards state capitalism took a great lurch forwards.

Economic problems remained serious. In 1975, a deficit of 13,548 million escudos was recorded between January and April. Gold reserves were dwindling, and emigrants were sending little cash home. Economic dependence on the EEC countries (which accounted for 45 percent of Portugal's imports and 16 percent of its exports) was critical and financial aid was badly needed. It is worth noting that a trade deficit with Russia also occurred during this period, despite the claim by the PCP that Russia was helping Portugal.

The Bank Workers' Union (affiliated to Intersindical) exposed the economic sabotage and malpractice of the large banking families. Accounts in false names or in the names of known right-wingers were mysteriously credited with money, which was then passed on to various right-wing parties including CDS and PPD. Money from the government to bolster employment was diverted to small companies in the colonies and false figures published to cover this up. Many of those involved in these practices, including the administrators of the banks, were arrested and imprisoned.

More serious in some ways was the news that ELP (the Army for the Liberation of Portugal) was preparing an attack on the country. Based in Spain and supported by Portuguese businessmen who had fled after April 25, this body had received massive financial support from some of the banking families. It had also been engaged in arms deals in Europe, and in large-scale gun smuggling. The ELP had advised against the March 11 attempt, asking Spínolist officers to await a more opportune moment.

Most groups (including the PPD and the PS) welcomed the nationalisations. MES, LUAR, and PRP-BR were "critical," adding that the nationalisations had to be accompanied by "workers control." Demonstrations in support of the steps taken were called by the PCP and by Intersindical. "Nationalised in the service of the people" was a slogan which appeared over many banks and companies throughout the country. The new administrators were military men or "left-wing" economists, belonging to MDP-CDE. The nationalisations made little difference to the workers' real struggles.

VIII URBAN STRUGGLES

BACKGROUND

Emigration has been a permanent feature of Portuguese history since the seventeenth century.[1] But an internal migration has also taken place. The shift from the countryside to the urban areas accelerated during the period of economic expansion, beginning in 1959. The flight from the land and the housing policies of the Salazarist regime led to the formation of shanty towns in the Lisbon suburbs and around Porto and Braga. Salazar's early promise of "a house for every Portuguese" had, by 1956, been reduced to discussions about "dualistic development." Sedas Nunes, a fascist author, could write that "two societies coexist in Portugal and the 'modern' is rapidly overtaking the 'traditional.'" The contradictions of capitalist development were attributed to the so-called traditional attitudes of the agricultural population, or "explained" by homilies about "habitual" poverty. Such concepts allowed the authorities to close their eyes to what was really happening.

In contrast the middle classes had it good, especially in Lisbon and Porto. Overvalued land sites and housing programmes devoted to the building of expensive homes had gradually forced the working class out into the suburbs. Schemes to create municipal housing estates were not only hopelessly inadequate in terms of need but merely camouflaged the relocation of workers in the outer districts. Boroughs (Bairros Camarários) designed to house state employees came to constitute some 10 percent of

---

1   In the century before 1968, some three million people from a total population of ten million left Portugal. Between 1900 and 1930, about 750,000 Portuguese settled in Brazil, while another 250,000 ended up in North America. Over half a million people emigrated between 1961 and 1967, and this figure probably doubled between 1967 and April 1974. During the last decade or two, Europe (particularly France) has come to replace the traditional destinations (such as Brazil and the African colonies). Perhaps a million Portuguese are at present in France. Most emigrants left the Northern provinces, the highest figures being recorded from the districts of Viseu and Bragança. (Carlos Almeida and António Barreto, *Capitalismo e Emigração em Portugal*, Lisbon: 1974).

the total housing provision in the country. Insecurity of tenure ensured control over the inhabitants.

Shanty towns: These had been built illegally, usually of wood or tin. Families of eight or ten would live in a single room. The land was often privately owned and a "landlord" would charge rent, which would vary from 200 to 400 escudos a month. The buildings would be erected either by potential dwellers or by people already in the shanty towns, to be sold or further rented as the "owner" wished. Misery exploited misery. Monopolies within the shanty towns were not unknown. Although predominantly a Lisbon phenomenon, shanty towns also existed in many other parts of the country

Sublets: A building would often be rented by an entrepreneur, who would then sublet it (on a room by room basis) making a fat profit in the process. The "landlord" generally cared little for the conditions in which tenants lived. Thus three or four families would be squeezed into an apartment of four or five rooms. This was the predominant housing pattern in Porto and Braga but was also widespread in Lisbon (in particular among families from Cabo Verde).

Property owners: Most new housing was put up by private companies. By limiting the amount built (and thus influencing rents) they dominated the supply situation. Only thirty-five thousand units were erected annually during the period 1960–70, while the deficit in 1960 required that over fifty thousand units be built each year. Rents rose as demand increased. Only the petty-bourgeoisie got anything from the new housing. The poor became yet poorer, in terms of what they could buy.

Working-class and petty-bourgeois housing: Because of high rents (new houses coming onto the market fetched up to 1,000 escudos per room, per month), working-class and poorer middle-class people had to make big sacrifices just to get or keep a roof over their head. Rent alone accounted for at least 40 percent of the family budget in the Lisbon area (and in some cases, much more). In old working-class districts rents could only be increased every five years, and only on a percentage basis. Here rents remained lower. In other areas new families moving in were exposed to the worst forms of exploitation. Many were forced out into the "dormitory towns," in the suburbs. Living there entailed all the hardships of poor transport, fatigue, separation, and internal pressure on the family unit itself. Workers would leave in the morning, spend up to an hour getting to work, return home at night tired and irritable, watch TV, fight with their relatives, and grow more frustrated every day.

THE OCCUPATIONS

April 25 saw an explosion of information as to the "state of the nation." The new government made feeble attempts to right some of the wrongs belatedly discovered. Departments were reshuffled. The "Junta for Internal Colonisation" became the "Institute for the Reorganisation of Agriculture." The FFH ("Fund for Housing Development") was restructured and purged. On May 14, 1974, the Junta issued a statement dealing with the spontaneous seizures of empty property which had taken place in the first few days. The "undisciplined occupations of houses" were seen as "reflex actions against the ineffectiveness of official departments which never found a solution to problems." The Junta "would not now call for their evacuation, but would not legalise these occupations either."

A decree (no. 217/74) froze all rents at what their level had been on April 24, 1974. A law was passed soon after, allocating some 5 billion escudos to housing and granting certain tax exemptions to builders. The government was clearly supporting the private construction industry as a means of coping with the housing shortage. It was hoped this allocation would result in an increase in dwellings of 10 to 25 percent in a year, but even this was hopelessly inadequate.

The workers' reply was a spate of further occupations in May and June 1974. This forced the government to introduce a new law, on September 12, limiting to 120 days the time during which any house could be left vacant. The authorities even spoke of publishing lists of empty houses. The landlords weren't worried. They easily got round the threats by producing a series of fake rent books and contracts. In November 1974, decree no. 663/74 was passed. It further subsidised the private building industry by granting it yet more tax concessions.

Following the reshuffling and purging of the FFH (Fund for Housing Development) certain "progressive" officials reorganised the Mobile Service for Local Control or *Serviço de Apoio Ambulatório* (SAAL), a semigovernmental agency, geared to "assisting the urban struggle" The local authorities in Lisbon set up the Cabinet for Housing (CTH) and the Empresa Publica de Urbanização de Lisboa (EPUL). These bodies, in turn, appointed Brigades for Local Support (BAL) in the Lisbon area. The original ideas behind both the semistate SAAL and BAL were similar: to defuse the explosive housing situation with a series of promises, and control things from above.

Many revolutionary militants joined semistate SAAL, radicalising it considerably. SAAL's unconditional support for occupations, for example, was not at all what the government had in mind. An endeavour to split the organisation took place in November 1974, with an attempt to set up a parallel but more reformist group (SAC). Despite its left image it was only after March 3, 1975, (and the purging of the new conservative president of the FFH) that SAAL actually sought to take on a mobilising role, helping in the setting up of Neighbourhood Committees. The semistate SAAL denounced the housing estimates issued by FFH (according to which only sixty thousand units needed to be built in 1975 and ninety thousand units in 1978). SAAL also criticised the proposal that the state should pay 40 percent of the cost of each house, leaving the future residents to pay the balance through loans repayable at 7 percent.

Occupations had two main purposes: to put a roof over one's head or to establish a political office. The second kind was usually supported by COPCON. One occupied and then phoned them. They in turn informed the police.

Squats were a very different matter. When on November 26 260 families from a shanty town moved into an empty apartment block at Chelas, near Lisbon, COPCON ordered them out. The families held their ground. COPCON had to back down. Other occupations quickly followed. The paper *Revolucāo* described statements made to it in Lapa, a mainly bourgeois area with a shanty town in its centre:

> Here some houses have been empty for eighteen years and are still in good condition. Eighteen families who occupied such houses have signed contracts with their landlords.
>
> But some landlords won't do it. Some get court orders. Some see their lawyers and decide to rent the houses. Rents vary from 500 to 1,500 escudos per month. If the Residents Committee (set up to defend the occupations) could be legalised we could summon the landlords and if they refused to turn up we could penalise them, even arrest them. But, as things are, we can't go any further as we don't have the powers. If they've kept their houses empty for so long and never made improvements it must mean they don't need the money. We are the ones who need the houses.
>
> We are on the brink of a revolution. In my view there is going to be bloodshed between landlords and occupiers. I have six kids and a seventh in my belly. I will go with all seven and a house will have to be arranged for me. The house I'm in now is owned by a guy who owns banks in Brazil. He says he wants to demolish it and has permission from the Council. This shows that the rich still have

the law on their side. They have influence inside the Council . . . Nobody, at this moment, should evict us. If the police tried or started shooting it would lead to riot, COPCON would then have to decide which side they are on.

In Bairro das Fonsecas shanties had been broken up by the police before April 25. A special "housing" police force backed by the PPS had been used. In Porto, where the sublet situation was critical, the residents of Block 402, Rua de D. João IV, put out a manifesto to the workers of the city:[2]

Sublets are still sanctioned by law and we can be put out of our homes. We are 15 families here: with 20 children, a total of 100 people. The building has no amenities. There is not even a bathroom; we have to go to the Municipal Baths to wash. The ceilings are falling in. There is only one toilet and no flush. It's wet right to the basement. A pig wouldn't live here. We pay rents of 600 to 1,000 escudos for small rooms where our families live. Our landlord, Maria de Costa Pereira, owns many buildings like this. She refuses to fix anything. The electricity in the house is very dangerous . . . We refused to pay the September rent saying we'd only pay after the necessary work on the block had been done. We put the money aside. She took us to Court and now we are faced with a dispossession order. We went to the FFH. We went to the government. They all said they had no authority, they couldn't do anything. They also said they thought we'd lose our case. They said sublets were legal. The law protects them, like it protects all those who exploit the workers. Is this fair?

Everyone told us to be patient, to be calm. They told us to write out "papel selados" (official petitions, on blue paper, bearing a government stamp). How can we be calm and patient when we've lived in this misery for so long? Only those with no problems can afford to be patient. We would like to solve the problem legally, but we see that the laws are not on our side. We have no time or money for lawyers. And anyway the laws defend the parasitical subletters, not us. This isn't a democracy: this is fascism. Given this, we shall make our own law and take our rights.

1) We won't allow anyone to be thrown out of the block.

---

2   This document was published by SAAL (Norte) and appeared in *Combate* 12, December 6, 1974. Parts also appeared in *A Capital*, (October 26, 1974).

2) We demand that the work be done quickly, starting with the electricity.

3) We want the end to sublets and a contract between us and the owner.

4) We want all workers to unite and fight for good houses.
Down with subletters and capitalists.

Rua de D. João IV, 402. Porto, 23/10/74

On October 26, the residents of this block invaded the Cámara (Council) in Porto, together with residents from other sublet blocks. Their rents were waived for the months of September and October.

House occupations increased during January and February 1975. LUAR and MES played important roles in obtaining buildings for "Workers' Centres," "infantários," "Crèches," and "Popular Clinics." The luxurious private clinic of Santa Cruz, near Lisbon, was seized by its workers and renamed "the Hospital of April 25." The local population and LUAR helped with the arrangements and certain doctors offered their services free. For a while the clinic functioned but eventually ceased to do so for lack of financial support. The workers, however, remained in occupation. Similarly FSP opened a "Popular University" in Porto, aimed at "helping the development of revolutionary groups and the discussion of political texts." There were no exams, no fees, no diplomas—but few workers enjoyed this kind of diet. Children and adults could attend. Mansions and palaces around the country were taken over by various groups as offices. In general the buildings had been empty for years. The occupations were not legalised and no rent was paid.

In Campo de Ourique (Lisbon) there were some four hundred empty houses and the local Neighbourhood Committee began to take them over. It fixed a "social rent," to go towards improvement. The government, alarmed at the extent of the occupations (which by April 1975 had reached five thousand in the Lisbon area alone) moved to a harder line. It refused to legalise some of the occupations. The Coalition parties (including the PCP) began to forbid their militants from taking part in this sort of activity. Nuno Portas, Secretary for Housing, ex-MES, ex-PCP condemned "spontaneous" occupations because they were "outside" of state control.

HOUSING STRUGGLES

Two types of autonomous organisation were thrown up in response to the housing crisis. The first were the Autonomous Revolutionary

Neighbourhood Committees (Comissões Revolucionárias Autónomas de Moradores, or CRAM). They were usually based on the older working-class and lower-middle-class areas. Although they had a general critique of private property, they were more concerned with how to use empty houses and with the setting up of community services such as crèches, etc. After March 1975, it was these Committees (some thirty-eight existed in Lisbon alone) who initiated most of the occupations. The Committees would be elected in General Assemblies grouping all the residents of a given area. The assemblies were usually large, up to five hundred people attending. They would discuss the problems of the neighbourhood and make suggestions as to what should be done. Clearly, party political struggles took place within these bodies. But most Committees were not dominated by any particular party. Such was the popular aversion to party-politicking that those elected to the Committees often had to hide their political affiliations.

The other organisation thrown up had a different origin and was a response to a more pressing need. The "Inter-Comissões de Bairros da Lata e Moradores Pobres de Lisboa" brought together delegates from thirty different shanty towns. It came to represent some 150,000 people and saw itself as the nonparty and independent organisation of shanty town dwellers.

"Inter" was critical of Revolutionary Autonomous Neighbourhood Committees (CRAM) whom it termed "bourgeois." This was not strictly true, though the respective areas of concern were clearly different. "Inter" would have nothing to do with "parties who come here to ruin the work which we ourselves have done." It consciously avoided being trapped into relationships or deals with local government offices, because "these only serve bureaucracy and talk, and are staffed by individuals who live in good houses and know nothing of our problems."

On February 15, 1975, "Inter" nevertheless presented a list of demands. It also came out against the government's plan for "self-help in building," whereby the authorities would provide free bricks to shanty town inhabitants to build their own houses. Inter's document speaks for itself:

> At meetings, it was seen that the Brigades (BAL) could not resolve our problems (drainage, water, refuse, etc.). Neighbours in some areas decided that the struggle would have to be taken into their own hands. They decided to occupy houses, even though the government had decided that such occupations were illegal. This was forced on us by necessity.

As workers we all know that it is we who produce the wealth of this county, and that despite this we have no right to a decent house which we could rent with our wages, no right to crèches, to schools or gardens for our children. Because of this thirty Neighbourhood Committees came together.

We demand that new boroughs be built in places which concern us, where we live today, and where most of us were born. Workers are being moved to the outskirts of the city because others want to build shops and offices in the centre. The government speculates on land. They offer to lend us 60,000 escudos per house, at an interest of 7.5 percent. 60,000 escudos won't get us anywhere, let alone pay back the interest on this loan. With respect to these subsidies we cannot forget that they represent only a tiny part of the surplus value which we produce daily at work, and of which we are robbed by the capitalist class.

We don't have to whine for what is ours by right. We demand that our problems be solved. And they must be solved without our need fattening those who exploit us. This happens when speculators and those who exploit land through indemnities help capitalist building firms. It also happens in the case of "self-help in building." People say that "self-help in building" is good, that we build our houses ourselves. In reality it means a double exploitation. After a day's work, filling the pockets of capitalists, we are expected to work up to our eyes building houses.

400,000 people are today unemployed, thrown onto the streets and into misery by capitalists. Work must be given to these brothers. Why not employ them in civil construction? Plans for housing cooperatives are a way out for the government. Through such plans the government can avoid having to pay for the building of new houses. It allows them to control our just demands . . .

The neighbours of various shanty towns and the poor of Lisbon and its suburbs are fed up with all the false promises to solve the housing problem. We reject all the antipopular measures which only seek I to con the people, and to delay the solution of our problems. "Inter," uniting the various Committees and cooperatives takes the following stand. We demand the following concrete measures:

1) That new boroughs be built in existing areas

2) The expropriation of free and occupied land, within existing boroughs, as a way to rehouse the people. We want a definite answer as to which lands can be taken over and when

3) A reply as to when work will start in the building of new boroughs, and what they will be like

4) The right to decide the type of houses to be built

5) The right to organise in cooperatives. Loans should be repayable at 2% over 25 years

6) In the case of boroughs which choose social housing, rents should not exceed 10% of the wages of the head of the family (without prejudice to those who can't afford to pay)

7) Information about funds to be allocated to the shanties by the council, with details as to what they are for, so that those concerned can control the funds

8) That all urgent cases presented by Committees (including BAL and EPUL) be immediately dealt with

9) A reply to demands already made by other shanty towns

10) That as long as adequate houses are not built, the occupation of empty houses be made legal

11) That a member of 'Inter' be present at the various meetings between the Lisbon Council and EPUL

12) That house distribution, either by the Cabinet, or by EPUL, or by Foundations, or by any other official body, be controlled through representatives of the inhabitants
We reject:

1) Self-help in building

2) Renovation or recuperation of existing boroughs, as well as the use of prefabs

3) The existing legislation about cooperatives, as merely a method to fool the people and delay solutions (for example the need to muster 200 members, etc., when the general law only requires 50).

Inter-Comissões, 15/02/75 [3]

Although widely referred to in the national press, the document was ignored by the government, whose members at this time were more interested in the elections than in concrete problems such as those being raised.

---

3   From a document published by SAAL (Norte), parts of which were published in the national press.

By the beginning of April, some twenty thousand occupations had been reported throughout the country. On April 14, 1975, the government, alarmed at its lack of control over the situation, passed a law (DL 198-A) that legalised all collective occupations (crèches etc.) but forbade squats.[4] The Left lined up against the Centre to fight this law.

The Autonomous Revolutionary Neighbourhood Committees (CRAM) called a demonstration on April 19. This was supported by various groups though none were allowed to carry banners. Another demonstration on May 17 called by "Inter," also condemned the new law and called attention to their demands of February 15. This demonstration brought some ten thousand shanty town dwellers into Lisbon, chanting "Houses, yes, Shanties, no."

INTER, CRAM, SAAL, AND THE SHANTIES

The differences between Inter-Comissões and the Autonomous Neighbourhood Committees are worth dwelling upon, for they illustrate the complex dialectic operating *within* the class. "Inter" fully realise that the situation of those it spoke for was different from that of workers already housed. But by its demands and organisation it revolutionised the latter. Other Neighbourhood Committees (whether related to CRAM or not) had a more mixed membership (embracing teachers, office workers, etc., as well as factory workers) and therefore tended to look at things differently.

For the shanty town dwellers, a house was crucial. More important, for workers already housed, were questions of the control (or abolition) of rents and of the control of space. Such workers could not be dismissed as "privileged" just because they had a roof over their heads.

Still deeper problems existed. The shanties were not united. Some owners of shanty "property" actually rented it out to others. Within the same town, black (Cabo Verde) shanties might exist quite separate from white Portuguese ones. The families who lived in shanty huts worked in different industries. In general they were workers without contracts, casual labourers, or navvies in the building industry.

While in many shanties the setting-up of Neighbourhood Committees was enthusiastically greeted, in other areas apathy prevailed. This can't be explained solely in terms of "habitual poverty" and other such reactionary

---

4   These laws can be found in the *Diário do Governo*, an official publication brought out daily while that government existed.

interpretations. Apathy might also imply that those concerned felt their struggle was being directed by others.

This was a dilemma which the "technical state helpers" of SAAL were well aware of. SAAL, after establishing the original contacts, generally lay low, rarely intervening in the assemblies. Those seeking to work through SAAL were limited by the whole slowness and bureaucracy of the state apparatus (in relation to finances, etc.). The manifesto of Inter was thus crucial in the development of the shanties.

CRAM faced different problems. The Neighbourhood Committees were subject to party political interference (from PRP, UDP, etc.) in the sense that those who were more "political" got into leading positions. Those on the platform would use a specialised "political" language which was off-putting for the others. Some refused to speak, because they would not talk this way. The party ideologues could thus rise to so-called leadership all the more easily. Even the Committees, manipulated from the platform, could take over meetings by rejecting or dismissing motions.

The issues raised during meetings of the Neighbourhood Committees were of a wider kind than those discussed in the shanties. In general the function of CRAM was to collect information on the area and then occupy all the available houses. But the PRP-BR's preoccupation with "building the Party" through the Committees (the PCP, MES and UDP were doing much the same thing) was hardly conducive to unity. In general these groups, while they helped in the sense of supplying paper for leaflets, calling meetings, etc., had a negative effect on the dwellers themselves. Once a Committee was felt to have been taken over by a particular group, many left.

The Neighbourhood Committees were moreover limited by the very structure of space and work in Portugal. The vast majority of workers lived in one area and worked in another. This allowed but little contact between the factories and the living areas. The Workers Committees were attended during the day, the Neighbourhood Committees during the evening, if at all.

Shanties surrounded by petty-bourgeois housing estates (like in Cruz Quebrada, near Lisbon) were often prone to bourgeois pressures. Here, individualistic solutions often lay just below the surface. In the Falgueiro shanty, for example, a woman who could not pay even the minimum rent (400 escudos a week) was criticised by the other dwellers.

A number of shanty town dwellers began to construct their own homes over the wooden structures. They would build one wall this weekend, another next, until a house was formed. This happened on a big scale near Odivelas, one of the Lisbon dormitories.

The shanties were the "great shame" of Portuguese capitalism. They were an obvious eyesore and everyone was intent on "getting rid of them at all costs." But thinking seldom went beyond this. What would the shanties be replaced by? What would the new communities be like? Such problems were hardly ever aired in the Assemblies. There was here a universal paralysis of imagination. Would the "pressures" in the new houses (if and when shanty town dwellers ever got them) really be less than in the old huts—or merely of a different kind? These questions were never openly discussed, because never openly admitted as relevant. The silence of the Left on these issues could be heard for miles around.

The shanty town dwellers wanted a quick solution to their problem. They wanted to keep their culture, built up over decades, intact. The conditions in which they lived (no water, no electricity, no drains, and all the pressures of living in overcrowded space) had to be changed for the better. But how and to what end? To make them "better workers," so that they could be more efficiently exploited? By getting them to accept ideas which allowed a greater extraction of surplus value from them by the ruling class (whether represented by the state or not), as in the various programmes for "self-help in building"?

At the beginning of June 1975, the overall situation was still open. The dominant class was still in power. But it was having difficulty in maintaining its rule. The working class (housed or not) continued to press for all it could get, as and when it could get it.

MACHISMO AND THE WOMEN'S MOVEMENT

No discussion about housing and urban struggles is complete without specific reference to women. In societies where most women stay at home, they bear the brunt of bad housing.

I will attempt to describe the situation here realistically and without false optimism, as it was riddled with contradictions. The urban struggles were very positive. The feelings of hope and joy which they gave rise to are difficult to describe. They had so many facets: freedom on the streets, freedom to come and go, tiny changes which made a great difference to everyday life. Many women felt this freedom. A woman from Tinturaria Portugália (a dry-cleaning firm), when asked about the greatest change she had experienced after April 25, said: "Before, I was locked up in my house. I don't know why. After, I came out onto the streets, in the demonstrations . . .

There's no describing the joys I have lived since April 25th." My ex-neighbour was also exuberant in her confidence. She began to criticise me for not having gone to demos she had attended. These were real changes.

But there was another side to the coin. Women were second-class citizens. The year 1975 may have been touted as "Women's Year" elsewhere in the world, but it was not so in Portugal.

The real problems of women in Portuguese society were immense. Before April 25, they were legally disadvantaged in many ways. Divorce was forbidden. Contraceptives could only be obtained on prescription, and were thus not available to the poorer classes. The glories of motherhood and fertility were widely proclaimed in an effort to supply future white rulers and soldiers for the colonies. I clearly remember a pregnant fisherwoman near Nazaré, before April 25, patting her belly and saying resignedly "This is for the war." Abortion was illegal, even when the woman's health was threatened.

Matrimonial relations were almost feudal. A husband could legally open his wife's letters. She couldn't leave the country without his written permission. All economic decisions were by statute in his hands. In law, she remained a serf to her husband's wishes.

Some things changed after the coup but it is difficult to imagine army officers being particularly sympathetic to women's problems. A movement to make divorce possible grew and campaigned throughout the country. MDP-CDE gave it support. The law was finally altered, although abortion continued to be illegal. Contraceptives could still only be obtained on medical prescription.

A decree passed soon after April 25 said that the state would henceforth be responsible for children: "the nationalisation of children," as one woman doing her shopping in the market called it. In fact the decree removed from the family (and from the father in particular) their right to do what they liked with the children. It established penalties for child-beating and ill-treatment.

Housewives were called *donas da casa* (the mistress of the house). Especially in the North, they were often called "the boss" by their men. This wasn't only condescension: it was real in a limited way. But because it was limited, it was derogatory. Many terms insulting to women existed in the language: a girl who slept with men was a *puta* (prostitute) while a man who had sex with girls was a stud to be admired.

Between 1969 and 1974, the number of working women increased rapidly because many potential male workers were abroad, fighting. But their wages were lower. Even after April 25, the CTs (work contracts, established for each trade) were loaded against women. In the PCP-dominated cooperatives (around Beja especially) the women worked from 6 a.m. to 8 a.m. in the house, then went to the fields, picking olives, etc. Between 7 p.m. and 10 p.m. they did more housework. Yet they were paid less than the men who worked from 8 a.m. to 7 p.m. In other, more independent, cooperatives, near Lisbon or in Setúbal for example, the women received equal pay for their farm work.

Macho attitudes die hard. The men often defended their higher wages by claiming that their work was more productive. But when the women pointed out that picking olives was a job the men wouldn't want to do, the argument seemed somewhat shallow. Such questions were never really resolved and machismo persisted.

On January 13, 1975, there had been a meeting in Parque Eduardo VII sponsored by the MLM (Movement for the Liberation of Women). About ten women carried posters and placards. This sparked off one of the most reactionary counterdemonstrations ever seen. The women had stated:

> We shall burn objects which are examples or symbols of the
> oppression of women. We shall destroy, for example, the Civil
> Code and the Penal Code of Portugal, which are now in force, as
> well as the Labour legislation. All of them endorse an inferior
> position for women and the subjection of women to men. We
> shall burn pornographic magazines which use the female human
> body as a sexual object; dusters and brooms which symbolise
> the women as slaves in the home, as domestic servants; books
> in which the image of women is presented in a totally deformed
> way, created by men, and in which she becomes everything he
> has made her; nappies as a symbol of the myth of the woman
> as mother-who-makes-all-the-sacrifices (the father is the
> lawmaker), who does the hard work, who faces the sleepless
> nights; toys which, from an early age, show children very clearly
> the roles in society to which they are destined, depending on
> whether they are boys or girls, toys which in boys are conducive
> to aggressiveness and violence (like machine guns and tanks) and
> which condition girls to the passive roles of mother and housewife
> (like dolls and little pots and pans) . . .
>
> We hope that 1975, International Women's Year, will at least
> call attention to the scandal which these facts represent, and to the

fact that half the world's population (53 percent in Portugal) are subjugated (controlled, mastered) just because they are women.

The proposed demonstration was publicised in the most trivial manner. *A Capital* (a serious paper on the national level and on most other subjects) treated the whole thing as a joke. It only announced the "bra-burning" episode. Like all other newspapers it promised a "striptease." The MDM (Democratic Movement of Women) (PCP-controlled) violently denounced the demonstration. Crowds of men turned up and began to boo. They jeered and taunted the girls. The women only escaped by a hair's breadth from being severely manhandled.

Reporting this demonstration, *O Século Ilustrado* (January 17) condemned the men: "it is probably the same people who applauded the glorious victories of Caetano, who spread flowers on the streets for the little dictators to walk on, who congratulated themselves on the massacres in the colonies and diligently informed the PIDE, who for half a century supported the brainwashing and the oppression, who are today opportunistically demonstrating for democracy. Good democrats, all."

The MDM, although involved in women's struggles, was more intent on defending the family than in discussing more basic problems of women. It directed struggles into channels which, while important for families (like crèches, financial assistance for children, parks and so on) were not primarily related to women themselves, or to the roles assigned to them in class societies.

After the break-up of the MLM demonstration radical women were genuinely frightened of engaging in further political action. A whole area of the struggle for liberation had been successfully gagged.

IX BEYOND THE ELECTIONS AND POLITICAL PARTIES

ELECTORAL ARITHMETIC

The elections to the Constituent Assembly, in April 1975, caused no surprises. With two Maoist groups (MRPP and AOC) and the right-wing PDC banned from the race, twelve parties lined up.

The initials of the contenders proved an eye-opener to the new labyrinth of Portuguese political life. In the twenty electoral regions people were offered a choice of eight Leninist parties (PCP, MDP, FSP, MES, LCI, FEC-ml, UDP, and PUP); two of a social-democratic type (PS and PPD); one right-wing party (CDS) as well as the monarchist PPM.

The main parties, PCP, PS, MDP, and PPD presented themselves in all twenty areas, the FSP in sixteen, MES in fifteen, FEC-ml in twelve, PPM and UDP in ten, PUP in seven, and LCI in four. People voted for parties rather than candidates.

A pact assuring the MFA—in advance—of power during the next three years had been signed by seven of the contending groups (the UDP, LCI, MES, PUP, and FEC-ml had refused to oblige). The signatories agreed to the institutionalisation of the MFA, recognising its Revolutionary Council as the highest political and legislative body in the country. The General Assembly of the MFA (reshuffled to include 120 lower-ranking members) was to have legislative powers, limited only by this Council. The Constituent Assembly, the composition of which would be decided by the elections, would have as its sole task the drafting of a new Constitution.

The first elections in forty-nine years were taken seriously by nearly everyone. Anyone over eighteen had to register, although voting itself (despite wide beliefs to the contrary) was not compulsory. The campaign itself was strictly controlled—"to maintain democracy"—and was restricted to just over three weeks. The opening act saw a frenetic rush by all concerned to hang posters and banners on every conceivable building (and quite a few inconceivable ones) all around the country. Every available wall, monument, window, pavement, or roof in Lisbon was plastered with slogans, exhortations, and graffiti, until the city looked as if it had been wallpapered. It was made illegal to tear down other people's posters: many Maoists were arrested for this "offence." The slogans were predictable. The CDS advocated "Progress in Peace"—the old slogan of the Caetano regime. The PPD recognised "Only One Way: social-democracy." The PS wanted "Socialism with Liberty" while the PCP urged people forward "On the Path to Socialism." PCP posters depicted very respect-able looking family groups and carried headings like "Women: in your hands lies the future of your children," a slogan criticised by the feminist movement. The PCP also used photos of working peasants and students. Other groups were less affluent and hence had fewer posters. They called for various brands of revolutionary socialism.

AOC and PCP-ml, driven by their hatred of the Moscow-orientated PCP, supported the PS. The MRPP threatened to sabotage the campaign, while PRP-BR and LUAR refused to have anything to do with it. Opting for "direct workers' control" they argued that the elections had nothing to do with the revolution in Portugal, and called for the setting up of Workers' Councils. Equal TV time was allocated to each of the parties. They came on three times a day made their promises, repeated their slogans, working up their daring and demagogy as the campaign progressed, in a revolutionary auction to outdo their rivals. The Maoist UDP and PUP always ended their speeches with "Viva Marx, Lenin, Stalin, and Mao." This caused derisive laughter in many of the cafés I visited.

The poll (92 percent) was the heaviest ever recorded in state elec-tions. The PS obtained 38 percent of the votes cast, the PPD 26 percent, the PCP 12.5 percent, CDS 8 percent and MDP 4 percent. Between them the also-ran gathered some 4.5 percent of the vote. At the bottom of the league came LCI, PUP, and PPM. The PS secured 42 percent of the vote in Porto (as against 5 percent for the PCP). In Lisbon the PS got 45 percent (as against the PCP's 19 percent). In Sacavém, Marinha Grande and Almada, industrial areas with strong Communist Party traditions, the PCP suffered almost total defeat. Why?

Two factors were responsible for this voting pattern. The first and most significant was the apparent option offered to the working class of a non-Stalinist solution to the Portuguese revolution. The PS was accepted by a widely-based and heterogeneous section of Portuguese society. Apart from support by the Maoist Left (which was small but noisy) the PS also benefited from the widespread realisation that the PCP was bureaucratic and Stalinist, a view tellingly driven home by various reactionary priests and local bosses. The highest poll for the PCP was recorded among agricultural workers in Beja, in the Alentejo. In the North the small peasant farmers opted for the CDS or PPD. The second major factor was the attitude of overseas workers and soldiers, who had not been involved directly in the revolutionary process in Portugal. About a million out-of-country votes (out of a total electorate of five and a half million) poured in from France, Sweden, and Angola. This was an overwhelming PS vote.

Only 7 percent of the ballot papers had been deliberately spoiled. This is low if one considers the campaign by the MFA to get people to register a blank vote, that is, to vote but not to show preference for any of the parties.

When the results of the elections were known the PS and the Right started denouncing the MDP and PCP for their disproportionately large representation in the state apparatus and in the media. Repeated attacks were made, at every opportunity. The whole coalition was threatened with collapse. It was in this atmosphere that the idea of the Councils was discussed and gained some impetus. The launching of the Revolutionary Councils had taken place on April 19, six days before the poll, and another meeting had been held in Porto on May 10, which Soldiers' Committees from the North had openly attended. (The whole subject of the Councils will be discussed more fully in the next chapter.) The main political parties responded appropriately. They decided to bury their hatchets, for the time being at least. A joint statement was issued on behalf of the PS, PCP and PPD. They would keep the coalition going.

But elections or no elections, coalition or no coalition, the struggle continued. Fifty thousand hotel and restaurant workers went on strike between May 10 and May 15. Chemical workers in the North had withdrawn their labour on May 6. Fishermen in Peniche struck for higher wages. Many small firms passed into self-management. Workers in the metallurgical firm of Corame arrested their managers and handed them over to COPCON, who accused them of exporting money illegally. Employees of the exclusive Lisbon tailors Candidinha (where the haute bourgeoisie had bought clothes for over a century) took the place over, and started producing low-cost clothing. Both CTT (the telephone company) and TAP (the national airline) were threatening strikes.

"POPULAR POWER" AND THE MILITARY

It was against this background that two suggestions emerged for bypassing the existing Political Parties altogether. They were first to be discussed by the General Assembly of the MFA on May 26.

The first (proposed by Rosa Coutinho and CODICE, and supported by the PCP) was to set up *Committees for the Defence of the Revolution* based on the old Juntas de Frequesia (Parish Juntas). It was a natural enough response to the PCP's electoral setback. The second was presented by delegates to the Assembly active in COPCON. It stressed the "organisation and exercise of power at the base." It emphasised "grassroots organisations" (especially the Councils) and the need for their coordination on a wide scale. It proposed the "creation of a popular army, democratic and revolutionary" and advocated a "real alliance" between the people and the MFA. It spoke of the "dictatorship of the proletariat" and mentioned Kim Il Sung's Korea as an example worth considering. It was suggested that, to start with, the Central Command of the new "popular army" should rest with COPCON . . . at least until such time as something else had been created. The proposals were supported by the Provisional Secretariat of the Revolutionary Workers' Councils, promoted by the PRP-BR. Otelo (as he was now widely known) spoke in defence of the second document: "Party struggles are causing extremely dangerous divisions within the working class, which are extending into the armed forces . . . Spínolist officers have formed a PS bloc—though the PS probably played no part in this . . . I am convinced that the dynamic of the Portuguese Revolution (given that the MFA is not lined up behind any political party) will transcend the great political parties altogether. We are not pledged to European social-democracy. We are not allied with any of the great imperialist blocs. We are not allied with China."

For the parties in the coalition, of course, all this was anathema. It threatened the entire base of their power. The PS and PPD attacked the pro-COPCON proposal outright, calling it dictatorship (which was never denied). The PCP also criticised it, though more cautiously: it was stealing much of their thunder.

The debate became public. MES criticised both proposals: the "Committees for the Defence of the Revolution" and the Councils. The revolution had not yet taken place, they argued, and it was therefore impossible to defend it. They saw the Councils as a specific PRP-BR creation, which detracted from the already existing popular organisations. Both LUAR and MES saw the future in terms of reinforcing already existing structures from the base up, and not in terms of a master-plan, decided in advance. UDP criticised the pro-COPCON document for other reasons: they saw themselves as an already established vanguard.

What was really being discussed in the MFA Assembly was whether any leadership role was to be left in the hands of any of the political parties or whether the parties should be bypassed altogether for a system of soviets or grassroots organisations. What was unreal about the debate was that it was taking place at all, that the revolutionary self-activity and self-organisation of the masses should have been deemed a suitable theme for the agenda of a military gathering. The discussion continued for several days. When the pro-COPCON motion was finally put it was defeated, though only just. Political parties were to continue.

The pro-COPCON proposal having been rejected, an MFA group called the "Cabinet for the Dynamisation of the MFA-Povo Alliance" (*sic*) produced a "Guiding Document" which was presented to the Assembly on June 8. The "Guiding Document" called for a strong state economy, for agrarian reform, for more *saneamento*, for decentralisation of administration, and for workers' control. To achieve this they proposed a structure in which Neighbourhood and Workers' Committees would form "local popular assemblies" which would elect delegates to municipal assemblies, which in turn would elect delegates to a National Popular Assembly. Within the barracks ADUs (unit assemblies) would support the civilian assemblies. The Council of the Revolution would oversee all this.

On June 21, the MFA (one of the most prolific literary groups of soldiers ever encountered) published a Plan of Political Action. It was an extension of the "Guiding Document" and opted for a pluralistic "socialism" centred on the MFA's own authority: "The MFA is a liberation movement of the Portuguese people. It defines its main objectives as the establishment of national independence and of a socialist society. By a socialist society we mean a classless society, the collectivisation of the means of production, the elimination of all forms of exploitation, and the equal right of all to education, work and promotion without discrimination on the grounds of sex, religious beliefs or ideology."

After these generalities, specific demands were spelled out:

- A pluralistic society, which allowed opposition parties
- Political administration independent of the Constituent Assembly
- The reinforcement of the authority of the MFA
- A law against armed clandestine groups
- Recuperation of Leftists and pseudorevolutionaries who, although well intentioned, created a climate of anarchy
- Austerity in consumer goods
- The dynamisation of rank-and-file organisations, as the determining factor in unitary power

- The creation of an official MFA newspaper
- Control of TV and radio by the state

The plan was well received by the four coalition parties and the CIP (Confederation of Portuguese Industry). The PS and PPD welcomed its "pluralism" while the MDP was pleased by the verbal endorsement given to "popular power." But as an attempt to solve real problems the proposals were hopeless, for they were all firmly grounded in class cooperation.

The Constituent Assembly had met for the first time on June 3. It had started its proceedings with an appeal to minimise party friction. But the Assembly was doomed, from the onset, to reflect the feuds raging outside it, if not to aggravate them. The PS in particular used the Assembly for political propaganda. The PCP sought people's attention by other methods. On June 10, Intersindical—in a sort of preemption of the kind of society they envisaged—called for a "Sunday of Work" to launch the "Battle for Production." Interest in the scheme proved distinctly lukewarm and remained confined to PCP-influenced areas like the Alentejo. The idea was criticised by many Committees who wanted to know *for whom* they were producing. The PCP Minister of Labour (and member of the Revolutionary Council) answered: "for the collectivity." He was to be vigorously criticised (by Lisnave workers among others) for his general lack of class understanding.

THE *REPÚBLICA* AND RÁDIO RENASCENÇA AFFAIRS

During May, June, and July 1975, both *República* and Rádio Renascença (RR) were to become focal points of struggle. The relevant events have been widely misrepresented or misunderstood in the international press, and are worth going into in some detail. They raise important issues concerning the role of information in the revolutionary process. So important were these developments, in fact, that they were to contribute significantly to the collapse of the Fourth Provisional Government.

On May 15, 1975, the Workers' Committee of *República* attempted to take over the paper. Throughout the years of censorship *República* had remained a lone independent voice. Under its director Raul Rego it had printed many CDE proclamations and criticisms of the regime. Its journalists were firmly in the PS camp and its main articles were certainly PS-oriented. After April 25, the paper had become the mouthpiece of the PS. In a statement the Workers' Committee said: "The majority of the workers of *República* want it to be a nonparty paper, and not a paper in the service of a certain ideology." On May 5, 1975, in a general assembly, the workers had elected a committee of 14. They had also called for the resignation of the director and of the editor. They printed their own edition of the paper, and set up pickets at the main gate. A separate meeting of the editorial and journalistic staff refused to accept the legality of the Workers' Committee and of its rulings. The PCP was held responsible for the occupation, despite the fact that all sorts of tendencies were represented on the Committee.

On May 19, Mário Soares and others handed out leaflets in the streets of Lisbon. These said: "You cannot ignore the people's will. *República* is not Cunhal's." At 7 p.m. the editorial staff entered the newspaper building. One of them, João Gomes, spoke to the crowds outside. Soon after COPCON representatives also arrived and were let in. A certain amount of confusion seems to have followed. A stone smashed one of the windows, to the accompaniment of shouts such as "Death to the CIA and KGB" (a slogan of distinctly Maoist flavour). The crowd sang the national anthem. More soldiers arrived. The crowd asked of "MFA, whose side are you on?" The MRPP chanted their own slogans: "Out with the social-fascists." PS members added, "Socialism, yes—dictatorship, no." When Soares too attempted to enter the building the workers inside refused him entry. One made a speech: "These aren't the PS offices. You and your colleague Cunhal should take a look at the people, at the force of the working classes, and not play games with us. Why don't you both go back where you came from?" Impasse continued. Towards midnight the TV and representatives of other papers were allowed in. An impromptu debate began from the windows. João Gomes, for the editorial staff, argued that it had been the typesetters (mainly PCP members) who had been responsible for the decision. A Committee member corrected him, saying that the decision had been taken by all the workers. He stressed that, over the previous months, fourteen members of the editorial staff had been sacked and replaced by PS members. The spontaneous debate, in the early hours of the morning, to a background of jeers, sloganeering, and applause from the large crowd in the street was in many ways typical of the direct democracy of the time. For the MFA the Minister of Social Communication (Major Correia Jesuino) said that the readers should decide what kind of paper they wanted. But at 2 a.m. the readers could not be contacted. A member of the Committee said it was up to all the workers involved to decide what kind of paper they were going to produce. These weren't matters for minorities (those on the editorial staff, or those belonging to a particular political party) to decide.

At about 4 a.m. another member of the Workers' Committee made a speech that best summed up the problem:

> As a worker I cannot ignore, nor do I wish to ignore, existing differences in the working-class struggle against the exploiting class. We all know that the production workers took no part in the dispute between the PS and PCP. It has nothing to do with us. Our aim is to transform this paper into something new: an objective and independent paper, owing no allegiance to any of the political parties. It is this which is causing resistance. It is those who want *República* to continue as a party paper who should be asked to leave. It shouldn't be the workers . . . who have to leave. It was the people, after all, who for a dozen years bought the paper and paid for it, not the PS.

Although it was raining heavily, the night was warm. The debate continued until 6 a.m., when workers and editorial staff both agreed to evacuate the building and to await a decision of the Revolutionary Council. On May 24, the Workers' Committee at *República* issued a statement of aims: "The struggle here is the culmination of a whole series of dissatisfactions which have come to the surface since April 25th. They range from internal censorship to the refusal of our demands, and include dismissals, drop in sales, a fall in subscriptions, protests by readers, nonpublication of certain letters, the arbitrariness of publishing certain articles, the choice of writers, and above all the taking over of the paper by a party political faction. República will not henceforth belong to any party, in the sense of reflecting that party's views. All the progressive parties will be given identical treatment, depending only on the importance of events."

For a long while there was deadlock. The issue was widely debated throughout the country. Then, on June 16, COPCON reopened the doors to the workers involved in the production of the paper. On June 11, these workers had issued their explanation of what was at stake. The text is interesting and important, despite illusions concerning unions and parties, for it calls into question the whole structure of class power in Portugal, as well as the legitimacy of political parties:

> MANIFESTO TO THE POOR, EXPLOITED AND WORKING CLASSES
> OF PORTUGAL
> The workers of *República* are a group, small in the context of the total force of the working class in Portugal. In the current

crisis concerning information we are reacting against reformist trends. We do not obey any sect, we are not subordinated to any party, and we are not of any fraternity. We extend our solidarity to all the exploited of Portugal and want information to be a collective activity . . . As workers we want a paper which helps the Portuguese to struggle, in full consciousness of their rights and of their dignity, against the demagogues and opportunists who regiment liberty . . . We workers of República are conscious of living in a society in which the masses are deprived of knowledge and education. We feel that political information . . . should give people the power of intelligence . . . It is now time completely to rethink our policy concerning information. We want to create information in the hands of the workers, free of all double-talk and party allegiances. As was inevitable, part of the bourgeoisie who at one time supported the exploited and poor—either in their songs (they have a good poetic sense) or with a view to building up a future clientele—gradually abandoned this stance. Today, after September 28 and March 11, they take up despotic and doctrinaire positions. Antifascists before April 25th, they became authoritarians after March 11. They seek to take over information, to inject into the people their own brand of ideology. Information should help transform the exploited classes into the dominant class. *República* should help in this process. Information, moreover, should not be permeated by spontaneous and sensationalist conceptions of revolution. It is not enough for Workers' Committees to appear and then disappear after a struggle. They must be stable organisms, united at the base. They must determine the actions of unions and parties. We declare to all workers that we struggle to ensure working-class control over information. We extend our solidarity to the poor of Portugal, to all who work in factories, in the fields, on the high seas, in the service industries and in transport. We struggle for a revolution in the interests of the workers themselves, and not of half a dozen men with ambitions of power, ever ready to betray the real soldiers of the revolution.

The *República* workers were supported by the Workers' Committees of various newspapers including *Diário de Notícias* and *O Século*. *A Capital* also supported them in the following terms: "Information cannot be left in the hands of journalists alone. All workers in the industry must participate

and we must protest against any elitist manoeuvres . . . Now, when everyone wants an honest dialogue, we cannot tolerate that privileged intellectual workers establish lines of separation from manual workers. Organs of
communication (like *A Capital*) who claim to be independent of the parties
and who seek to build socialism must be at the service of the working-
class. They must never favour party feuds which give the reader negative
ideas about a dictatorship over information."

The question of "dictatorship over information" was widely discussed in all the papers. In capitalist countries there clearly exists a class
control over news. But weren't 150 workers just as likely to constitute a
dictatorship, bourgeois or proletarian? What distinguished the workers of
República was their refusal to relate to any particular party or organisation,
and to trust to their own class instincts and interests. This is how they saw
it themselves: "Let us put it clearly. The organs of decision-making are
either on the side of the dynamic elements of the revolutionary process:
the Workers' Committees, the Neighbourhood Committees, the organisations of popular power. Or they relate to the political parties, are yoked to
those parties which in most cases don't defend the interests of the workers
at all. The question is who is to have political power in this country? Is the
MFA interested in the construction of a socialist society? Or is it interested
in bourgeois democracy? We are only 150 workers but in a sense we are
representative of our class, of millions like us. What is at stake is political
power and knowing in whose hands it is. Is it to be in the hands of the
bourgeoisie and of those who defend its interests? Or is to be in the hands
of workers and of those who defend the interests of the workers?"

The issue at Rádio Renascença was somewhat different, although
it raised many similar issues. The radio station had been owned by the
Catholic Church. Gradually, during May, the workers concerned had
taken it over, disliking the line being pushed. Their communiqué of June
6 outlined what was at stake:

> The complete history of our struggles at RR would bring together
> arguments and documents which a simple communiqué cannot
> hope to cover. When our story is written many positions will
> become clearer, as will the ways in which they relate to the
> overall politics of the country. The Portuguese people will then be
> able to judge the counterrevolutionary politics of the bosses, the
> immoralities of all sorts committed in the name of the Church, and
> the many betrayals carried out by capitalist lackeys in our midst.

. . . In their latest delirium the Management Committee (i.e., the Church) completely distorted our struggle and attacked the MFA. Of 127 lines, 73 were devoted to denouncing the government . . . When they speak of the violent occupation of the radio station they forget to mention that the only violence was when Maximo Marqués (a member of the Management Committee) attacked one of our comrades, who didn't respond to the provocation . . . The management argue that we are a minority of 20, whereas 30 would be more correct. Rádio Renascença is a private company, owning a radio station, a printing press, a record shop, two cinemas, buildings and office blocks, etc. In the station we are about 60 workers. The management say we are trying to silence the Church's mouthpiece, and prevent it from reaching a large section of the population. If by this they mean we are trying to silence fascist voices, they are right. Words like truth, justice and liberty lose all meaning when they come from the RR administration. We remember the time when the priests managed the station and censored encyclicals, Vatican texts and even the Bible (!!)

We propose that the management show their concern for liberty by supporting the current liberation of RR, now in the service of the workers and controlled by the workers.

The workers of RR. June 6, 1975.

The struggle at Rádio Renascença was widely supported. The options were fairly clear: to side with the Workers' Committee or with the Church. Vasco Gonçalves and other members of the Revolutionary Council decided to hand the station back to the Church. The decision was bitterly opposed by some one hundred thousand workers. A demonstration was held on June 18, during which Lisnave and TAP workers stood outside the gates and warned that RR would only be returned to the Church "over their dead bodies." Four hundred Catholic counterdemonstrators had to seek refuge in the house of the local Patriarcado. The determination of the workers caused the Revolutionary Council promptly to reverse steam. It found a way out: to decree the nationalisation of all newspapers, radio stations, and television networks.

Both the *República* issue and the issue of Rádio Renascença have been described at length to challenge a whole mythology. The issue was one of control. The division was not between the PCP on the one hand and the PS or Catholic Church on the other. In both cases, to be sure, there were sympathisers of the PCP among the workers who occupied the premises. But there were also sympathisers of the PS, the PRP, the UDP, etc. Most of the workers involved in both "occupations" were not party militants at all. The division was essentially between those who supported direct democracy and workers' control over the means of production and those who desired a liberal-capitalist type of parliamentary socialism.

The crisis of early July 1975 (with CTT, TAP, and TLP workers on strike) produced a mighty mobilisation on July 4 in support of the struggles at *República* and RR. The strikers had established direct links with one another. They also supported the workers of RR and of *República*—who returned the support. Two separate calls had been issued, one by Inter-Empresas and the other by the strikers. As a communiqué from the workers of Siderurgia put it, the demonstrations were "to show the bourgeoisie the power of the workers." Workers from Timex, Sapec, Petroquímica, Guérin attended. Men even came from the Soda Póvoa works at Vila Franca de Xira, forty kilometres from Lisbon. The workers of Lisnave and Setenave gave massive support. "Death to Capitalism" was the main slogan on this largest "nonparty" demonstration since February 7. Forty thousand people took to the streets, the first demonstrators to march through the Chíado (the bourgeois shopping centre). Two main factors had prompted this massive turnout: the struggle over information at *República* and RR, and the news that some ninety PIDE agents had escaped from a security prison at Alcoentre. RR broadcast appeals throughout the day: "Only working class unity can help the workers take power. The struggle at RR has taught us that the workers can win when they rely on their own strength, on their capacity for class solidarity. This solidarity is born in struggle."

The PS reacted strongly to all this. What was at stake was not only the fate of *República* but of bourgeois democracy itself. On July 7, Mário Soares spoke out: "We are ready to call demonstrations and paralyse the whole country so that we can extend the revolution in freedom. We don't want new forms of alienation. There is no battle as important, at this moment, as the battle for a free press." He added that attitudes to *República* were "a barometer." The whole thing was presented as a defence of "democracy" against Stalinism. A vast PS wall painting said: "No to Stalinism. Yes to Popular Democracy." But the PS critique came from the Right. On July 2, the PS had called for support for the owners of industry. On July 5, they had called for "the right to private property."

The situation was very complex. Although the channels of information were being controlled by Workers' Committees a great deal of party influence still existed. The Workers' Committees of the two morning papers (*Diário de Notícias* and *O Século*) were overwhelmingly PCP. The PCP supported the workers of *República*, whereas they had condemned the militancy of *Jornal do Comércio* as recently as September 1974. The evening papers were more open and less sycophantic. They were less prone to "socialist realist" headlines and articles. But because they were dependent upon state funding they were also less critical than they might have been. *A Capital* had, from the beginning, published dissenting views from the Left and continued to do so. But many aspects of struggle never got reported. As an editorial in *Combate* put it (in an article entitled "The state of information and the information of the state"): "Whoever has power over information subordinates to it, and makes dependent upon it, almost everything in everyday life and local experience. Information creates a commonplace, a consensus, a mediation which tends to make uniform all our individual reactions and provides 'alternatives' which never question the existing order."

It will be seen that the decision to nationalise the press was taken by the government during a moment of extreme crisis. The decision, in a sense, had been forced on the government by the workers. It suited all those concerned with the retention of information in the hands of "responsible" people. The only losers were those who wanted the control of information by the base. The government's decision was therefore loudly applauded by most of the left parties, from the PCP to groups of Christian Marxists. At a price, it even let the PS off the hook. A legitimate working–class struggle had once again resulted in a further extension of state capitalism.

COPCON AND THE MRPP

In the wake of the elections of April 1975 the MFA and government had had many problems on their plate. The challenge to their authority had grown steadily. Not only were base groups taking over the channels of information but "subversive" proposals were being voiced within their own structures and institutions. It is against this background that one must look at one of the most bizarre episodes of the Portuguese revolution: the arrest of several hundred Maoist MRPP militants by the forces of COPCON. COPCON was very much the creation of Otelo Saraiva de Carvalho, as he himself never tired of reminding people. It had been set up as the "armed intervention" section of the MFA, in an attempt to recover some of the power originally vested in Spínola, following April 25. The

September 28 events were in some respects the result of a power struggle between this section of the MFA and the Spínolists.

COPCON's role increased as the political crisis deepened during the summer of 1975. Given the "neutralisation" of the National Republican Guard,[1] COPCON became the main operational police force in the country. But it is important to remember that both COPCON and the MFA were minority tendencies within the armed forces as a whole. As such they walked a tightrope. This was to prove particularly true of COPCON. The group needed mass support if it was to continue to exist. Although in the last analysis COPCON was part of the armed forces, which were a prop of capitalist society the workers felt they could exert considerable influence on the lower ranks of both organisations. COPCON was forced to support many occupations of land and houses.

COPCON achieved a certain popularity in many sections of the working class, despite the fact that it had helped break a number of disputes (for instance the TAP strike and the dispute at *Jornal do Comércio* in August 1974, and the strike of municipal workers in Santarém in October 1974. The latter, being public employees, were not officially "allowed" to strike.) Nevertheless COPCON sought to cultivate a popular image. Working people often turned to it in unexpected ways. In December 1974, for example, one of my neighbours—a woman whose tongue could be like a whip on anyone unfortunate enough to be pitted against her—went to the fish market one morning. A list of prices had been printed in the newspapers but the dealer was paying no heed to them. She phoned COPCON. Sure enough, within ninety minutes, two soldiers and a sergeant turned up in a Jeep. They forced the dealer to abide by the published prices.

By the early months of 1975, COPCON was being called out for pretty well everything—marital disputes being high on the list. At 3 a.m. a battered housewife would phone for help and COPCON would duly appear on the scene. There was a case, in Ajuda, of COPCON being called to rescue a stranded kitten.

During the summer COPCON began to lose some of the goodwill gained earlier. This was the so-called Gonçalvist period of the MFA and people didn't like it. In Dafundo, for instance, a family had occupied a six-roomed house. But they hadn't done so through the Neighbourhood

---

1   It had been to the GNR (National Republican Guard) headquarters that Caetano had fled on April 25. It was to the GNR that Spínola had entrusted the task of controlling the radio stations on September 28. And it was from these headquarters that the coup of March 11 was to be directed.

Committee and the CM told them to leave. They dragged their feet. So COPCON arrived at 1 a.m., broke down the door and ordered everyone out. While most workers in the area had criticised the original occupation, they now began to side with the family against COPCON. There were hundreds of such cases. Workers began to wonder whether there might be some substance to the MRPP's statements that COPCON was acting like a new PIDE.

The MRPP, of course, attacked COPCON systematically—largely, one suspects, because they couldn't manipulate it. In the process they made some correct points but also some more dubious ones. They accused COPCON, like the MFA, of being controlled by the PCP. The MRPP then began arresting certain soldiers and civilians whom they claimed were fascists. They would hold them for a while, beat them up, and then hand them over to RAL-1—taunting the MFA "Left" to take sides on the issue. On the night of May 28, COPCON couldn't take any more. Using old PIDE files they arrested over four hundred MRPP militants in the Lisbon area. Old addresses known to the PIDE but long since abandoned were raided. COPCON tried to explain things as follows: "Since April 25th the so-called MRPP, who in their majority are young students, have demonstrated against the constituted revolutionary authorities. The MRPP is more like a religious sect. They have little implantation among the workers. They are completely isolated from other national parties and are used by counter-revolutionaries . . . COPCON accuses the MRPP of the following: on May 15 the MRPP kidnapped ex-fusilier Coelho da Silva who was then beaten up by their militants. On May 18, three further individuals were beaten up. In Coimbra on the same day they kidnapped and beat up Maximo dos Santos."[2]

The arrested MRPP members were released a few weeks later though their office equipment and other items seized were not returned until August 1975. There is no doubt that the MRPP also practiced terrorism on their own militants (in particular on those who wanted to break with them). Given a choice between supporting COPCON and defending the MRPP, many people chose COPCON. This was a fact—whether one likes it or not. To mention it is not to praise COPCON so much as to comment on the regime within the MRPP.

The arrests had a profound effect on the MRPP membership. They became convinced that the "persecution" had been instigated by the

---

2   *A Capital*, May 29, 1975.

"social-fascists of the PCP." They resorted to the most unprincipled alliances, working not only with the PS but with right-wing groups. The MRPP even welcomed the burning down of PCP offices (see the next chapter) as instances of "popular vengeance against the social-fascists." Almost inevitably, the MRPP began being used by openly counterrevolutionary tendencies, unable to get an implantation of their own among the workers. The arrests reinforced both the MRPP's paranoia and its elitism. They were being persecuted, they said, because they were "the real vanguard." An introduction to Charles Reeves's Portuguese edition of his book *Le Tigre de Papier* clearly describes the "irreparable psychological damage done (to the Portuguese Maoists) during the years of clandestinity."[3] Events like the arrests of May 28 did little to heal this damage.

A criticism of a different order could be levelled at COPCON. COPCON's very existence as a "left" tendency within the MFA reinforced the whole MFA mystique. If COPCON existed to help them why should the workers even begin to think of autonomous military organisation, on a class basis? In this sense COPCON was an obstacle to the development of self-led groups concerned with workers' defence, groups which might have formed the nuclei of a workers' militia. COPCON was aware of this contradiction. The document on popular power, presented to the General Assembly of the MFA early in June had spoken of the "eventual arming of the working class." Although the "arming" was always for tomorrow, the rhetoric mesmerised most of the left-wing groups. They nearly all supported COPCON, and not very "critically" at that. Their illusions were to be shattered on November 26, 1975, when COPCON was disbanded on orders from above—without as much as a squeak from its leading personnel.

---

3   *Le Tigre de Papier: sur le développement du capitalisme en Chine* (Paris, Spartacus, 1972– Série B No. 48).

X THE GREAT NONPARTY

From July 7 to 9, 1975, the General Assembly of the MFA institutionalised the "pact" between the MFA and the people. It endorsed "popular power" as a means of defence against right-wing attacks and as a means of solving economic problems. It spelled out a complicated system of relationships between the MFA, the government and the grassroots organisations. In defining popular power it called for a decentralisation of the state machine. It advocated the handing over of power to Workers' Committees, neighbourhood committees, village councils, cooperatives, collectives . . . and to the League of Small and Medium Farmers. It called for local assemblies to federate into municipal assemblies and for these in turn to federate into what would become known as the National Popular Assembly, which would replace the government. Fighting talk. Military anarchism had appeared on the scene. "The present norms are not rigid," the MFA concluded. "Their application should depend on local situations and on the dynamics of the revolutionary process."

The decision to institutionalise popular power was applauded by all the left parties. Only the CDS, PPD, and PS opposed it. On July 11, the PS decided to leave the coalition over the *República* issue. "What is the PS doing in a government which does not govern?" Mário Soares asked. "It isn't our leaving or not leaving which will determine what the government is to be. We were in the government to govern. Since it doesn't, and can't, there's no point in remaining there." The PS decided to retain its positions within the Constituent Assembly. It indicted the PCP as the "chief manipulator behind the crisis in authority" and called for an end to what it described as "communist dictatorship."

On July 16, as expected, the PPD followed the Socialists out of the Fourth Government. Only the PCP and its "front," the MDP, were left within the coalition, together with some independents. Basically the PS endorsed some of the conditions made by the PPD for its continued presence in the government but, ever conscious of its image, the PS hadn't quite the courage to say this openly. Both parties wanted the old press laws (which vested authority in the editorial staff) to remain. The other PPD demands had been:

1) All-party participation in radio and television;
2) One newspaper (North and South) for each of the coalition parties;
3) Publicity for the PPD position in relation to the guiding document of the MFA;
4) Eviction of squatters from all houses illegally occupied;
5) Nonintervention of the military in matters that were not their concern;
6) Revocation of all Councils improperly elected;
7) A date to be set for local elections;
8) Limits to be defined between public and private sectors;
9) Guarantees for small and medium property-owners;
10) Immediate assistance for the textile, construction, and shoe industries.

Most of these conditions were, of course, rejected. The only concession made was to declare illegal the occupation of the houses of emigrants. The PPD and PS moved into opposition which—as a PRP-BR communiqué put it—"was their proper place."

The collapse of the Coalition had both internal and external repercussions. The parties of the Second International (especially the Socialists of Spain, Italy, and France) blamed the PCP. France vetoed all FEC aid to Portugal. Inside Portugal both party feuds and class struggle intensified. The Bishop of Braga, in the North, called a demonstration which was attended by ten thousand Catholics. Offices of left-wing groups and PCP headquarters were attacked all over the country. The four hundred Maoists arrested by COPCON on May 28 were released unconditionally. Arnaldo Matos, the leader of the MRPP, boasted that the government "needed the MRPP to rout the reaction." On July 15, about twenty thousand people marched in a demonstration calling for the resignation of Vasco Gonçalves. The PS leadership, surprised at the right-wing pull their party was exercising, tried to calm the crowds who now shouted "the people are not with the MFA" and "Otelo to Mozambique. He is not Portuguese." Soares had to reaffirm the "alliance" with the MFA and to tone down his criticism. "We must not and cannot forget that without the MFA there would have been no April 25th." Asserting that the socialists were no new "silent majority," he asked that the people's will, "as shown in the elections," be respected.

On July 16, a demonstration in Lisbon called by Inter-Comissões (the Federation of shanty town Neighbourhood Committees) was joined by three tanks and by armed soldiers, the first time that troops in uniform had marched in this way, in a popular demonstration. When they met the tanks of RAL-1 and of RIOQ the crowd chanted: "Workers of field and factory, soldiers and sailors, united we shall win." The troops replied through their megaphone "The RAL-1 soldiers have come to support your struggle." The applause was deafening. Climbing onto the *chaimites* (armoured cars), the demonstrators continued through the streets of Lisbon.

"We must transcend the false divisions which the counterrevolutionaries, the parliamentarians, the 'doutores' (literally: doctors) and their parties have created among us," one of the leaders of "Inter" proclaimed, addressing the crowd. "We must unite the true revolutionaries, leaving all sterile sectarianisms behind. The Workers' Committees are the organs which must advance the revolutionary struggle. We must put an end to this government of class collaboration, to this government which cannot cope with our problems. The government contains within it those who conspire, those who hesitate, and those who don't want revolution. The bourgeois Constituent Assembly must also be abolished, because it is there that the CDS fascists, the right-wing PPD and the false socialists join hands to halt the revolutionary process; our unity will dump them into the dustbins of history."

A proposed PS march on Lisbon, planned for the weekend of July 18, was denounced by many left-wing groups. Rumours were rampant. On July 18, barricades went up all over the country to stop the anticipated march. Armed soldiers guarded the main roads and all entrances to the town were blocked. On the April 25th Bridge returning beachgoers hooted their annoyance, queuing while their cars were searched by young militants. The march never took place: the PS moved into semiclandestinity. On July 28, 1975, Mário Soares made a speech which if uttered by someone less obviously compromised would have been very telling indeed: "The PS, conscious of its responsibilities, is prepared to take to the streets and to show its convictions . . . What divides us is not Marx or the construction of a classless society . . . what divides us is Stalin, the totalitarian concept of the State, the all-powerful single party, the right of man and the problems of freedom . . . what divides us is not the Neighbourhood Committees or other forms of direct democracy (these are included in our program) but the question of their democratic representation."

AUTONOMOUS WORKERS' STRUGGLE

The MFA support for the new institutions of popular power, and the momentary working-class successes at Rádio Renascença and *República* gave impetus to further struggles. A purge of an institution run by the Catholic Church took place. It was an old people's home in Setúbal. Six Franciscan nuns were thrown out by the inmates (helped by other workers) and accused of "inhuman practices." The old people were very badly fed and some had little or no clothing although they were being charged 1,000 escudos a month for their keep. The local population, horrified at what they found, immediately began to clean the place.

So strong, at this stage, was the feeling against manipulation that every group, party or organisation attempted to play down its own role. But this only helped them to mask their manoeuvres still better. The story was being told of how, when the two great "nonparty" demonstrations crossed on July 4, many workers had asked why there wasn't a united march, as the aims of the two processions seemed to be similar. The marches had stopped, while the hidden "leaders" of each emerged to discuss whether or not to join forces. The demonstrators had remained passive, manipulated, and depressed. They had come on a nonparty class demonstration, hadn't they? So why not join forces?

Why not, indeed? The answer lay in the explosive proliferation of messianic vanguard groups after April 25. This proliferation in turn was related to two basic factors. Faced with the impossibility of radically changing things through official channels, would-be revolutionaries found Bolshevism an easier option than self-organisation. But this in turn reflected the depth of penetration of bourgeois ideology, which saw society as "naturally" divided into leaders and led. This attitude had deeply permeated the Left itself, where it assumed the Leninist form of believing that the workers "could only develop trade union consciousnesses." Everybody wanted to provide leadership. The more sophisticated groups, sensing the popular revulsion against manipulation, attempted to play down their own existence and sought to relate more directly to the workers' organisations, trying to dominate them from within.

Not always, however, as the following episode shows. Some Maoists were demonstrating in Porto, shouting "Viva a *Grito do Povo*" ("Long live the *Shout of the People*," the name of their paper) A group of workers join in, misheard things, and—no doubt voicing their hopes for the future—begin shouting "Viva a Rico Povo" (Long live the people made rich). When the Party militants explain that this slogan is "incorrect" the workers answer:

"Ah, what does it matter? It's good to be shouting!" They could have added: "And which is more real, anyway?"

The real movement developed considerably during the summer of 1975. In Marinha Grande, seven hundred workers had occupied the factory of glass manufacturer Manuel Pereira Rodão. They purged the administration and were running the concern on their own. The Ministry of Labour had paid some arrears of wages and given help to the tune of 3 million escudos. The workers had rejected any party control within the factory. At the Yogurt Bom Dia plant, nineteen workers occupied the installations and set up a system of self-management. They received no help from the government. The Turiaga company, which had both tourist and agricultural interests, had also decided to purge the administration. The government gave no assistance. On June 26, 150 workers came to Lisbon and went on hunger strike outside the Prime Minister's residence at São Bento "to show the country."

In May 1975, in Unhais da Serra, the 1,100 textile workers of Penteada and neighbouring firms owned by the Garrett Brothers decided to set up a Workers' Committee and take over the management. After calling for government help the Garretts (one of whom had been an ANP deputy) had a meeting with the Workers' Committee and the PCP Minister of Labour, who called for a compromise. The workers went on strike and the talks broke down. A farm of some three hundred hectares owned by the same brothers was taken over by the workers who set up a "precooperative." COPCON sent eleven soldiers to "protect" the occupation. The workers at the textile plant were told by the Garretts that because of the farm occupation the wages due could not be paid. A certain division ensued between factory and farm workers (militants of FEC-ml played a role in this, supporting the farm workers). The Workers' Committee on the farm, along with the eleven soldiers, decided to march against the bosses. After a meeting between the two Workers' Committees a solution was worked out whereby the factory workers would pay the wages of the farm workers as long as the latter received no financial help from the Institute for the Reorganisation of Agriculture (IRA). Both occupations had the support of the entire population. The bosses' house was closed until an IRA inventory could be drawn up. The foreman's house was taken over by the workers. The Garrets fled to Spain.

Near Avó, in central Portugal, the factory of Manuel Dinis Dias employing forty workers went into self-management. In Porto, Manuel Esperança Viera, a synthetics firm employing sixty workers, did likewise.

So did the biscuit factory of Guetara de Pombal (90 percent Mexican capital, fifty-five workers). The Clana Mining Co., in Loulé, employing a hundred workers, went into self-management and received 500,000 escudos from the government. In Setúbal, workers at the Sapec factory (which made fertilisers and agricultural products) kidnapped two of the administrators and held them captive "to show the government how bad the situation was." The company had wanted to move to Brussels.

In Évora, the café Arcada (a busy restaurant employing forty-seven people) was occupied because the workers had received no pay. They began to run the place on their own, eventually receiving a government loan of 175,000 escudos. The Baheira Hotel at Sagres was occupied on June 11 and managed by its staff.

These were just some of the hundreds of struggles which took place all over the country. It was mind-boggling, the extent of the occupations and sometimes the fervour in which they were carried out. Most of them were done out of need, by factors such as not receiving wages, bosses fleeing with capital, and so on, but it was the total atmosphere which was greater than the sum of its parts. Occasionally you had to pinch yourself to see if this was really happening. By the beginning of August 1975, it was estimated that some 380 factories had passed into self-management. It is worth taking a specific example and looking at some of the practical problems involved:

Empresa Fabril de Malhas was a textile factory in Coimbra, employing thirty-two people. A worker explained what happened: "When April 25th took place we were on a four-day week. A minimum wage (3,300 escudos) was decreed in May (1974). The boss then decided to close the place down. The workers wouldn't have it. The factory was occupied and we posted pickets. In July we decided to sell existing stocks to pay wages. The boss's partner, Maria Clara, threw her lot in with us. After March 11, the women organised night pickets because they were afraid that something might happen. Maria helped us open the filing cabinet and safe. Most of the workers felt that the boss (Aires de Azevedo) should be locked up. The MFA arrested him on May 15, 1975."[1]

Support was offered by the Textile unions and by Intersindical, but the workers thought Intersindical was a *cúpula*, or clique. They also criticised the PCP Minister of Labour for being "legalistic." Their Workers' Committee or CT was felt to be much nearer to them than the union. The

---

1   *Combate* 27, July 1975.

company itself was having all sorts of financial problems: the whole textile industry in Portugal was in crisis because Asian countries could produce things cheaper.

The CT had been elected by different sections within the factory. At first it comprised ten members, later five. A "management committee" was set up which included Maria, the old business partner. The Committee had to present weekly reports to a plenário of all workers. The idea of forming a company with shares, etc., was discussed but rejected. The workers "didn't want to become little bosses." There were negotiations with the Minister of Labour for a loan of 180,000 escudos, with which it was hoped to create another ten jobs, including the hiring of a guard who would take over the role of the pickets. "We received promises but no cash." The partner had been overruled on many points relating to the running of the factory, including her idea of all the workers being business associates, and the idea of making profits and sharing them out. The workers believed that their situation was not one of "workers' participation" but of "workers' management." But they were also conscious of all the limitations of attempting this in a capitalist society. They had no idea of how to solve this contradiction, except by "all revolutionary workers uniting and fighting together." But that would have meant overthrowing the system.

This pattern was fairly typical in factories of this size (though the ex-partner joining in with the workers was exceptional). Workers were very conscious of living in a capitalist society, of having to obey all the rules of a market economy imposed upon them. They repeatedly rejected "elitist" organisations entering into or seeking to direct their struggle, or telling them they were exploited and had to abolish the wages system.

There were many instances of delegates being purged by the workers—or even of whole CTs being revoked during General Assemblies. At Provomi (a cattle fodder factory) near Alverca, the whole CT was purged for having attempted to hide information from the workers and for having tried to increase their own wages. Because of the crisis and of the general political situation it was difficult for the CTs in smaller factories to establish themselves as "new managers," or to separate themselves too much from the workers who had elected them.

INTER-EMPRESAS AND THE UNIONS

In January 1975, almost all the left groups had supported the struggle for *unicidade* (monolithic union structure). The obvious soon became obvious even to them, namely that unicidade meant domination by Intersindical and by the PCP. Meanwhile the reformism of Intersindical, along with its harassment of certain working-class struggles (Timex, CTT, Mabor, TAP, *Journal do Comércia*, Carris, etc.) caused workers to maintain their own CTs.

The demonstration of February 7, 1975, in the face of increasing unemployment and a possible NATO threat, was the culmination of meetings between various CTs. After that Inter-Empresas—which had called the demonstration—weakened, and for good reasons. It was the obvious place to be (or to get into) for any vanguard party worthy of the name. Every Leninist group in sight (and some invisible ones) made for Inter-Empresas, with offerings of gold, frankensteins, and mire. Inter united nobody and had very little to do with trade unionism. A witty slogan on a wall ("Inter: 2 - Sindical: 0") summarised things well, in this football-crazy country.

At first certain delegates from Intersindical (who had also been elected to their respective CTs tried to form a block within Inter-Empresas. Through them the PCP sought to push its "battle for production" within the portals of Inter-Empresas itself. The result was that many CTs stopped sending delegates to general meetings. This facilitated the manipulation of the Inter-Empresas skeleton by PCP delegates or other Leninists (PRP-BR, MES, MRPP, FEC-ml), and contributed to its further desiccation. The CTs were more genuinely representative of the workers. They existed in parallel with the unions. The unions, as already stressed, were numerous and ineffective despite certain dynamic "leaders" or "personalities." In TLP (the Telephone Company) only two members of the fourteen members of the CT were union delegates, and this was typical of many enterprises. Thirty-two different unions existed in TLP without any real unity.

Despite their democratic nature, most CTs could still be manipulated by anyone intent on "capturing" them and using them as a political base for "struggle" within Inter-Empresas. In Efacec-Inel the Maoists had worked hard. By getting themselves elected onto the *Journal de Greve* (the Strike Newspaper) they had secured a firm implantation within the industry. Their position was stated quite explicitly in issue 55 (July 6, 1975) of the paper: "The fact that a true Marxist-Leninist party doesn't exist in Portugal should not impede the actions of true communists and revolutionaries in the unions. To abandon the unions to the reformists is an utterly anarchist position."

The Maoists had a perspective of controlling the unions. They wanted their own, more "radical" version of Intersindical. To achieve this they needed a stepping stone. And if one wasn't immediately to hand they would create one, by capturing certain CTs and using them as an instrument in their power struggle. While the PCP used the most populist language imaginable, the MRPP used more worker-oriented slogans. In the last analysis both approaches were very similar.

The MRPP was not the only organisation attempting to capture or to manipulate Inter-Empresas. They were all at it. Siderurgia (the great iron smelting works just outside Lisbon) employed 4,200 workers. During June and July 1975, the UDP obtained a footing there. Thereafter the ideology of the UDP became associated with Siderurgia CTs within Inter-Empresas. On June 4, 1975, the General Assembly of Inter-Empresas heard a proposal from Efacec delegates to form a "new Inter-Empresas." What certain Maoists couldn't do through a takeover of the Secretariat, they were attempting through the creation of a new organisation of the same name. A delegate from Melka (textiles) analysed the participation by Inter-Empresas in the demonstration called by Marxist-Leninist groups on May 1. She criticised the Secretariat for not having publicised the assembly point of the demo and for not having appointed stewards. Other critiques of the Secretariat were for not having contacted the organisers of the demo to insist on the slogans which Inter-Empresas had decided upon ("Not one more dismissal, all to be reinstated" and "40 hours per week, yes! 45 hours, no!"). These slogans had been replaced on the demonstration by "Against Unemployment: 40 hours per week." This had caused friction.

The critiques led to a demand for the reorganisation of the Secretariat. Divergences appeared about how some working-class groups should be represented. The Efacec delegates, who had played an important role in Inter-Empresas during its short history, hadn't managed to impose their views on the other delegates. At this point it was announced by a delegate from the CDDT (Committee for the Defence of the Rights of the Workers, one of the committees set up in Efacec after their strike) that some workers of Efacec were meeting to review their position in relation to Inter-Empresas:

> So, comrades, what is happening—and we have proof of this—is that
> the Efacec-Inel delegates are deliberately seeking to create a split in
> the ranks of Inter-Empresas, given that they are already thinking
> of organising another "Inter-Empresas." These Efacec delegates
> will continue their 'struggle' until the end: the creation of another

Inter-Empresas. They are trying to divide the workers by contacting and inviting other comrades or CTs. Besides assuming the name of Inter-Empresas, they claim that this one has ended. They say that the new Inter-Empresas will be the fruit of the old one. At the same time they slander working-class militants . . . All this shows the point reached by those who say that they are the friends of the workers but who really do everything possible to divide them. Since as yet nothing has happened we can only ask why and in whose interests they are attempting to split the organisation of which they themselves are a part and which struggles out of necessity and class feelings.

The name of the comrade from Sotécnica (a Lisbon electronics firm) who reported this meeting may never be known. He or she no doubt had illusions about "revolutionary unions," but the description of the Inter-Empresas meeting hit the nail on the head. Inter-Empresas was being manipulated by groups of CTs of similar party persuasion. The left-wing factions were doing their utmost to see that its autonomy was smothered.

The pattern was repeated many times. CT delegates would appear at Inter-Empresas meetings, making party declarations. Here is one, of slightly different parentage: "The working class cannot hide from politics. Unlike the fascists the CTs claim that politics must enter the factories through the gates. The CTs know that they can only take power if they are conscious. They know where their interests lie. This is different from defending a political party, which they shouldn't do. The CTs are organs which act autonomously against the bourgeoisie and against capital. Unlike the unions, they are not conditioned by the laws of the system. The CTs should be against the unions, or at least seek to bypass them, or even to establish themselves as parallel organisations. The CTs and the unions are working-class organisations when they are under working-class control, despite the fact that they have different objectives."

Then the punch line, giving away the Leninist authorship: "The CTs should not sow illusions in the working class that it can come to power without a Party. But the Party cannot replace all the organs of the class. The CTs have a structure which is genuinely their own. Democratically elected and revocable, they can assess the various political lines within the struggle and analyse the various ways of responding to practical problems. They can do this like a true Party of the Working Class."

THE "REVOLUTIONARY WORKERS' COUNCILS"

In April 1975, both the PRP-BR and LUAR had warned people not to be surprised by a liberal result to capitalist elections. Throughout the campaign, the PRP had been talking about "Workers' Councils." On April 19, (six days before the poll) they organised a large meeting in Lisbon with militants from Inter-Empresas and various Workers' Committees. Delegates from Lisnave, TAP, Setenave—and others from the building and textile industries—met to discuss the setting up of a new type of organisation. Representatives from Soldiers and Sailors' Committees also attended, in uniform. Members of the PRP-BR were, of course, also there—in strength. A programme was agreed. The meeting launched the Conselhos Revolucionários de Trabalhadores, Soldados e Marinheiros (CRTSM or Revolutionary Councils of Workers, Soldiers and Sailors).

In Marinha Grande, workers had organised a Council and (given the historical associations of this town—and of this idea) the PRP-BR decided that this was the form of organisation most appropriate for the workers in general. They were mesmerised by the word "council," despite the fact that workers in the São Pedro do Covo mines had, for example, already set up a "revolutionary centre," and that workers everywhere had—without prompting—set up their own CTs. What the PRP were advocating was a particular brand of institution. Living reality had to be poured into the moulds of the past.

The council structure proposed was outlined in some detail. Local councils based on enterprises, boroughs, and barracks would elect representatives to zonal councils. These would elect a regional council, and regional councils would elect a "national revolutionary council"—which would be the embodiment of working-class power. The functions of the councils were defined as the political clarification of the workers, the control of the economic and financial aspects of various enterprises, *saneamento*, and the arming of the working class.

Crucial questions concerning the real locus of decision-making in this four-tiered structure were evaded. Were the councils the embryo of a new form of social organisation? Were they to embody a fusion of economic and political power or would there be parallel political institutions as well? Little thought seems to have been devoted to the more difficult questions such as the specific weight and nature of the representation of agricultural workers, of women, of young people, of the population as consumers (as distinct from producers). How often would the "revocable delegates" report back? Would delegates remain at work during their tenure of office? How would functions rotate to ensure that bureaucracies based on monopolies of information did not arise? These questions were surely crucial to ensuring genuine—as distinct from purely formal—working-class power. While blueprints were premature, it was alarming to see the details with which organisational forms had been thought out and to compare it with the total lack of imagination (or even awareness) about relevant content.

The political confusion underlying PRP thinking about the councils was enormous. The PRP had never really understood the nature of state capitalism and of the agencies that would bring it about. "Working-class parties" to the Left of (but including) the PS had been invited to send delegates to the Provisional (procouncil) Secretariat. They would bring in "the masses." But it was naive and dangerous in the extreme to expect the cooperation of Soares and Cunhal in the council movement because this movement was aimed at destroying the very basis of their power. The participation of Social Democrats and Stalinists would not have been "neutral." It would have been profoundly counterrevolutionary. The PS and PCP would have been the conscious agents of the centralisation of the economy, in a state capitalist direction. The whole weight of their respective party machines would have been used to destroy the autonomous organisations of the working class. The councils would soon have been converted into typical instruments of capitalist recuperation.

Another area of ambiguity was the relation of the proposed councils to the MFA, seen as composed of "progressive officers," of "right-wingers," and of those "still undecided." The MFA was never explicitly analysed in class terms. CRT documents even boasted of the "support" their movement enjoyed among officers in high positions.

The idea of the councils gained publicity when Otelo and COPCON rallied to it. "I see no danger at all in these congresses or councils," Otelo said in an RTP interview. "I consider them, like the Neighbourhood Committees, to be the essence of the Portuguese revolution. I consider them similar to the Russian soviets of 1917 . . . The anarcho-syndicalists are very humorous when they write slogans on the walls such as "A portuguesa só temos cozido." (The only thing that's Portuguese is the stew). It's true enough. We must construct our own socialism. I give my whole-hearted support to these revolutionary councils."

On May 10, a meeting of Councils was held in Porto, openly attended by soldiers and sailors in uniform. At another plenário the provisional secretary (Vitor Crespo, a metalworker) said: "We should start by making the CRTs the organisation of the Portuguese people, an organisation which can exercise power, an organisation in which everyone has a say. In each factory the workers should get together to discuss problems and to elect bodies which will implement what the workers want."[2]

On August 2 and 3, 1975, the Second Congress of Councils was held in Lisbon's Technological Institute. But a change was already noticeable. Whereas at the First Congress there had been a genuine working-class representation, the second was primarily preaching to the converted. A number of enterprises were "represented" but members of the PRP-BR and their friends and contacts constituted the bulk of the audience. Banners on the walls sought nostalgically to recapture the atmosphere— and even the vocabulary—of the Petrograd of 1917. "Fora com a canalha! Poder a quem trabalha." (Out with the scum! Power to those who work! Long live the Socialist Revolution.). The Congress discussed at length certain resolutions concerning the MFA-Povo Alliance, none of which openly called for a clean break with this mystifying concept. The relations between COPCON (especially Otelo) and the PRP were very close at the time, and it was essential not to tread on anybody's toes. The perspective was clearly spelled out in a leaflet distributed at the Congress: "The Councils are the proposed organisation of the workers at their place of work, in their neighbourhoods, in the barracks. The Councils seek to form structures to take power, both political and economic, in order to establish socialism. The CRTSM can't become the tool of any particular party because of the way they are elected. But this is not to say that they can't play an important role in the socialist revolution. Theirs is the task of ideologically organising the militants and of presenting proposals to the class. It will be up to the class, and the class alone, to decide what they want."

The PRP-BR didn't have to call demonstrations under the name of Inter-Empresas in order to create a "nonparty" structure. "The Councils are our organisation," they claimed, "and it is not just because a party launched them that they can be accused of partyism. Council members are elected at their place of work and are at all times revocable by the workers."

In a formal sense this was true. But the Councils nevertheless provided a good field for party manoeuvres. They had "appeared" at the very moment when, after the fracas at Inter-Empresas, the workers were feeling their way towards new forms of organisation. But they were not

---

2   *Expresso*, May 17, 1975.

born directly in struggle. Their creation was contrived. As *Combate* put it (July 17, 1975): "It is in the moment of impasse in the autonomous workers' struggle when people are saturated with party politics—but also at a time when the workers haven't yet created autonomous organisations relating various struggles to one another—that this wide open space for opportunist adventure appears."

The space appeared—and the PRP colonised it. Councils implanted themselves in a few companies: Lisnave, Setenave, Efacec, Cambournac, etc. Their demonstrations certainly had an effect on Otelo, and on the "left" of the MFA in general. Because of this the CRTs could support COPCON and the "progressive" wing of the MFA without serious thought being given to the whole question of state capitalism.

As a reality in the life of the class, the Councils hardly existed. They were significant only in the minds of PRP planners and intellectuals who had made a fetish of the "council" form, (i.e., who had a traditional perspective). While workers participated in demonstrations organised by the CRTs, these bodies had few roots in the factories, where they were seen as yet another party political faction. Of the 7,300 workers in Lisnave only two or three dozen actively supported the Councils. Other workers, searching for new means of self-expression, supported the Councils temporarily, as on the May Day demonstration of 1975. Most workers soon reverted to their original instruments of struggle: the Workers' Committees. Throughout, the Councils remained more an idea than a real movement.

THE COOPERATIVE MOVEMENT

Some three hundred "cooperatives" had been formed by August 1975 and another two hundred were set up in September. In general, these productive units (whether industrial or agricultural) had appeared either when a boss had abandoned his company or when he had declared himself unable to continue running it as a profitable venture. Fewer than half were ever "legalised": they existed in a certain limbo between established capitalist companies and enterprises under workers' self-management. A federation of cooperatives came into being and gradually sought to define itself, both in terms of structure and of functions. Let us look at the problems of a specific cooperative. The seventeen workers at Termo e Sol (Lisbon) had been engaged in the assembly of air-conditioning equipment. Because of difficulties in paying the minimum wage the boss had abandoned the firm. The workers took it over. Through much sacrifice and many hours of overtime they managed to alter the type of production from the assembly of air-conditioning equipment to the assembly of drainage and electrical components, considered more important. A management committee was set up to deal with all aspects of finance. No decisions were taken without plenário. In August 1975 one of the workers described the situation to me as follows:

> In terms of red tape, it would have been easier to set up a limited company than a cooperative. The cooperative had not yet been legalised though it was formed in November 1974. Different wages are paid, but everyone has equal responsibility. It is impossible to go back. If it proves necessary to take up arms to defend the cooperative, I and others would be prepared to do so. The boss is claiming indemnity which isn't fair. Many bosses have joined various cooperatives. I don't mind this, since they too have to eat. At first there were 22 workers here, but 5 refused to join (the cooperative). The reason, I think, was that they were afraid. There are great difficulties in making socialism in a capitalist world, but the cooperative movement is a step in the right direction. Of course I am still a wage earner but what other way is there, here and now, of resolving the problem? The cooperative has made a contract with a Neighbourhood Association in a shanty town (in the borough of Falqueira, in Amadora, Lisbon) . . . Our offer was the cheapest that the Neighbourhood Association had received. It was to do the plumbing and electrical wiring (some 5,000 escudos per house as against 7,000 or 9,000 which others would have asked).

LAND OCCUPATIONS

Unpublished official statistics showed that by August 8, 206,645 hectares of 330 different *herdades* and *latifundias* had been occupied by some 6,000 workers. The main regions affected were the Alentejo, the Ribatejo, and the area around Castelo Branco (Centre). The organisation of this land into cooperatives and collectives was less amenable to left-wing manipulation. The government instrument for social change in the countryside was the Institute for the Reorganisation of Agriculture (IRA), teams of agronomists and specialists working from its eight Regional Centres. At Évora, the IRA was running an eighteen-hour day schedule. On May 17, 200 hectares in Alentejo (the farms of Mantargil, Leitões, Pipas de Baixo, etc.) were occupied by about a hundred workers. The occupation was supported by both IRA and MFA, and fertiliser was promised. The workers required fifteen tractors to start work. With the area in full production they might need thirty.

On June 11, the Quinta (farm) da Torre, near Cabanas, was transformed into a cooperative. The IRA gave support. The land had been abandoned by its previous owner, the Count of Tojal. The occupation was carried out with the help of the local Neighbourhood Committee. Machines were taken from a nearby factory to help clear 30 hectares. Houses on the land were to be part of the cooperative.

The 300 hectares of the Quinta de Alagoas near Lagoa (Algarve) were turned into a collective (named "Red Star"). The Quinta of Sousa de Sé, near Évora, was occupied. Some 2,000 hectares were involved. Twelve *latifundiários* attacked the workers with guns. One man was wounded. On July 16, the Quinta de São Pedro in the village of Cuba (Alentejo) was also occupied and a cooperative set up.

On July 25, some 10,000 hectares in the district of Santarém were occupied by 354 workers and declared a collective. Other workers carrying pick-axes had climbed onto trucks and helped the agricultural workers carry out this massive occupation. Together they had taken over farms at Engal (2,000 hectares and twenty-three workers), Monte Couco (3,000 hectares and sixty-two workers), Esparteiro (300 hectares and forty-five workers), Faias (350 hectares and forty-five workers), Aguas Belas (700 hectares and sixty-two workers), Aldeia Velha (1,100 hectares and fifty-nine workers), Courela dos Barreiros (500 hectares and the same number of workers as the preceding farm), Palma (300 hectares and nineteen workers), Monte Novo (1,000 hectares and the same workers), and Ruivos (700 hectares and forty-eight workers).

In July 1975, through some friends who were now working in the Institute of the Reorganisation of Agriculture, João and also Gloria, I was able to visit some of the land occupations in Alentejo.

By July 1975, a clear pattern was emerging. The most noticeable fact was that there was never talk of dividing up the land. The land was to be worked collectively and owned by the village as a whole. The availability of workers was never in question, but the lack of machinery caused endless problems. The Bank Workers Union (affiliated to Intersindical) had helped ensure that credits were granted to occupied farms. But the agricultural banks insisted that the loans be invested under the guidance of the Minister of Agriculture, Baptista, and through the IRA Regional Centres.

Immediately after an occupation teams from the IRA would arrive and discuss things with the workers. Decisions would only be taken if the workers agreed. Credits would be allocated to the new cooperatives at the current bank rate (6.5 percent). The credits included an emergency fund from which wage arrears could be paid. Many cooperatives took over stockpiles of cork and wood and sold them to pay wages.

The law on Agrarian Reform had set a ceiling of five hundred hectares on personal land holdings. This gave the government power to take over land needed by cooperatives. In many areas the IRA Regional Centres would immediately legalise an occupation. The task of these Centres was to service the cooperatives, not to manage them. Workers at the Centres had constantly to remind agricultural workers of this fact.

Apart from the cooperative movement there also existed a "League of Small and Medium Farmers." They were puzzled by the occupations and afraid that their lands would also be taken over. Most were secretly if not openly against the movement.

In the Évora district some hundred occupations had already occurred. In August 1975, new occupations occurred daily. Again let us look at a specific case: the cooperative of Safira, near Montemor (Alentejo). Having occupied two farms (covering a total area of 1,100 hectares) the eighty-nine workers involved elected a Committee which immediately contacted the IRA Regional Centre. The occupation was registered. The Committee, meeting in a barn, decided to ask for a loan of 300,000 escudos to get the farms going. Zé, the most articulate member of the Committee spoke to me of some of the problems:

> The owners of the land came round at night, with the intention of removing some of the machinery left on the farm. Because of this a night picket has been set up. Another farm nearby lost two tractors through a lack of vigilance. Most occupations are guarded by armed workers. People know it. They don't come this way at night.
>
> Another problem is the continued capitalist mentality of the workers. Our neighbours at Infanta have two machines which we would like to borrow. But instead of lending them to us, they want to hire them to us at 400 escudos per day. A meeting of the two cooperatives has solved the problem by analysing the politics of such a transaction.
>
> A small property is stuck right between the two occupied farms. Although they have no particular respect for its owner, the men want to rent his place from him, and for the government to pay the rent. They have invited this individual to join the cooperative but

he has refused. The problem remains unsolved. It will depend on the line of the League of Small and Medium Farmers, of which this man is a member. The workers on the cooperative have received no wages for seven weeks. No emergency monies have been paid to them. We cut some 24,000 tons of cork and seized another 25,000 tons when we occupied the farm. We intend to sell this to pay ourselves.

Zé also spoke (and here he was interrupted by other members of the Committee) about the number of wild rabbits roaming the fields. Because of the general opposition to hunting rabbits (a predominantly aristocratic pastime, and one of the reasons why the land was not cultivated) there was some confusion as to what to do.

The workers from the Regional Centre in Évora advised the men to do whatever they thought fit. They alone knew the problems. As one IRA worker put it: "For forty-eight years, you have had people making decisions for you. If we were now to do that, everything would stay the same. You have occupied the land, now do what you want. Shoot the rabbits if you want to." In general, this was the attitude of the IRA workers. There was little red tape and the only control by the Centre was in the allocation of loans which were, in most cases, automatically granted. Yet there was a great class divide between the Committee and the IRA technical helpers. The IRA team asked the workers to criticise the Centre. Zé spoke of two grievances. The first was a certain disorganisation. When he went to the Centre he met different people all the time. Secondly, what one IRA worker said didn't always correspond with what another said.

This, of course, wasn't surprising. Within the Centre there were all sorts of political technocratic tendencies. They ranged from PCP to MRPP and even included "libertarians." In general the role of the IRA was one of recuperation. Just as COPCON helped promote the myth that the working class didn't need to be armed, the IRA promoted the myth that the working class didn't need to take control of the total juridical and financial power. No matter how much the IRA repeated that the workers had friends in the Centres, the existence of the IRA as a lifeline to power impeded the setting up of parallel and autonomous workers' organisations, at this level.

XI CRISIS LOOMING

Between June and August 1975, it became increasingly difficult to speak of a government or indeed of an opposition. Real power was coming to lie more and more in the streets. With the departure of the PS and PPD from the Fourth Government the PCP and MDP were left in virtual control of the state. The "Gonçalvists," as the military wing of the PCP were called, dominated the Council of the Revolution, while the PCP and its sympathisers controlled most of the ministries. But their basis in the country was narrow and certainly showed no signs of broadening.

The PCP had spearheaded the response to March 11 and both the "moderate" wing of the MFA and the PS had had to follow in their wake, accepting nationalisations as a price to be paid for their participation in office. Between March and June, the PS (and the social-democratic wing of the MFA) was disorganised. They were to remain in a minority position, despite the "support" for the PS which the April elections had revealed.

The newly formed Fifth Government was opposed on all sides. It would be simplistic to view all support for it as "revolutionary" and opposition to it as "reactionary" a view held by the PCP. "The Fifth Government was born dead," according to Arnaldo Matos (MRPP). But it also inherited all the dead governments before it. The same forces opposed the Fifth Government as had opposed the Third or Fourth. But there were other oppositions, too, which were now to take on a violent form.

BACKLASH IN THE NORTH
The fire-bombings which were to spread throughout the North began in earnest in Fafe (near Porto) on June 11, when a grenade exploded in the PCP offices. Most of the terrorist actions which followed were clearly the work of the Right. In Póvoa de Varzim (near Porto) leaflets were handed out saying that the MDP had planned to kidnap the local priest. In Trofa, on June 16, CDS sympathisers organised a demonstration against the PCP.

The class structure in the North was complex, in many ways it was like a different country. A different attitude was needed which given the revolutionary situation was difficult; things seemed to orbit out of Lisbon TV stations and the South. The Left had really little implantation in the North, the right wing had used their influence to send thousands of poor Northern farm workers to the colonies etc. The Church was in control.

On July 1, the workers of Moleflex (mattresses) downed tools and marched from S. João da Madeira to the army barracks in Porto. Some two hundred of the two thousand workers claimed that the PCP was manipulating the Administrative Council (which had been appointed by Vasco Gonçalves) and that their CT was completely controlled by the Party. In Lourinhá, in the centre of the country, most small farmers and workers had supported the social movements after April 25. The local PCP criticised a local innkeeper for renting his hall to the PPD for a meeting. The man was popular in the area, having hired his hall to most of the workers at one time or another for marriage feasts, etc., even charging less to the poorer workers. When the PCP called him a "fascist" and a "reactionary," the local small farmers and agricultural workers rallied en masse to support him. Their demonstration, like many such, was as much against the local PCP cell as in favour of the PPD (or CDS, etc.). During the demonstration fire-bombs were thrown. The only response by the PCP was to label the entire local population "reactionary and uneducated." This paternalism was rampant. In order to explain divisions within the class the left groups were reduced to talking of the backwardness of the proletariat. This inflamed the "backward proletariat" still further. While at a certain theoretical level groups like UDP and PRP-BR discussed among themselves problems such as those of agricultural workers and tenant farmers, at the practical level their behaviour showed the worst form of cliquism.

The backlash continued nonstop throughout July and August. In Santa Comba Dão, over the weekend of July 26, a crowd raided a local National Republican Guard barracks where an ex-PIDE was being held prisoner. In Bragança some ten thousand people turned up to hear the Bishop say Mass and began shouting, "Down with Otelo, Otelo to Mozambique." In Agueda and Esmoriz the PCP headquarters were completely destroyed. On July 29, the MDP offices in these towns were burned to the ground to cries of "Long live the CDS." In Lourinhá, where the Lisbon papers had been burned during an "anticommunist" demonstration, some three hundred small farmers and local businessmen marched to one of the nationalised banks and called for the saneamento of three PCP members who worked there. They claimed that agricultural credit was being granted according to party colours, and that information concerning the political beliefs of customers was being fed to the bank by local PCP workers. When the PCP was accused by some thirty members of the "Committee for the Extinction of the PIDE" of using PIDE files to blackmail people into supporting them, the PS called for an enquiry. That the PS (or others) would also have used them, given half a chance, is beside the point. The scandal helped discredit the Fifth Government even more.

By the end of August, most of the groups (with the exception of the most orthodox Maoist ones) had been attacked. They included Intersindical (trade unions), PCP, MDP, FSP, MES, UDP, PRP-BR, FEC-ml, and various front organisations controlled by these groups. To understand this wave of fire-bombings in the North and Centre, one must look at the social and cultural peculiarities of these areas. It was not the first time that a Lisbon-based regime had been frontally attacked from the North. In the famous wars of the Patuleia (1846-48) riots had spread from Porto, directed against reforms introduced by the right-wing Cabralist regime. This regime, established through a bloodless coup, had been opposed by the main classes in society (aristocrats, artisans and peasants) and by a variety of political tendencies (monarchists, generals, clergy, and left radicals). The revolt at that time (also known as the revolt of Maria da Fonte) was certainly popular, although its internal contradictions were just as sharp as were to be those of the opposition of 1975.

Before April 1974, PCP and MDP theoreticians and economists had only seriously attempted to analyse the situation in the South, where capitalist contradictions were more blatant. They drew up their plans for dismantling the great latifundios and monopolies through agrarian reform. The North, almost forgotten, was now staking its claims to be remembered, and with a vengeance.

The structure and problems of the North were quite different from those of the South, as a few figures can easily show. In Évora 71 percent of the existing farms comprised of less than four hectares. But together these numerous farms only covered a minute part of the land (6 percent). The rest was in the hands of the owners of large estates. At the other end of the spectrum, in the region of Viseu, there were very few large estates and some 92 percent of the land was covered by plots of less than four hectares. Also, all the major labour intensive factories in Portugal were in the South, twenty one of forty-nine factories employing over a thousand workers were in Lisbon and Setúbal.

Agrarian reform in the South presented few problems. The *lat-ifundiários* fled the land (or were driven from it) and the agricultural workers merely walked in and occupied it. In Évora, 90 percent of the population engaged in agriculture were wage-earners. In Viana in the North, the figure was only 27 percent. The unevenness of industrial development was associated with a very uneven development of agriculture.

In the South there was a certain support for the policies of the PCP and MDP: they opened a door whereby the workers could occupy land and take over the machinery and houses on it. The *latifundiários* (through the PIDE and the National Republican Guard) had kept a tight hold on their workers. The miserable wages paid had engendered a real solidarity and hatred for the great land-owners. Nationalisation of the banks and the centralisation of credit were the obvious PCP responses to pressures from below. Support for land occupations and acceptance of the "cooperatives" was also necessary, at least in the first stages.

The North was a different matter. Most peasant families there rented their small farms from local land-owners who had a hold over them far more powerful than anything encountered in the South. The "rent laws," which dated back to the early 1940s, allowed the landowners to refuse renewal of leasing arrangements to any family, at a year's notice. This law was changed by the Fourth Government. Almost no landowner could now evict a tenant within eighteen years of having signed a contract. The new rent law—typical of the new legislation—was a compromise with the local landlords. On the one hand it helped tenants while on the other it legitimised the whole concept of agricultural rent, confirming the landlords' "right" to the land.

The Northern peasants had provided whatever "mass basis" the previous regime had enjoyed. The demonstrations in support of Salazar after the Second World War were however often farcical affairs: Northern peasant farmers were shepherded into buses and brought to Lisbon (being paid a massive twenty escudos for the day). Local authorities arranged the lists of demonstrators, helped by the clergy in the churches.

Northern families often lived entirely off the land, eating vegetables, bartering for essentials, seldom using or needing money. In some parts it was like living in the nineteenth century. Certain villages were so remote that news that a coup had taken place in Lisbon took a considerable time to sink in. The "cultural dynamisation" programme of the Fifth Division was carried out in many areas in a manner offensive to these peasants. The local power structures were difficult to dismantle, attempts being met by the combined resistance of rural bosses, a very influential clergy and the police.

Generations of ignorance had been fostered by the Catholic Church. Even today spokesmen for the Vatican continue to wield influence both in the North and in Lisbon. Cardinal Cerejeira, the right hand of Salazar, was allowed to move freely in the capital while his friends, leaders of the PIDE, were arrested. But all this only provides a partial explanation. Half a century of Salazarism had never engendered as much anticommunism among ordinary people as eighteen months of PCP participation in various governments. The real roots of power in the countryside had in no way been threatened by the MFA. Of the PIDEs arrested by the First Provisional Government, 75 percent had been in the South and only some 6 percent in the North, according to a Lisbon journalist related to the PCP. No priests had been arrested, North or South.

THE ROAD TO STATE CAPITALISM

The story of the Manuel Gonçalves's factory in Famalicão, in Braga in the North, shows some of the problems facing the workers as a result of the international ramifications of capital. The factory had been nationalised soon after March 11, its boss being implicated in the attempted coup. From Spain this man had written to international suppliers (a Swiss company) instructing them to withhold raw materials unless he personally signed the orders. The workers were out of work for four weeks, without pay. Manuel Gonçalves was of poor origins himself. He had built a swimming pool in the factory for the workers and had provided them with a new canteen. The wages paid were miserable but were better than none. Members of the Gonçalves family within the factory began campaigning to have the boss reinstated. When two hundred of the workers (led by these members of the Gonçalves family) called for new elections to the CT, the PCP led CT refused, calling it a "reactionary manoeuvre." A demonstration into Famalicão in late June was to lead to the fire-bombing of the PCP headquarters there, in July.

Some of these workers stressed that nationalisation had brought them nothing but hardship. What they meant was that their new boss (the state) was no better than the old one (private capitalism). Indeed state capitalism was in many ways worse: all the previous hardships remained, to which was now added the threat of losing their jobs. Within the factory, labour relations had not changed. Wages hadn't increased. Only insecurity had mounted.

The only groups to support these workers were the CDS, PPD, and PS, and they only did so by attacking the new PCP-dominated management. The workers were confused as to what they wanted or how their problems could be solved. After a demonstration in the town of Famalicão in August (under the slogan "Down with the Workers Committee—Long live the boss") I spoke to some of those involved outside the local cinema, where they were meeting. Their wages were lower than the legal minimum defined by the government. Their anger was expressed as anticommunism.

The bombings and terrorist attacks continued. It is true the weather was dry, but the number of forest fires registered during the summer months was vastly in excess of what was usual. Groups like ELP (Army for the Liberation of Portugal) spearheaded many of the attacks. But it would be evading the real issues to attribute to them the fact that twenty thousand people turned up to a demonstration in Braga, early in August, to listen to a speech by the Bishop denouncing the countries "behind the Iron Curtain."

The economic problems were serious indeed. Some quarter of a million Portuguese was out of work and without real means of support. The unemployment fund set up by the Third Government was ineffective in great parts of the country. Some three hundred thousand Angolans were to arrive by October, and more later. Many companies had been abandoned by their bosses because they were no longer profitable, and taken over by the workers because they needed work. Of the deficit in the balance of payments between January and April 1975, 75 percent was with EFTA and the EEC countries. External and internal markets were closing up. Something had to give in.

THE CRISIS AND THE EMERGENCE OF THE "GROUP OF NINE"

On July 21, Vasco Gonçalves made his own analysis of the situation. "The creation of the conditions whereby the workers can progressively come to power implies the existence of a vanguard capable of developing a socialist practice." He then voiced the state-capitalist policies of the PCP. He had reservations concerning the Left. "Voluntarism and idealism have limited relevance to the building of socialism . . . Leftism is objectively on the side of the reaction . . . its development lies in the failure of the powers-that-be to fulfil the requirements of the revolutionary process."

This was one of the first acknowledgements that mistakes had been made, and that the PCP was in danger of losing ground unless these were rectified. Costa Gomes warned that the "Lisbon column was in danger of being cut off from the rest of the country" and that "the revolution was taking place at a pace which the country could not follow." The division building up within the Revolutionary Council reflected the divisions outside. Vítor Alves was later (*Expresso*, September 20, 1975) to say that the Council had broken down altogether, and that it was because of this that it had been decided to concentrate power in the hands of a triumvirate. The triumvirate consisted of Vasco Gonçalves (PCP), Costa Gomes ("the Cork"), and Otelo (populism). This move was not to solve the divisions but only to aggravate them. On August 7, a group of officers on the Council produced a pragmatic document which became known as the "Document of the Nine." The Nine were: Captains Vasco Lourenço and Sousa e Castro, Majors Costa Neves, Canto e Castro, Melo Antunes and Vítor Alves, Commander Vítor Crespo, and Brigadiers Francisco Charais and Pezerat Correia. The last two were Commanders of the Southern and Central regions (Corvacho, who supported the PCP, was responsible for the North). Vasco Lourenço had been the spokesman for the Council of the Revolution while Melo Antunes had written the first programme of the armed forces. He had also drafted an economic plan before March 11, a plan which was to be discarded with the nationalisations. Crespo and Alves had been members of the "Movement of the Captains" from its inception, and had been deeply involved in subsequent events. With their supporters they formed a powerful bloc in the Council of the Revolution.

The essential point in the "Document of The Nine" was that the revolution was taking place too fast, as a result of which the social and cultural fabric of the country was being damaged. The state apparatus was "degenerating into anarchy." "The country found itself defrauded of the hopes of April 25th," it said, "and daily the gap was growing between those in Lisbon and Alentejo—and almost the whole of the rest of the country." Refusing both the Eastern European model of bureaucratic organisation and leadership and social democratic models from the West, The Nine claimed that the problems of Portuguese society required something new. Stressing the "left" nature of their project they asked for links to be set up with the EEC and EFTA countries, as well as with "socialist" and Comecon countries, in short with anyone prepared to do business with Portugal. "It is necessary to denounce," they said, "the fascist spirit of a project which claims to be socialist, but ends up with bureaucratic dictatorship against the inert masses of the citizens."

While signs of social agitation grew daily, the left groups (from the PCP to LUAR) condemned the document. The signatories were immediately suspended from their duties in the Council (whose democratic-centralist practices they had violated by making the document public). But they continued in their military duties. The PCP sympathisers on the Council and in the Fifth Division had not the power to demote or cashier them, much as they would have liked to. The chorus against the document was almost unanimous from the Left, only certain Maoist groups (like the PCP-ml and the AOC) supporting it, as opposition to the "social-fascist" politics of the PCP. The PS saw their opening. They rushed in with their own programme "to safeguard the revolution and overcome the crisis" which, along with the "Document of The Nine," they proposed as a basis for a new government.

Four days later, on August 13, a group of COPCON officers published their own interpretation of the crisis. Their document strangely resembled texts that had been circulating within the PRP-BR and UDP for over a month. Titled "A Working Proposal for a Political Programme" (and subtitled "A Self Criticism of COPCON"), it blamed the political parties in the coalition (and particularly the PCP) for generating the crisis. The PCP practice of occupying the Parish Juntas and of allocating grants according to party colours had worsened the situation of the small farmers. Cultural dynamisation had been carried out, the document argued, without due respect for the cultural habits in the villages. The PCP was not alone to blame, for all the coalition parties were responsible for governmental policies. The solution didn't lie in concessions to the Right. The document pointed out that liberals who made concessions to the Right were, historically, always the first to suffer. It called for "reinforcement of the alliance between the MFA and the people" and for the strengthening of the organs of people's power. Dependence on imperialism had to be terminated and Portugal had to be made self-sufficient. In order to do this, agriculture had to be developed. Rents would have to be frozen and speculation in housing abolished. Socialised medicine and generalised education would be instituted. Power, according to the COPCON document, would have to be maintained in the armed forces until the formation of a Popular Assembly at the national level. The election of officers was the only way of maintaining discipline.

None of the political vanguards could hope to carry out this COPCON programme. None of them had the mass base necessary. Part of the crisis lay in the ambiguities concerning *who* would organise the masses for "socialism." People were discussing matters which have haunted the communist movement since the Russian revolution. Was "the Party" necessary? Would "the vanguard" come from within the class or "from without"? In the minds of some, the organs of "popular power" provided the bricks with which "the Party" could be built. By manipulating the CTs and CMs (while retaining control of them wherever possible) the various Leninist groups hid their own vanguardism. The class had other ideas. The numbers of nonparty demonstrations show this clearly. On such demonstrations, when political groups tried to raise their party banners, they were shouted out: "Here, there are no parties."

The signatories of the two documents ("The Nine" and COPCON) met over dinner on August 14 to work on a third document which might combine the essentials of the other two. Charais and Pezarat (Southern and central Commanders) claimed that many of the COPCON proposals were impossible. The talks broke down. Many units supported the COPCON document in Assemblies, but many officers and even ADUs (Democratic Unit Assemblies) supported "The Nine." A high-ranking officer from the South said that army discipline was disintegrating and that he no longer felt in command of his own unit.

The PCP-influenced Fifth Division criticised the COPCON document and called for an enquiry into the activities of Vasco Lourenço and "other officers manipulated by the PS against Vasco Gonçalves and the representatives of the MFA." But their attempts to concoct a credible plot failed.

The PS and PPD launched a new offensive against the Gonçalves government. They called demonstrations which brought ten thousand people onto the streets chanting "Out with Vasco," "For a government of national salvation." A PCP meeting had to be called off in Porto because of threats. On August 13, soldiers in Braga refused to protect the MDP headquarters, despite orders to do so from PCP Northern Commander Corvacho.

On August 18, Vasco Gonçalves made a speech in Almada, across the river from Lisbon, which was to become his epitaph. His language was becoming indistinguishable from that of the PCP. He proclaimed his belief in state capitalism as the next step in the transition to "socialism." He stressed the need for a strong vanguard based on the unions and for strong centralised power, which he identified with the Fifth Government. But, much as he called for such a "vanguard" and for such "power," they simply didn't exist. Neither Intersindical nor the Fifth Government was trusted by the vast majority of industrial workers, either North or South, or by the peasants and agricultural workers in the North. Undeterred, Vasco Gonçalves went further. He said that if it was necessary to carry out his programme with "reduced forces," he was prepared to do so.

On the same day the PCP called for a half-hour general strike. This was all but ignored. At the same time some PRP-BR and UDP Neighbourhood and Workers' Committees called a demonstration on August 20 "in support of the COPCON document." Throughout August 19, Rádio Renascença kept its channels open to groups who supported the demo. The movement snow-balled: in the end some 200 to 250 Committees gave formal support to what became one of the biggest demonstrations in Portugal since the "unicidade" demo in January 1975. Some seventy thousand people marched to São Bento: agricultural workers streamed into Lisbon from the Ribatejo and Alentejo, in tractors and trailers, carrying banners proclaiming "Agrarian Revolution."

After this virtuoso display of political acrobatics the PCP eventually "supported" the demonstration, which they had denounced a week earlier. The main slogans were: "Immediate application of the COPCON document"; "Death to ELP and those who support it"; "An end to the misery of country people"; "Soldiers, sailors, workers of factory and field, united we shall win"; "Against fascism, against capital, popular offensive"; "Against the imperialisms, national independence"[1]; and "The right to work." The whole emphasis of the demonstration changed. It had originally been planned as a demonstration "in support of the COPCON document." It was now becoming one in support of the Fifth Government. The episode was a clear illustration of the mobilising power still wielded by the PCP, whose attitude seems to have been "if you can't oppose them, join them." Many leftist groups were playing the same game. They were supporting the Fifth Government in an often uncritical way. They "defended" the PCP-MDP (to a greater or lesser extent, depending on the group) at the expense of open and honest discussions of class problems. Their attitudes were a strange mixture of opportunism and sectarianism. Some even claimed that no discussion with small farmers was possible—because they were small farmers. Many of these farmers were aware of class division, and some even put the interests of the proletariat above what seemed to be their own immediate interests.

On August 25, FUR (the Front of Revolutionary Unity) was set up. It was to prove one of the briefest political flirtations (between tile Communist Party and the far-left) in history. Apart from the PCP the "Front" comprised such strange bedfellows as the MDP, FSP, PRP, MES, LCI, LUAR, and the Maoist First of May Group. All the leftist groups doubtless felt that through the "alliance," they were getting a step nearer to political

---

1   That the PCP was prepared to accept the use of the plural here shows how desperate it was in its search for alliances.

power and they were all prepared to allow the PCP to make the running for them in this particular direction. Despite its criticisms of the PCP the Left was prepared to support the Fifth Government, when the cards were down. They justified this, saying that the Fifth Government would be better than any conceivable Sixth, and therefore needed support.

On August 26, the day after it had been formed, FUR called a demonstration. The theme was to be "the continuation of the revolutionary processes." Before the march got under way the Maoist First of May Group abandoned the Front. The PCP then introduced slogans other than those agreed and the demonstration proved a fiasco, with PRP and MES walking out. The following day the PCP was thrown out of FUR, which thereby lost its only chance of entering the government.

The Fifth Government was doomed, despite a trickle of support still coming in from officers in the Fifth Division or in the Navy. Most officers supported "The Nine," and many units did too. The Fifth Government, as though realising that its time was up, rushed through a series of laws which included further nationalisations (such as that of the giant monopoly CUF).

In the North the burning of PCP offices continued without respite. The PS and PPD began talking about another government. Accusations and counteraccusations flooded press and radio. In Leiria, in the Centre, PCP and MDP offices were attacked. PCP militants who came in, armed, from nearby towns to defend their headquarters were arrested. In the South and Centre, units called for the resignation of right-wing officers, while in the North some units called for the saneamento of their PCP Commander, Corvacho. The real balance of forces was difficult to gauge accurately. All sorts of dubious communiqués were appearing.

The PCP first reacted to all this by producing more and more of its "MFA-VASCO-POVO" posters, attempting to personalise the revolution in the figure of Vasco Gonçalves. But when Otelo finally broke with Gonçalves at the Tancos MFA Assembly (see below) the triumvirate collapsed. Much of the basis of MFA support for the Fifth Government collapsed with it. The PCP, having realised it was on an unsafe ticket with the Left, on the streets—and finding Gonçalves a liability—began negotiations with the PS and PPD with a view to a place in a Sixth Government.

THE SIXTH GOVERNMENT AND THE ADVANCE OF "THE NINE"

The Fifth Government resigned on September 9. Ten days later, a Sixth took office. An important shift in the locus of military power had meanwhile taken place. At the MFA General Assembly in Tancos, on September

6, the "Group of Nine" around Melo Antunes had succeeded in persuading a majority of Army delegates not to accept the reelection of Vasco Gonçalves. The delegates from the Air Force, who were mainly to the Right, had then forced a showdown. Having lost his majority Gonçalves resigned. The repercussions of these events were to affect the whole power structure in the MFA.

With the departure of ten members close to Gonçalves (including Eurico Corvacho, the Northern commander, and Costa Martins, ex-Minister of Labour) the twenty-nine members of the Council were reduced to nineteen. It was decided not to replace the departing officers. Of the nineteen members of the new Council, seven would be chosen by the President and twelve (Navy: 3, Air Force: 3, Army: 6) elected from the three branches of the armed forces. The political make up of the new Council greatly favoured "The Nine."

The PCP-Gonçalvist hegemony which had developed during the Fourth and Fifth Governments now lay shattered. The PCP even had difficulty in constituting itself into a meaningful opposition within the MFA. They had played the power game and lost, being literally evicted in the process from the higher echelons of the military apparatus. Having been pushed off the top of this particular ladder, the PCP started supporting and manipulating rank-and-file groups in the Services, seeking thereby to pressurise the MFA into reintegrating some of its members.

The new Council didn't fare much better. Its first attempted action was a total flop. It forbade all units to issue texts or manifestos, unless they had been okayed by the Council. The instruction was widely condemned in the press . . . and the units merely ignored it! It was aimed at stopping groups like SUV (Soldiers United Will Win) which had come into existence early in September from making political statements. It soon became obvious that this order could not be enforced.

Admiral Pinheiro de Azevedo became Prime Minister of the Sixth Provisional Government. He had been a member of the original "Movement of the Captains" and had led the assault on the PIDE offices on April 25. The regime still needed its radical image, if only to coat the pill of what it was now to propose. The aims of the new administration were spelled out, unambiguously:

1) To establish its own legitimacy
2) To guarantee the functioning of the Constituent Assembly
3) To decentralise the administration

4) To avoid purges taking an "arbitrary" form
5) To create conditions in which the courts could function.
6) To promote legislation which would punish armed civilians.
7) To reanimate the private sector and restructure the state sector
8) To strengthen relations with the EEC and EFTA countries

The Sixth Government comprised four PS ministers, two PPD, one SEDES, and one PCP. The four "military" seats went to officers who supported "The Nine." The two independents were "right of centre." The creation of the new government was hailed by both the PS and PPD as a "victory for democracy." It was well received by the ruling classes, internationally. The U.S. and EEC promised massive aid. But the problem of governing Portugal was not to prove so easy.

XII THE SITUATION IN THE CLASS

While the North was exploding in a spate of "anticommunist" actions the South was evolving quite differently. The political crisis was deepening. The newly formed Sixth Government and the "Council of the Revolution" were opposed by wide sections of society and from many directions simultaneously. In many respects the Sixth Government only had a nominal reality. Not one but several "parallel" states existed in Portugal at this time.

The breakdown of the state apparatus had two immediate results. The first and most important was that the workers (both industrial and agricultural) could exert greater pressure on employers. The second was that the various groups, to win support, treated all demands in a completely demagogic way. The press manipulations, the front organisations passing themselves off as "united, nonparty groups," the "triumphalist" lies on the radio and in the press (an optimism gone crazy) all increased.

The PCP had a foot in the Sixth Government but was also opposing it from the outside. FUR and the UDP, in their different ways, issued calls for a "Revolutionary Workers' Government." Their projects of state capitalism (FUR) and of "national independence" had more force at the level of the media than in terms of real support. The platform of FUR, decided upon on August 25, 1975, saw the COPCON document and a PCP document "Lines of programmed action and the tasks of transition" as a basis of common action. After the split with the PCP, FUR could still explain the need for its own existence as follows: "Now that the revolutionary process is in a certain impasse . . . it is necessary to close ranks and prepare for combat. The bourgeoisie is trying to regain ground lost after March 11 and we must oppose the reactionary forces with a revolutionary offensive. At this moment, when reactionary forces are spreading confusion and disunity amongst the workers . . . it is necessary to unite the revolutionary forces against social democracy and fascism."[1]

---

1   *A Capital*, September 12, 1975.

For FUR the greatest enemies were the PS, the PPD and the extreme Right (which used these groups as cloaks). Reaction was undoubtedly on the offensive. There were reports of CIA money pouring into Portugal (*New York Times*, September 25, 1975). False $20 notes were being passed round to the tune of $7 million. Vast amounts of Russian money were also reaching both Portugal and Angola.

Land occupations were increasing. By the end of September, 393,000 hectares had been taken over by 10,800 workers.[2] By November, it was to be over a million hectares. Thus during two months the number of occupations had more than trebled. The main reason was the lack of state control. The bureaucrats and officials had been slow in establishing their inventories and in developing their state capitalist policies for agricultural production. The National Republican Guard (always the mainstay of stability in the countryside) was partly neutralised. In this context, the agrarian revolution surged forward. Workers took the law into their own hands. They went ahead and occupied, without worrying about the "necessary" formalities, that is, without being unduly concerned about legal "requirements" such as getting the support of the IRA. The feeling was that this was the time to occupy, as the National Republican Guard was weak. Hundreds of agricultural workers forced through occupations in the regions of Beja, Portalegre, Évora, Setúbal, Santarém, Lisbon, Faro, and Castelo Branco. The weakness of the state apparatus enabled the technicians of IRA promptly to legalise most of the occupations.

The names of the new cooperatives speak for themselves: "Go to hell," "Now or never," "New souls," "Wall of steel," "Shining star," "Liberty or death," "Soldier Luís," "Otelo Saraiva de Carvalho," . . . but also "Red star," "Freedom or fascism," "Vasco Gonçalves" and even "Bento de Jesus Caraça" (an old PCP militant and brilliant mathematician).

POPULAR ASSEMBLIES

The base groups, in many areas, fully appreciated the need to coordinate their struggles. Parochialism was not one of their weaknesses. They were also deeply aware of the need for self-defence which, on their own, they would have had difficulty in providing. Soldiers and workers alike attempted to set up contacts at a nonparty level. The various Leninist

---

2   The IRA technicians were facing a crisis. Threats of sackings caused them to ratify occupations quickly and tried to "legalise" as many occupations as possible over September, October, and November of 1975.

groups functioned within these autonomous organisations but had to hide their party colours if they wanted to take part.

In Marvila, near Lisbon Airport, the troops of RAL-1 met with the CMs and CTs. Some twenty-three such committees, collectives, and cooperatives set up what became known as a Popular Assembly, which defined itself and its tasks as follows:

The Marvila Popular Assembly

1   Is the organisation of workers and local inhabitants of Marvila. It is autonomous and nonparty, and seeks to represent their interests at all levels.

2.   Recognises the CTs and CMs already elected.

3.   Will reinforce the alliance between the popular masses and the MFA, guaranteed by the CMs and CTs and by the ADUs (Assemblies of Unit Delegates) of RAL-1.

4.   Aims at mobilising for a socialist society, contributing to the solution of the most pressing problems.

5.   Represents the class aspirations and organisations of the workers.

6.   Should progressively replace the organs of the state apparatus, already decrepit and inefficient, taking into its own hands the power to legislate, at a local level, over all problems which affect the workers. The Marvila Popular Assembly is composed of CMs and CTs, with one representative of the Parish Junta and one representative of the Social Centres. There will be one delegate from the collectives of Marvila with less than 200 members and two delegates from collectives with 1,000 members. There will also be representatives of the ADUs of RAL-1.[3]

The first action of the Assembly was the collection and sifting of information about the area: companies in difficulty, cases of economic sabotage, problems of housing, transport and sewage disposal, etc.

Many other Popular Assemblies were coming into being or were being planned at this time (early September 1975). Most were in the Lisbon area but Assemblies had appeared in Faro, Coimbra, Porto, and Braga. PS members participated in certain areas but on the whole party involvement was limited to groups to the left of the Socialist Party.

---

3   *Movimento: boletim informativo das Forças Armadas* 25, August 14, 1975.

Houses were occupied, parks created. Social centres sprung up where none had existed. In general a great explosion of energy was witnessed. Even in Northern towns, condemned as "reactionary" and "anticommunist," self-activity aimed at improving people's own living areas was not totally absent.

In Setúbal the Popular Assembly decreed a ceiling on monthly rents of 500 escudos per room. This "social rent" was practiced throughout the town. A kitty was set up to improve neighbourhoods, build recreation centres and plan parks and common grounds.

The coming together of soldiers from the ADUs and of delegates concerned both with work (from the CTs) and with housing (from the CMs) represents an interesting attempt to break down the barriers traditionally separating these functions. But as in so many other areas, forms alone were insufficient. The most active militants in the Popular Assemblies were Leninists of one kind or another—with all that that, implies in terms of behaviour and concerns.

EVERYDAY LIFE IN THE COOPERATIVES

There can be no meaningful revolutionary upheaval without a change in how people live. If one compares everyday life in 1975 with what it had been in 1973, or even 1974, there was clearly a difference. The external signs were obvious enough. Politicians toured the villages in the South, holding three to five large meetings per day, in which they would "turn nice Marxist phrases round in their mouths." The radio stations blared out songs of "revolt." But the gestures and cultural habits were also in upheaval and it is here that the most important changes were taking place. It was in the depth of this feeling that the real revolution was seeking to develop. It is much easier to change regimes than to change lives.

If the workers struggle successfully, the only person to lose out is the boss. It is he who panics, flees, has a heart attack, or immigrates to Brazil. The workers are dazed, left to start anew. Their stories sometimes tell in a few lines what pages of statistics cannot possibly convey. Myself, Teresa, and some of our friends from the "Institute of Agricultural Reorganisation" visited some of the cooperatives at this time.

The agricultural cooperative of Casebres was set up in February 1975 and comprised almost four thousand hectares. In many ways it had been a model occupation and it now promised to be a model cooperative, an example to others. The old bosses had left the land fallow, using parts of it as hunting grounds for Portuguese latifundiários and their German and American friends. Now the soil had been turned and was growing a variety of crops. The Workers were full-blooded communists: the land and everything on it was for everyone, they said. In March 1975, they erected a large sign at the entrance proclaiming "the Dictatorship of the Proletariat."

Álvaro Cunhal was to visit the cooperative and a troop of aides went ahead to sound out the reception. The sign at the gate was "ideologically correct," the PCP explained, but would have to come down. "The elections had to be won." "But it's in your writings," one of the workers argued. "We saw it there." "There's some mistake," the PCP delegate explained. "Our Seventh Party Congress voted against the dictatorship of the proletariat." "See, it's here," the workers insisted, taking out a well-thumbed copy of *The Works of Marx and Engels* to prove it. The PCP militants from Lisbon were completely at a loss.

This story shows a deep sense of class justice and communist principle. In an RTP interview carried out by a PCP crew with workers from a cooperative near Évora, the commentator was interrupted as he was repeating the usual slogan: "the land to those who work it." A worker said the slogan was incorrect. It should be "the land to all who work." He then explained how the cooperative functioned: "this man takes more because he needs more, that man takes less because he needs less."

There were darker sides too. In a cooperative with two tractors there were often squabbles over who should work them. At Aveiras de Cima, a self-managed farm about forty kilometres north of Lisbon, this problem was to lead to fighting between workers. Other problems related to the division of labour were also, at times, at the root of bitter disputes. Housework was a case in point. In the canteen of the "Comuna" (a nineteenth-century mansion belonging to the Duke of Lafões, which included a library, meeting rooms, a school and a medical centre) a sign bluntly proclaimed, "He who leaves his dirty dishes in the sink for someone else to wash up leaves behind his socialism." A meeting had criticised the lack of initiative of the men in this area and a "strike" by the women had forced the work to be divided more evenly. Despite this, and despite their complaints, the women continued to do the housework and washing up.

The allocation of tasks varied from cooperative to cooperative. In the better organised ones a rota was set up. But often work was not done, when it should have been. In most instances it was just left at that. But there were cases where workers disciplined other workers.

Another problem was drunkenness. After France, Portugal is the country which consumes the most alcohol per inhabitant. At least that's what the OECD says. But with all the home-made brews (both wines and aguardentes) Portugal might well consume more. Most of the wine is drunk in the countryside. In cooperatives near Évora many men consumed up to 5 litres of wine per day. Some drank even more.

At the cooperative of Torre Bela, in the region of Azambuja (north of Lisbon) the women held a meeting to discuss the drinking habits of the men. It was decided that they were drinking too much and that a limit had to be set. A compromise was worked out: the limit would be four litres!

Drunkenness often highlighted sharp divisions. There were fights and rowdiness, and production suffered. In many places the house of the ex-owner had been occupied, together with his land. As many as eight or ten people would move in. The men sat around the fire, drinking and talking late into the night and causing others to lose sleep and feel tired the following day.

The Nefil furniture factory near Porto had gone into self-management late in 1974. Shop-floor relations improved greatly and one of the most popular "improvements" had been the construction of a bar on the premises. The only problem was that the workers began using it. Production slumped. When a member of the CT was found snoring merrily under one of the machines, a meeting was called and resolved to close down the bar. The workers later rescinded this decision and voted to keep the bar open—during certain hours. This case was not unique.

Drunkenness often produced amusing results. During the election campaign of April 1975, it was made illegal to tear down other people's posters. Many MRPP militants were imprisoned in Lisbon for doing this (they concentrated on PCP posters). One middle-aged member of a cooperative was rounded up by the police for tearing down a PS poster. The man was obviously drunk. He had used the poster to wrap up a piece of chicken. When the police searched him, they found . . . a membership card of the Socialist Party.

Many party militants took the electoral campaign with a seriousness bordering on mania. Legalistic attitudes were rampant throughout Portugal. Everything is tied up in bureaucratic red tape and endless signatures are needed to complete any legal business. Many parties began their campaign early, an hour or two before midnight. Some people, busy tearing down the posters of all parties, were threatened by PPD militants: the police would be called. The poster-strippers pointed out that there were still ten minutes to go and that the regulations didn't yet apply. The PPD militants felt outwitted and left. Others took things in a less docile manner. Street battles were fought at gunpoint between the MRPP and PCP. On one occasion UDP militants dumped an MRPP member, found tampering with one of their notices, into the river. He couldn't swim and drowned. In general the forces of COPCON turned up to "restore order." In most cases they gave more support to the PCP than to the "illegal" MRPP.

The state capitalist parties to the left of the PCP were often extremely puritanical. The Maoists were notorious in this respect, idealising asceticism and monogamy and being very heavy about extramarital relations. There were many young workers who left the MRPP because, as the Portuguese say, they "liked their glasses." The parties in a sense reinforced the traditional moralism in the country at large.

Despite all the freedom to demonstrate and go to meetings, everyday attitudes and relations hadn't changed all that much. Men still went to the tascas, and women, while they could now go to meetings, usually remained at home. There had been more change in the rural cooperatives than in the cities.

Clearly the mode of living was not altered overnight. The setting up of crèches which was taking place all over the country was something positive. It was not an outcome of state planning. It liberated women from child-minding. But the level of unemployment being some 12 percent it didn't just "liberate" them in order to drag them into the factories. Crèches were on the whole organised by local women, often helped by progressive teachers and other young professionals, through the Neighbourhood Committees. Many parks were also built.

Within the cooperatives and self-managed factories working relations changed in a definite way. Workers had more freedom to come and go. In many cases they could come late and go even later. What was important was not being parasitical on the work of others. But this awareness varied from place to place. In some instances the CTs began to behave as though they were the new bosses. Decisions were not always taken in common and members of some Committees occasionally went around snooping on the workers. The textiles factory of Jotocar in Vila Nova de Gaia near Porto was a case in point. The CT, which consisted of members of the Union of Textile Workers, spent more time doing "national" political work than concerning itself with problems of the factory. For this it was "fired" by the workers, who accused it of being party-orientated (PCP). In many other cases the workers weren't so vigilant and the CT became a bureaucratised organisation having little contact with its base. At the agricultural cooperative of Torre Bela (where the mansion had belonged to the Duke of Lafões) Camilo Mortigna, leading CT member and ex-LUAR militant, had commandeered the master-bedroom. But he also spent more time on other cooperatives than on his own.

Such cases, and the frictions they produced, caused an upheaval in everyday life. Attempts to resolve the subsequent problems provided a rich lesson in understanding.

The cooperatives were what their members made them. Some were far more radical than others. Cooperatives with names like "Red Star" or "The Steps of Lenin" functioned through instructions received from the "Union of Agricultural Workers" in the PCP stronghold of Beja. Life there changed very little, though the work was organised communally and members could not avoid some of the problems inherent in this. Other, more autonomous, cooperatives tried to establish quite different working relations to deal with their problems.

Take for instance Argea, a village of about three hundred inhabitants, twenty kilometres from Santarém. The cooperative there was set up initially by a group of intellectuals from Lisbon. Because of the level of unemployment in the village it quickly integrated many of the local inhabitants. The latter, in fact, soon became a majority. The initial suspicion with which the inhabitants had viewed the cooperative was eventually transformed into enthusiastic support. A collectivised butcher's shop was set up in the village (to the annoyance of the resident butcher who was forced to lower his prices). A communal canteen was established. People not connected with the cooperative could eat there, provided they helped in a rota of duties shared by all supporters.

Perhaps the most difficult problem of all was the organisation of living accommodation on the occupied farms. Space was scarce and when only two or three houses existed they had to be shared. The family unit underwent a certain change. The idea of individual families struggling on their own was overcome: the economic survival of the cooperative was a communal preoccupation.

At a cooperative in Unhais da Serra, the workers asked for troops to be sent to protect them from an expected attack by the bosses. The two soldiers "just hung around all day with their G3s (automatic rifles)." When it was discovered that they were having affairs with some of the wives, their welcome was cut short. One of the workers said that it had been wrong to ask for outside help and that it was up to them to defend themselves.

Attitudes to sexual matters always provide a rich insight into the fabric of everyday life. In Portugal sexual moralism was rampant due to the influence of the Catholic Church. There are many expressions of derision in Portuguese, usually directed against women. Women were held responsible for "loose morality" rather than men.

There were also class responses to sexual problems. When in the late summer of 1975 the whole of Portugal was inundated by "revolutionaries" from all over Europe they often brought with them problems which the Portuguese workers could have dispensed with. Emigration to Portugal had always been a predominantly bourgeois phenomenon and foreign residents in Portugal rarely spoke to the natives. They lived in their Algarve villas or in their Estoril and Cascais "ex-pat communities." The new "revolutionary tourists" were different. They came to Portugal to see the revolutionary process. Many visited the agricultural cooperatives, to "work" alongside the workers there. They stayed for a month or six weeks, and then moved on. At first they were welcomed.

In some ways these visitors created more problems than they helped solve. Many had little respect for the autonomy of the workers and little understanding for the deep, personal meaning of their struggles. In many cases they went so far as to tell the workers how best to manage their problems. At Torre Bela, for example, the workers decided to limit the number of "assistants" to six. The eight foreigners who were there at the time held a meeting of their own and "decided not to agree with this decision." The workers were annoyed, but tried to explain the situation in class terms. "You, in your German university, may have certain problems. We help by sending good wines and cheeses to you. During your holidays you can come here and work. But do you think we can go to the director of your university and tell him how to run the place?"

In the late summer of 1975 some Swedish leftists visited Portugal, staying in various cooperatives, including "Estrela Vermelha" and "Torre Bela." The women often appeared in the fields scantily dressed. The contrast between these girls, naked under their jeans and tee-shirts and the heavily-clad, browbeaten working wives was enormous. When sexual relations began to develop between the men and these girls, the women of the cooperative felt hurt and betrayed. They met and discussed the problem and decided to throw these bourgeois girls out. Whatever comments one cares to make about the "opportunism" of the men, the behaviour of the girls was experienced as a form of terrorism by the other women.

Many such problems were thrown up in the day-to-day lives of the workers. They were resolved (or not resolved) in a variety of ways.

Discussion in any case was rampant, sometimes formal, sometimes not, and here the richest experiences were lived.

Things at times reached surrealist levels. A *latifundiário* in Elvas happened also to be the owner of the local taxi company. His lands had been occupied and his drivers thought this was a good example. They turned up in force at the Centre for Agrarian Reform, and asked that the takeover of their taxis be legalised.

People's behaviour did not always follow a "rational" pattern. Many workers were upset by this, but that was life. When a cooperative was faced with chaos because of internal problems, some of the older workers threatened to leave. Some did. They went back to their villages and sought work there. Some later returned and were reintegrated. Others never came back.

BEYOND LOCAL WORKERS' COMMITTEES?

Many of the seven hundred cooperatives only survived because of the overtime being worked or as a result of loans granted by the government. The cooperatives faced all the problems confronting private companies . . . and more. Boycotted by international enterprises and denied markets they survived by two interrelated methods.

Firstly, through credits. It was estimated by one of the leaders of the Confederation of Portuguese Industry that paper money in circulation during the last six months of 1975 had increased from 1.1 to 3.7 billion escudos. Many of the companies in self-management would have gone bust had it not been for the steady growth of bank-lending. Such an increase in paper money meant an inflation rate of between 50 and 100 percent. The granting of credits to both industrial and agricultural units was a political manipulation of the highest order. PCP cooperatives could be sure of credit from the Fifth Government, while PS cooperatives had to wait for the Sixth.

The second system of support for the cooperatives came from the workers themselves. By "dealing among themselves" they provided a parallel internal market. The "Cooperative of April 25th" started building houses for the shanty towns, having won an order for six hundred units. Lisnave shipyard workers gave their order for boiler-suits to companies in self-management. Agricultural cooperatives organised markets through Neighbourhood Committees and sold their products directly to the population. The Setúbal Federation of Neighbourhood Committees got their products from the agricultural cooperatives in the region of Azambuja, while Neighbourhood Committees in Lisbon supported the cooperatives of Alcácer and Évora.

But if the Workers' Committees were to provide a real alternative to capital they would sooner or later have to face up to some political and institutional problems. The most important was how to organise themselves into a larger federation. This was talked about on many occasions, but it was usually the political parties who were behind such moves, not the workers themselves. "Politics" couldn't be divided. One couldn't help relating, in one way or another, to all that was going on. Workers' Committees made political choices every day, either meeting in plenários or taking initiatives themselves. Literally thousands of communiqués by all sorts of Workers' Committees were published in the papers. Here is one example, published in *República* on September 27, 1975. The workers of Entroposto (Setúbal EIA, Lda—a car repairs unit) met in an assembly on September 22 and decided to:

1) Support the people of Porto in their struggle against fascist laws used by the civil governor of that city in an attempt to close down the Municipal Council.

2) Support the manifesto of SUV (Soldiers United Will Win) and the demonstrations called by that organisation.

3) Support the rural workers of Alentejo in their revolutionary struggle.

4) Support the just struggle of disabled ex-servicemen, victims of the shameful colonial wars waged by the fascist regime against both colonial and Portuguese people.

5) Support the struggle of the workers of República and Rádio Renascença in defence of popular power and of information at the service of the workers and their organisations.

In some instances (as at Auto Succo) workers occupied the Lisbon branch of a firm and sent telex messages to the Porto section. Timex workers made international phone calls, asking for solidarity, but their enthusiasm was damped when managers, rather than workers, answered at the other end of the line. But what was noteworthy in all cases was the class solidarity, the support given by workers to other workers.

Inter-Empresas, formed in December 1974, had now fragmented into various "Inters," controlled by different political factions. They even fought over the salvage of the fragments. On September 13, some fifty CTs in the Lisbon industrial belt held a conference in the Copam factory, the general theme being "Advancing the Revolution." One of the decisions taken was to call a "rigorously nonparty" demonstration on September 18.

The factories taking part included Copam, Fima, Robbialac, Corame, Volvo, Lever, Luso-Italiano, Autosil, Sorefame, J. Pimenta, H. Parry & Son, etc. The demonstration wouldn't end up in São Bento, where the Constituent Assembly sat, but in the Parque Eduardo VII.

During the demonstration (supported by the PCP) certain elements, devoid of much imagination, began shouting "Vasco, Vasco." The demonstration was then recognised as having been a PCP demonstration, which was unjust to those workers who took part in it and didn't belong to the Party or didn't agree with it.

Another attempted regroupment was the "Federation of Covilhã." Covilhã was a town in the Centre, in which many textile factories were concentrated, and which had a rich history of workers' struggles. Here, over ninety CTs met during the weekend of September 26-27, 1975. Some fifty-two of the CTs represented had been mandated by their plenários. The basis of representation (i.e., the voting and speaking rights) at this Congress of Factory Committees was worked out as follows:

Enterprises of fewer than 100 workers	1 vote	Right to speak
200–1,000 workers	2 votes	Right to speak
1,000–4,000 workers	4 votes	Right to speak
Over 4,000 workers	6 votes	Right to speak
Neighbourhood Committees	0 votes	Right to speak
Soldiers and Sailors' Committees	0 votes	Right to speak
Unions	0 votes	No right to speak
Political parties	0 votes	No right to speak

Topics discussed at the Congress included: Workers' Control (forms production and working hours, unemployment, control exercised by CTs over consumption, self-management, etc.), arming the working class, purges, workers-peasants alliances, nationalisations, etc.

The secretariat of the Federation accused certain Workers' Committees of sectarianism in relation to the Congress: "We are nonparty but still insist that the question of the party of the working class is a question which must be resolved. Our position is clear: the Congress is open to all delegates of organisations which, by their programme, politics and practice, support the organs of popular power, realise their importance and defend these organs ... These CTs have their own political significance. What is important is the simple fact that they are meeting in a National Congress to discuss, not just the problems of their own factories or economic sectors, but a whole spectrum of general political problems of importance to the working class."

The secretariat condemned the fact that the PCP had organised a boycott of the Congress by organising a picnic in Coimbra for the same weekend, through the auspices of the Southern Textiles Unions.

> While at the level of Intersindical they defend unicidade, at the level of the Workers' Committees they can take such an attitude (as boycotting the Congress), ignoring the fact that this Congress is open to all Workers' Committees which are freely elected and revocable.
>
> We doubt that the demonstration of September 18 was rigorously nonparty. We know that most of those CTs belonged to a well-defined political tendency. But if they were democratically elected in their factories, if they accept the principle of free revocability, if they defend the fullest democracy in the plenários, meetings and ideological discussions within their own factories, then those CTs are representative. We don't consider it incorrect to defend a political line. What is incorrect is for them to have a sectarian attitude in relation to our secretariat and to Inter-comissões, and that they play party politics, hiding under the cloak of nonpartyism.
>
> We think the political situation calls for the unification and centralisation of the organs of political power. Today everyone talks about the return to fascism and about swings to the right. The question, for us, is knowing who is politically responsible for this. The responsibility must fall on the political forces who participated in government until now, and who continue with their pacts, conciliations and betrayals of the interests of the people. It is they who open the door for a return to fascism.
>
> These elements are now trying to recover the political initiative, trying to manipulate incentives of this kind, covering them with a nonparty cloak while mobilising certain CTs.
>
> It is important to stress that we are not against these CTs having a political line. This line seems to us to be incorrect, but if these CTs are representative of the working class then this line must be discussed.
>
> Secretariat of Inter-Comissões (Inter-Empresas)
> September 27, 1975

This Covilhã Congress was, however, supported by the Maoist MRPP and thousands of their highly characteristic red and yellow "nonparty" posters had appeared all over the country, publicising it in factories and public places. The MRPP had infiltrated the original Inter-Empresas and through such CTs as Efacec-Inel were now attempting to infiltrate all the other Workers' Committees related to this "Inter." The above document criticised the PCP and Intersindical but failed even to hint at the MRPP's own role in the whole project of coordination. The Congress elected a new secretariat which included the factories of Hoechst (Porto), Celnorte (Viana do Castelo), Cravinhos (Covilhã), TAP (Lisbon), Cambournac, Efacec-Inel, Timex, Plessey, Sacor, etc. The CTs of Cambournac, Efacec-Inel, and Celnorte were heavily MRPP-orientated.

Another attempt at federation was the attempt to create TUV Committees (Workers United Will Win) based on the SUV model. This attempt was more propagandistic than real, being launched by the PCP-controlled Diário de Notícias.

The weakness of the state apparatus, and the discredit in which the political parties found themselves, left the task and burden of self-organisation firmly in the hands (and on the shoulders) of the workers. Both the state and the political parties were aware of this reality and attempted to manipulate it by creating supra-party structures. The PCP was most notorious in this respect, the MRPP coming a close second. The PS too, realising its falling support within the working class, were present in Covilhã.

These experiences provide rich lessons in the techniques of manipulation—and in methods of resisting them. But these lessons were not assimilated fast enough. The majority of the workers who wanted to fight capitalism never took the lead themselves. It was during this period that they could most easily have taken the initiative—but they didn't. Some, admittedly, were moving in this direction. Party banners were prohibited on demonstrations (there were workers who forced groups like LCI to take down their banners and shouted "Here there are no Parties"). People moved from a situation which ridiculed the claims of particular vanguard parties to a situation where they were openly saying that there were too many vanguards. What was needed was to go a step further—and see that vanguards were superfluous. If the parties could not bring about radical change—and if radical change was what one wanted—one would have to consider alternative means of achieving it. If the dream was to become reality, self-mobilisation on an enormous scale would have to be undertaken and certain new institutions created. Throughout the whole of the Portuguese revolution this remained the biggest problem of all. And it remained unsolved.

XIII DE-SOCIALISATION

When Zé Diogo, the agricultural worker arrested for having killed a *lati-fundiário*, was declared innocent by a "popular tribunal" held outside the civil court of Tomar, the Association of Lawyers denounced the verdict. "Judicial power in the country has been insulted," they said. "Democratic authority has been overtaken by the delirium of people who have the absurd notion that even a man's right to his life is a bourgeois right."

The event was typical of the dwindling authority of the central organs of the state. The Sixth Government, in office since September 19, had little or no basis for its rule. To impose its decisions a state needs an army or at least a police force. But the National Republican Guard had been neutralised and the military apparatus was in shreds, incapable at this stage of being mobilised against the Left. The government was a government in name only. Although both ministers and the Council of the Revolution got together regularly, their writ hardly extended beyond the walls of the room they met in.

The army still existed. But, at every level, it was torn with conflict. There was a government but street mobilisation threatened its every decree. The state was weak. Who then was in power?

The answer depended upon where one was. In Alentejo, the Agricultural Workers' Union (PCP) was without doubt the main force. What it said, went. The trouble was that it didn't say much. It had a tremendous power of mobilisation (and demobilisation). In the North power was in the hands of local bosses: the landowners called the tune through the village clergy, the local officials, the teachers. In the South such voices were now less distinct. In the cafés and tascas the once vociferous and opinionated critics of the Fifth Government were keeping quiet. More and more of the PCP's "popular power" posters were appearing. Workers who had worn PS badges discreetly took them off. Some café owners, just to be sure, kept PS and PCP posters up, side by side.

In the North the Right was in full advance. PCP and FUR offices were burnt down, usually by small groups of four to five right-wing activists, while the local population just looked on, neither preventing nor assisting the arson. Local clergy called political "Masses" which echoed the views of the local bosses (CDS or PPD almost to a man). The Bishop kept a close eye on potential dissidents among the tenders of the flock.

The "Group of Nine" attempted to strengthen its position in the MFA by creating a new police force to counter COPCON. They also sought to silence the media, which were conducting a sustained campaign against the Sixth Government. They were in militant mood but—despite the result of the elections—couldn't compete with the PCP or with the Left when it came to mobilisation. To vote PS or PPD was one thing; to go into the streets to defend these parties was quite another.

To carry out its programme the new government had to control: a) the means of communication; b) the armed forces; c) the workers. In each of these areas its endeavours met with very mixed results.

THE MEDIA OF CONTROL AND THE CONTROL OF THE MEDIA

In an *Expresso* interview (November 15, 1975) Major Aventino Teixeira claimed that if Lenin had had access to television the October Revolution would have taken place in September. The major, an MRPP sympathiser, had been the military director of the morning paper *O Século* in the months after April 25, and was later to be a member of the MFA Council for Information. His attitude was typical of many on the left towards the media. All believed that whoever controlled the media controlled the way people thought. The struggle to control the media was one of the fiercest ever fought. After March 11, it was the Left, particularly the PCP, who controlled the radio, TV, and most of the newspapers.[1]

On August 22, 1975, when the Fifth Government was about to collapse and talks were going on in the MFA between COPCON (roughly, the Left),

---

1   The two morning papers *O Século* and *Diário de Notícias* were controlled by the PCP. The latter, as the "journal of record" was the most important because of its nationwide distribution and it was the only paper with a sizeable advertising section, and as a result, it was on display in many cafés and institutions. The five evening papers printed in Lisbon were all in the hands of PCP-FUR, with the exception of *Journal Novo* (which was social democratic) and *A Luta* (mouthpiece of the right of the PS after *República* had been taken over by the UDP and PRP. *Diário de Notícias* had the largest circulation. Then in declining order came *A Capital*, *Diário Popular*, *Diário de Lisboa*, *Journal Novo*, *A Luta*, *O Século*, *Journal de Notícias* (the Northern morning paper which had hardly changed since April 74), and *República*. Apart from the dailies, there were also influential weeklies like *Expresso* (PPD-MRPP-Independent), *O Journal* (PS-PCP), *Tempo* (CDS), and a variety of magazines.

the "Gonçalvists" (approximately, the PCP) and "The Nine" (by and large, the PS), the newspapers gave different versions of events.

The headlines were interesting. "The Revolution triumphant" exulted *Diário de Lisboa.* "The Nine and COPCON in disagreement" warned *A Capital.* "Socialist Party proposes economic transitional programme" trumpeted *Jornal Novo.* "Decisive hours for the Revolution," pontificated *República.* People bought the paper which they hoped would bring them the news they wanted. Middle-class people began tuning in to foreign stations (BBC, etc.).

Newspapers and radio indulged in an orgy of propaganda. The truth was the main victim. The Sixth Government, after much travail, altered some faces in certain ministries, but little else changed. The Minister of Communications, Almeida Santos (PPD) had virtually no control over the papers or TV. The PCP still dominated *Diário de Notícias.* With one foot in the government, it attempted to undermine it at every step, "hunting with the foxes and running with the hares," as one journalist put it. One had constantly to read between the lines, always remembering whose interests were at stake. As a chronicle of what was happening most newspapers (especially the national ones) were useless. Many journalists were so carried away by their power to create events that many began believing the myths they themselves manufactured.

The PCP-FUR opposition was based on the manipulation of the spectacular. Massive coverage was given to things which hardly happened. Extensive space was devoted to organisations which existed in name only. The ephemeral was presented as enduring, the established as evanescent. All this was an attempt to create "support" or a vantage position from which to bargain for power. Demonstrations were often reported as having numbered thousands (and to have been supported by hundreds of CTs and CMs) when in fact one had seen with one's own eyes that barely a thousand people had been there, with perhaps a dozen CTs. Journalistic enthusiasm fed on the need to believe that the movement was larger than it was. Popular confidence was drowned in the waves of a self-defeating triumphalism.

The headlines of *Diário de Notícias* during September and October 1975 were a constant tirade against the Sixth Government. The government's own deliquescence both encouraged and sustained the campaign. Rádio Renascença kept up a patter of revolutionary songs, some Portuguese, others from Chile, Cuba, and the France of 1968. In the morning, the station (which had a radius of about sixty kilometres) broadcast to agricultural workers in the Lisbon area. At night it had a special pro-gramme for other workers. There were news items from soldiers' organi-sations in France and Italy, commentaries from *Lotta Continua* (Italy), and communiqués from CTs throughout the country. RR was now firmly in the hands of the UDP and PRP.

The rulers could not rule, confronted with such opposition. On September 29, while Costa Gomes was on a state visit to Poland, Prime Minister Pinheiro de Azevedo ordered the military occupation of all radio stations. The action was directed not only against RR but also against Rádio Clube Português, which had opened its channels to the disabled ex-servicemen when, in defence of their claims, they had occupied the bridge over the Tagus. Threatening a state of siege, Pinheiro de Azevedo justified his move on the grounds that an "emergency" existed. COPCON forces were ordered to carry out the occupations but they made it clear that they weren't going to allow themselves to be used by the Sixth Government for this purpose. The RIOQ Infantry Regiment (many with FUR stickers on their rifles) refused to comply with the order. They first occupied, then withdrew from Rádio Clube Português.

At 2:30 p.m. a demonstration organised by the Lisnave shipyards and supported by two thousand workers in the Lisbon industrial belt marched to the radio stations (where it left contingents) and then on to the Foz Palace near Rossio, where Otelo was discussing matters with the PPD Minister for Communications. The workers called on him to take a "class position." For two hours Otelo hesitated. The moment of truth had come for the darling of the PRP. Speeches by various workers were heard to the effect that Otelo was basically a social-democrat. When Otelo finally came to the window after having received a delegation he spoke of how hurt he was to hear such accusations. He claimed that the Sixth Government "had not been given a chance." The Lisnave workers began booing. Confusion spread through the crowd and Otelo looked worried, as well he might. "Go and put your demands to the Prime Minister at Belém," he said. "Lead us there!" the crowd responded. Otelo, more on the spot than ever, finally decided to lead a demo to Rádio Renascença ("which was much nearer than Belém anyway"). There he ordered the troops of CIAC which were in occupation to withdraw. RR began broadcasting again.[2]

---

2   A later report in 1976 said that the PRP had tried to persuade Otelo that the time was right for an armed uprising. The UDP, also present, said that the time was not opportune. Otelo agreed.

The demonstration left a strange impression. I was glad of the crisis in state power but really I felt a spectator, a lost leftist. A friend from Évora I met told me heartening stories of what ordinary people had done there. He had helped as best he could. He wanted nothing in exchange: no promises, no rewards, no appreciation, no votes. He was fighting for his own liberation.

But the media made a mockery of this type of autonomy and falsified it. They lapped it up, and then regurgitated out the pieces, lining them up behind this or that party in conflict. "Only the truth is revolutionary," one newspaper headlined using Gramsci's famous slogan to justify themselves. It was confusing, depressing and sad. An IRA worker I knew turned up. I knew we shared aims and motives, that she hated the "cúpulas" (cliques) and only felt at ease with the base movement. She was sincere (even though she had a government job). She had submerged her own problems in the general mêlée. She too felt depressed. But it was almost impossible to shake off the cúpulas. The demo had been stage-managed, like so many before and after. The difference between those who attended on behalf of their party and those who came because they felt that a revolutionary movement was possible or necessary was almost palpable.

There were many of the latter. Even the leaders had difficulty in controlling them. The Lisnave workers began shouting when the LCI, totally insensitive to all this, raised their banner. They felt desperate when external elements (to whom they were hostile) turned up and sought to take over the demonstration they themselves had organised. The speeches— from the top of a bus shelter—were sincere and pressing: "It is the workers and the workers alone who can demand what the workers want." The speeches were clear and to the point. In contrast to those of party militants, or even of Otelo, they were alive and real.

But such voices from below were soon buried in the headlines of *Diário de Notícias* or smothered by the well-formulated leaflets of FSP or MES, widely quoted by the media, and especially by Rádio Renascença.

Within six hours of being liberated, RR was temporarily reoccupied by commando troops under Jaime Neves. The station became a focus for many of the struggles which were to engulf Portugal in the following, weeks (SUV demos, metalworkers' and building workers' strikes, etc.). It was both a slogan and a crucial reality, a theme and an obsession. A demonstration by young leftists (including many foreigners) went to the transmitter at Buraca on October 16 and reoccupied it, when the commandos withdrew. RR went on the air again . . . at 3 a.m.

The stories of RR and *República* underline a tendency, apparent throughout most of the struggles in Portugal. Initiatives taken by workers would be jumped upon by political groups, who then began to manoeuvre things from behind the scenes. The real struggle would be drowned in the all-too-familiar leftist rhetoric. The initial issues would get lost in the swamp of the "leftist movement."[3]

RR was without doubt the best of the radio stations. But it couldn't resist the onslaught of the leftist groups. It created a mythology, propagated it, and then began to believe in it. It created a "folklore" of revolution which was at odds with the real, radical strand of Portuguese history and politics. It created a Disneyland of revolutionary fantasy. It boosted superrevolutionary personalities. And when the bubble burst all concerned were surprised to discover that little of all this existed. The failings of RR were the failings of FUR-UDP, an overoptimistic belief in their own power. FUR's strength was in the Lisbon area, and RR was the blood that circulated it. No wonder that certain papers like *Expresso* began talking of the "Lisbon Commune."

RR pushed the slogan of "popular power." But it was mainly wind. There was little discussion as to what it implied. No attempt was made to get to grips with people's anxieties and fears of the unknown in order rationally to overcome them. Fundamental (yet immediately relevant) issues such as the structure of work, the internalisation of hierarchy, the relations of manual and intellectual labour and various other problems that would confront a communist society were all avoided. Instead: just revolutionary trumpet calls. At times it was even tiring: revolution, revolution, revolution, morning to night. After a hard day's work one wanted to relax, just a little. One had to shut it off, get it out of one's ears, or treat it as background noise. People turned to other stations. Sad, because despite its shortcomings (ambiguous attitudes to Third World issues and to the state capitalist countries for instance) it hit hard at the local technocrats and rulers. So hard that their only solution was to blow it up.

MILITARY FACTIONS

Following their break with the Gonçalvists at Tancos, "The Nine," with a pack of reactionary officers behind them, moved in for the kill. Military

---

3   When we look at the occupation of RR we can in fact discern two "occupations." The first was carried out by RR's own workers. The second was a "colonisation" (both ideological and physical) of the occupied premises by political tendencies such as the UDP.

power was rather diffusely distributed. There was the Council, now dominated by "The Nine." It had rejected "popular power" and was seeking to
repudiate the orientation taken in July, in the "Plan of Political Action."
There were also the forces of COPCON, with Otelo in charge. COPCON
supported the "Left" and swore to "defend the workers." Their main
constituency was in and around Lisbon. Then there were the Gonçalvists.
Although they had lost much ground they still existed as a force within
the ministries and media. A series of purges culminated in the saneamento of Corvacho, the Gonçalvist Northern Commander. In general
the Gonçalvists supported COPCON against "The Nine." To the right of
"The Nine" were a number of extreme right-wing officers, increasingly
alarmed at the growth of indiscipline in the ranks and at the erosion of
the army hierarchy. The MFA as a bloc no longer existed.

Essentially what had happened was that the various state capitalist
projects, latent within the MFA from the beginning, were now no longer
capable of being contained within a single organisation. People joked about
an MFA, an MFB, and an MFC. The original organisation was breaking up
into its component parts and tendencies, all claiming to be "the real MFA."
What differentiated them were not so much the ends they had in mind as
the means they were prepared to use to reach and defend those ends.

1) The COPCON faction was based on some of the most heavily armed
units in the Lisbon area: RAL-1, PM, EPAM, 1st Engineers, EPSM, the
Beirolas barracks, the fort of Almada. These units more or less controlled the Lisbon and Southern areas. In the Centre they also controlled the
Infantry regiment of Abrantes.

2) Then there was what remained of the Gonçalvist faction—the ex-
Fifth Division which still controlled CODICE (the Central Committee for
Dynamisation) and the SDCI (Service for the Detection and Coordination
of Information—which many called the new PIDE). There was scattered
"Gonçalvist" influence among officers in certain COPCON and paratroopers units. The Navy, under Rosa Coutinho, could be counted on (Pinheiro
de Azevedo, the Prime Minister, was himself an admiral but had little
influence in the Navy). The Artillery unit at Vendas Novas, under Andrade
e Silva, was also considered "Gonçalvist."

3) Among "The Nine" were those original MFA officers loyal to Melo
Antunes and Vasco Lourenço. "The Nine" could count on CIAC (Cascais),
on the Infantry units of Mafra, on the Cavalry at Santarém, to a certain
extent on the Cavalry of Estremoz as well as on large sections of the
Northern officers.

4) The Right, following in the wake of "The Nine," was based in all those officers—and they were many—who had never identified with the MFA. The commandos in the Lisbon area were their main strike force but it had firm support from most Northern units (now under Pires Veloso) and among units in the Azores and Madeira (who threatened to secede from Portugal unless military discipline was restored). They also had support in many of the air bases (though here the sergeants' movement was an important obstacle to them).

5) There were also certain autonomous, rank-and-file groups, although here it is more difficult to draw lines. Among these were many of the COPCON units, CICAP–Artillery Regiment of Serra do Pilar in the North, RI in Abrantes, and the SUVs everywhere insofar as they went beyond UDP–PRP control. But as in civilian struggles any autonomous movement was soon jumped upon by one or other of the main contending forces.

It was against this background that the "party of the working class," evinced from the corridors of bourgeois power by those more versed than itself in the arts of manipulation, began to look to the lower ranks for allies. SUV came into existence. Some hundreds of soldiers and lower officers met in a pine forest on August 21, between Porto and Braga, to discuss the military and political situation. The meeting decided to set up its own network, built from the base up. There had been previous attempts at such an organisation (ARPE, CUV–RA) but these had only functioned in the sense of leaking information to the rank and file concerning military operations, planned manoeuvres, etc.

The influence of SUV soon spread to Coimbra and Lisbon. It was not initially a creation of the PCP, although the PCP jumped on the bandwagon as soon as it got moving. The three regional organisations of SUV (North, Centre, and South) differed slightly in their make up and in terms of the groups seeking to push them. On September 8, SUV issued its first communiqué:

> For more than six weeks it has been clear that the reaction is
> raising its head in the barracks. Many facts show this: the purge of
> left-wing soldiers in CIAC (Artillery Instruction in Cascais), CIOL
> (Centre for Instruction and Special Operation) in Lamego, RIP
> (Porto Infantry Regiment) in Viana and other areas; the attacks on
> comrades who struggled for popular power in the barracks, the
> fact that the ADUs are being turned into disciplinary instruments

which condemn comrades instead of being what they should be:
organs which discuss and struggle for the interests of the workers
in uniform, for pay increases, free transport, purging of reactionary
elements in the barracks, links with the base organisations . . .
Confronted by these manoeuvres we ask all to unite . . . Increase
our miserable pay. Reactionaries out of the barracks. Portugal will
not be the Chile of Europe. Workers, neighbours, soldiers, always,
always, on the side of the people.

SUV called a demonstration in Lisbon on September 11. Some thirty-
three units from all over the country were represented. FUR, UDP, and
many Neighbourhood Committees supported the demo. The PCP also
gave support, but when they tried to introduce their own slogans, they
were stopped. A banner read. "It is the soldiers who are in control. We
obey no secretariat."

Another "military" organisation to hit the headlines at this time was
RPAC, the MRPP's "front" among the soldiers. On September 13, about
300 PMs (Military Police) supported by some five hundred Maoists (the
papers said thousands) demonstrated noisily against being sent to Angola.
The war in Angola was correctly denounced as an interimperialist conflict.
Political insight on this issue didn't, however, generate a wider wisdom.
The MRPP crudely manipulated the soldiers' movement. In the North they
sought to pressurise a plenário of PMs by packing it with members of
Neighbourhood and Workers' Committees sympathetic to their outlook.
But the PMs, meeting again the next day, decided that their meeting had
been manipulated and that it therefore hadn't been representative. Points
3 and 4 of their communiqué stressed that "all forces which support our
struggle are welcome, as it is only within the people that contradictions can be resolved" and that "everything which divides these forces is
demagogic." They denounced the "antidemocratic attitude of CMs, CTs
and unions" present at their assembly. These "merely represent one type
of opinion . . . other workers and neighbours are also willing to help us."

The question of weapons was much talked about. While the workers
might have counted on certain units to support them should civil war
break out, and it seemed more likely every day, it was clearly essential for
the workers themselves to be armed. *A Luta* estimated that twenty thousand guns were in the hands of civilians, while *O Século Ilustrado* (October
11, 1975) put the figure at forty thousand. The paper carried an interview
with workers who had been "offered" G3s by soldiers. Many civilians still

had guns from the colonial wars hidden away, and many other weapons had been "redirected" from various barracks.

A spectacular "shrinkage" had been arranged by one Captain Fernandes. Fernandes, a thirty-three year old Angolan, had been in the "Movement of the Captains." He was one of the authors of the COPCON document. He was found to have "redirected" some 1,500 G3 automatic weapons from the barracks at Beirolas. "The arms were not given out according to political ideology or affiliation," he explained, in justification of his action. "They were only given to workers clearly interested in the development of the revolutionary process." It was widely believed that PRP, LUAR, and UDP had been the main beneficiaries and that they had buried their allocations.

Some time earlier Otelo had made his widely publicised remarks to the effect that the main mistake of April 25 had been its failure to fill the bullring with fascists and shoot them.[4] When asked about the "leakage" of weapons he said the guns were "in good hands."

On September 26, SUV held a vast demonstration in Lisbon. The march ended outside the military prison at Trafaria, where two soldiers had been incarcerated for handing out SUV leaflets at the military school in Mafra. It was an enormous gathering (some estimates mention 120,000 participants). Messages from soldiers' groups in Italy and France were read out. But the demo also showed something of the insecurity of the whole situation: when it reached Parque Eduardo VII a rumour spread that the commandos and RIOQ were on their way to break it up. Someone had to point out that most of the RIOQ contingent was already on the demo!

To cope with what it described as "anarchy spreading within the army," the Sixth Government badly needed a new police force. Somehow or other COPCON's wings had to be clipped. The AMI (Groups for Military intervention) were set up. The RAL-1s, Military Police and the Coastal Artillery Regiment all refused to have anything to do with the new organi-sation. The commandos and a unit of fusiliers and paratroopers accepted the role and were eventually to form the core of this new Military Group. The new police force came into existence on the eve of September 27 (the night the Spanish Embassy was burnt down). It was rapidly expanded

---

4   "I lack political coordinates. If I had these I could have been the Fidel Castro of Europe but I have a limited culture . . . This is the first revolution that I've been involved in in my life," Otelo said on his return from a visit to Cuba. Otelo had been invited to become President in August 1975 but had declined.

after October 1, on which date the PS papers had warned of an imminent left-wing coup by the RAL-1s.

At this stage the paper *O Século* managed to get hold of a secret document (later widely known as the "Plan of the Colonels") and leaked it to the public. The document revealed the strategy behind the government's moves. The plan clearly had the backing of the Revolutionary Council, though this was to be officially denied. The ten main objectives were:

1. Control of SDCI (Service for the Detection and Coordination of Information)
2. Control of the "public relations" of the MFA
3. The creation of AMI (Groups for Military Intervention)
4. The creation, within AMI, of a riot police force
5. A change in attitude towards the MPLA
6. The military occupation of the radio and TV
7. The disbanding of certain "progressive" military units, especially RAL-1
8. Absolute control to be in the hands of the Revolutionary Council. Otelo and Fabião to be purged
9. Members of "The Nine" to be placed in key positions
10. The República and Rádio Renascença issues to be settled once and for all.

Every one of these aims was to be achieved by the end of November.

It is important to see the background against which these objectives were conceived and implemented. Not only did the army not look like one any more (long hair and beards now came with the uniform) but it no longer behaved like one. The struggle of the disabled ex-servicemen highlighted the breakdown of military authority in some units—its preservation in others—and the total absence of a meaningful structure of command.

Some one hundred thousand civilians and thirty thousand soldiers had been maimed or badly injured during the war years. Many had lost an arm or leg and were unable to work. For a private the pension was 2,000 escudos a month, for a sergeant 4,000. A captain got 8,000 escudos, and a general 18,000. The disabled ex-servicemen had been active since November 1974, when they had demonstrated in front of the presidential palace. Despite promises they had received no increase in their pensions.

On September 20, 1975, they again marched, hobbled, or pushed themselves in their wheelchairs to São Bento. They were ordered to disperse by a commando unit, an elite corps still organised along strongly disciplined lines. The demonstrators refused. The commandos then brought up an armoured car, intending to drive it up to the front gate of the palace. A wheelchair was placed in their way, with a disabled commando in it. The commandos hesitated for a moment. At that instant the forces of RIOQ arrived on the scene. The commando officer gave the order to advance. The RIOQ troops fired over their heads. Only then did the commandos withdraw.

The demonstrators meanwhile held their ground. They waited until 11 p.m. and then decided to set up barricades across the nearby railway line which runs along the river Tagus, as well as across the Marginal, the main road running parallel to the track. Throughout the whole of the following day they forced all trains to stop for several minutes, while a manifesto was read out over the public address system. The government still failed to respond.

The ex-servicemen then decided to occupy the bridge across the Tagus. The toll was abolished. The situation lasted a whole week. Rádio Clube Português handed their station over to the ex-servicemen for half an hour a day and all the papers supported them. At the end of the week, after a conference held in the "Voz do Operário" (Voice of the Worker) hall under the auspices of *República*, the ex-servicemen decided to levy the toll during one night and donate the proceeds to the paper. This was the last straw. The government sent in troops to take over the bridge. The troops refused. The government capitulated.

During this period the political allegiances of various commanding officers were to play a key role. Many units held general assemblies to discuss the situation. They even held elections to appoint delegates. But they retained their hierarchical structure. As units, they remained cohesive. Many soldiers were proud of their regiments or battalions. This "schizophrenic" attitude was perhaps normal enough. Even in the units of RIOQ, sent in to defend the demonstration of disabled ex-servicemen, there was an uncritical attitude to rank. The soldiers would say what a good officer they had, because he played groovy music over the walkie-talkies when they weren't in official use. Soldiers could be mobilised by the sacking of progressive officers. While they condemned the uses to which a bourgeois army was put they retained its structure. The officers— even those who supported FUR—fostered these attitudes. The soldiers, by and large, obeyed their officers (progressive or whatever). They often acted without really thinking about the consequences. The tradition of obedience did not encourage critical thought.

SUV gathered a momentum which no one could control. When Brigadier Charais (of "The Nine") visited a barracks, a SUV group commented: "Charais visited our quarters. To answer the anxieties of the soldiers? No. To threaten them. To announce even more repressive and more sophisticated ways of purging the Left. To prepare more violent forms of repression."

In a transport unit near Porto the struggle reached a high level. CICAP was a military driving school. It had played an active part on April 25. The new Northern Commander (Pires Veloso, a right-winger) decided to close it down. Some of the soldiers described what happened:

> CICAP is being turned into a bulwark of reaction in the Northern military Region. All our victories have been neutralised. At the end of July three comrades were cashiered. Then came the August holidays and the devil was let loose. Reactionary officers and sergeants held constant secret meetings. Without consulting the democratic bodies we had set up they decided to send Captain Morais, a Spínolist, to the Assembly. With him went Captain Loureiro (ex-Mocidade Portuguesa).[5] They didn't wait long to start the purge of progressive soldiers . . . We announced a SUV demonstration. The commander did all he could to stop it, to threaten it. We were still many. On September 11, slap in the middle of our normal parade, we held a minute's silence for the Chilean people. The "ringleaders" were sought out. We complained about the food. But they weren't interested in improving the food. They just wanted a scapegoat. They expelled a conscript. We opposed these purges. On the parade ground we shouted: "Reactionaries out of the barracks." They didn't wait long before trying further purges, this time in a legal and more subtle manner. We said: "Enough." Well into the night we held a meeting. We asked for an explanation of the purges. Everything was done to disrupt our meeting. But in the end we managed to have a vote. The result was 312 votes for the dismissed men to stay, and 6 abstentions. No one supported the expulsions. Hundreds of people waiting at the gates applauded our victory . . . The immediate effect was to close down CICAP, on direct orders from Pires Veloso. But just as this was taking place, another unit took over their barracks in solidarity with us.[6]

5   Fascist Youth Movement.
6   *Soldados em Luta* 1, Publication of Artillery Regiment of Serra do Pilar, October 15, 1975.

The other unit was the Artillery Regiment of Serra do Pilar (RASP), near Porto. They took even more radical action. They defiantly brought civilians into the barracks:

> We began our struggle with one objective: the reopening of CICAP and the reintegration into the barracks of all purged soldiers. Today, a week later, rich with extraordinary experiences, strong from unbreakable unity, our objective remains the same, only more pressing. Why are we struggling? The closure of CICAP must be seen in its true dimension. The intention of whoever gave the order must be condemned. The closure of CICAP was a high point in a campaign which had led to the expulsion of many dozens of progressive soldiers and military personnel from units in this region; more than fifty from RIP, from CICAP, from ClOE in Lamego, Braga, Vila Real, etc. The closure of CICAP is a deliberate attempt to throttle those who say "no to militarist discipline." . . . An army manipulated and controlled by reactionaries will sooner or later attack the workers . . . CICAP will not belong to Veloso. It will belong to the people.[7]

When the RASP men occupied their barracks they brought civilians into the place and held a week-long festival. They showed films, talked, argued, discussed, held sing-songs and enjoyed themselves. Gradually other units started voting solidarity motions in favour of the PCP-oriented Fabião "to work out a compromise," that is, to reestablish "order," "discipline," "normality." After discussions, Fabião promised that Veloso would be overruled and that CICAP would not be disbanded. Artillery Regiment of Serra do Pilar then suspended their occupation. As in civilian matters, the PCP was being used to defuse crises. In industry they did this through Intersindical, in the Army through their few remaining "Gonçalvist" officers.

When the commandos withdrew from the Buraca transmitter of RR on October 16, the station began broadcasting again. It remained on the air for a mere three weeks. On November 7, a group of police specialists and a squadron of paratroopers paid a night call to the installations, ordered everyone out, and placed a bomb in the building. The paratroopers later said they "hadn't realised what they were doing." They said they thought the orders had come "from the left." One should neither laugh nor weep,

---

7   Ibid.

but seek to understand. Is it sufficient to dismiss their action as due to extreme political naivety? Why did this correspond to the mental image of the Left that they held? The question was never to be answered. A unit of fusiliers, contacted for the job, had refused. Vasco Lourenço, for the Council of the Revolution, later "explained" things. The Council, he said, had had three alternatives:

1. To give RR back to the Catholic Church—but he doubted they could hold it.
2. To occupy the station militarily—but he doubted the troops would comply with the order.
3. To blow it up.

This duplicity ("you can say whatever you like, so long as we're sure no one can hear you") and terroristic vandalism ("if we can't control it, we'd rather no one did") on the part of the state were deeply resented. They were to have unexpected repercussions among the "politically backward" paratroopers. It so radicalised some of them that they played an important role in the events of November 25. But in many ways it was the political groups who had propagated the myth of the "MFA-Povo alliance" who were responsible for the debacle. In the maze of folklore, the real limits of the situation had not been grasped.

TOWARDS BREAKING POINT

The advent of the Sixth Government did not halt the bombings in the North. But it changed their character. They became more overtly terroristic. In Porto, cars with French number plates were found to contain explosives on September 16; a few days later, the Municipal Council was bombed.

In Alentejo the PCP-controlled Union of Agricultural Workers were very much in control. On September 17, they called a strike which paralysed the province. Only the frontier regions like Elvas (which was predominantly PS) were not affected.

The left groups continued to fight among themselves. Running gun battles took place in Lisbon and Porto between PCP and MRPP or UDP, and between UDP and MRPP. Depending upon which unit intervened the situation was "sorted out" more or less rapidly.

A horrified reaction swept through Europe when, on September 27, a moribund Franco ordered the execution of five political prisoners. In Lisbon and Porto large demonstrations marched in protest. In Lisbon both the Spanish Embassy and Consulate were set on fire. The crowds sang the Internationale as the flames rose to the sky. The feeling was vicious. Not even the UDP (who tried) and the RAL-1s (who refused) could control the crowds. Even the firemen who turned up joined in the singing and limited themselves to stopping the fire from spreading. The Sixth Government immediately promised to pay compensation to the Spanish state. Melo Antunes denounced the attack on the embassy as "vandalism." The Minister of Foreign Affairs explained that 30 percent of Portugal's electricity came through Spain. It was important to maintain good relations, etc, etc. *República* wrote: "Spain, the horror. Spain, the death. Spain, our sister and comrade. The revolution attacked: the torture, the police, the hangmen. Revolutionary and heroic Spain, from whom we have learned so much. We shall crush fascism. We shall leave nothing surviving of this world of hell, which was ours and which still threatens us. The assassin Franco will die. We want no king. The people in struggle will take their destinies into their own hands. Capital and its weapons will be destroyed in the melting pot and red glow of Europe."

The division between PCP-FUR on the one hand and PS-PPD on the other was meanwhile gaining momentum. A journalist commented that during this period there were only "huge" and "gigantic" demonstrations. All this tended to overwhelm any autonomous moves which anyone made. Most of the demonstrations were said to be "unitary" and "nonparty," but just about everyone now knew otherwise. The PCP was exerting more and more pressure through organisations like SUV (South and Centre) and through the CTs of the industrial belt of Lisbon. Certain bureaucratised CTs like that at EC Esteves (industrial transport) worked hand in hand with the Transport Union, which worked very closely with Intersindical, which was at one with the PCP. A secretariat based on such CTs was set up. Many of the Committees affiliated to this secretariat were not, however, PCP-dominated. Nor were the workers in them. The bureaucratic system just trapped them in its mesh.

In this sense the metalworkers' strike of mid-October was led and manipulated by the PCP unions. The PS tried their own tactics to challenge this dominance in SUV and in the media. On October 1, they warned of a "left-wing coup," due to be led by RAL-1, and called for a general mobilisation of their militants. The response was pathetic. If a coup had been planned it would easily have succeeded.

A reference to "coups" became a mobilising theme. On October 25, COPCON warned of a right-wing putsch and set up barricades on the main roads into Lisbon. Young soldiers searched cars. But the searches were half-hearted. Four days later another organisation, the "Air Force Committee for Revolutionary Vigilance" (this time related to the PCP) warned of yet another right-wing coup. Both *O Século* and *Diário de Notícias* published the warning in bold type on their front pages. The previous day the Agrarian Reform centre in Setúbal had been bombed and the local population had immediately responded with more occupations, including the takeover of the palace of the Duke de Palmela which was converted into a new Agrarian Reform centre. What was rumour? What was reality? One woke up in the morning and—if one believed the papers—one discovered that so many coups had taken place and that so many had been foiled. Behind all this manipulation of the spectacular was the need to create and maintain an atmosphere of political insecurity. On October 31, some MRPP workers occupied *O Século*, seeking to outflank the PCP-dominated Workers' Committee within it. They produced their own version of the paper for a week.

The threats continued. On November 3, there was a further warning from the Air Force Committee that a coup was planned for the weekend of November 7–9, to coincide with military manoeuvres in the Centre. Again *O Século* and *Diário de Notícias* gave prominent headlines to the story. Otelo was seen more and more at PCP meetings, an RR sticker on his lapel. He called for these manoeuvres to be cancelled.

On October 30, the soldiers of the main Arms Depot were ordered by Gonçalvist officers to "swear allegiance to the working class." In response, both *A Luta* and *Jornal Novo* published (on November 4) a communiqué of the Frente Militar Unida. (This organisation, which included the MRPP, Melo Antunes . . . and Ramalho Eanes, was supposed to be a rank-and-file vehicle for the political ideas of "The Nine.") The PS–PPD then called a joint demonstration in Faro in support of the Sixth Government. It was in this context that the Soares–Cunhal television debate took place on November 6 with the aim of "defusing the crisis." Of course, it resolved nothing. On the same day the Council of the Revolution reiterated its support for the Sixth Government. The bitterness grew daily. On November 7, the Ministry of Social Communication was occupied by its workers who accused a leading official of being related to PIDE. After having fired into a crowd outside, the National Republican Guard reoccupied the lower part of the building. They didn't manage, however, to evict the workers who had barricaded themselves in upstairs.

On November 9, the PS called an enormous demonstration in Terreiro do Paço. It mustered strange supporters: PPD, CDS, AOC, PCP-ml. The sight of the packed square shouting "Discipline! Discipline!" was both sickening and frightening. PCP-ml burned an effigy of Cunhal. On the following Sunday, November 16, the PCP-influenced CTs of the industrial belt of Lisbon retaliated with yet another "unitary" demo. In each about seventy thousand people turned up (although figures of two hundred thousand appeared in various papers). The only difference was that there were more tractors, cement-mixers and trucks on the PCP demo, which was also more colourful. Cynically, the parties moved their crowds like pieces on a chessboard.

The languages of revolution and counterrevolution became increasingly difficult to untangle. Authority was crumbling. Some six hundred thousand hectares were occupied between October and November 1975 — twice as much as between March and September. The number of factories passing into self-management also more than doubled. But this very weakness of the state drove the contenders for state power to increase their demagogy and to raise their stakes.

The demonstrations of November 9 and November 16 revealed something of the polarisation. But hidden beneath them, unseen and unrecorded, were the pent-up frustrations of many CTs and individuals who genuinely wanted revolution, but could not organise outside of the established groups. FUR was confronted with the same dilemma of its own making. When not demonstrating with the PCP, it was giving it critical support. It was too late to resolve this "contradiction," which had deep roots in history. In a sense it was not a contradiction at all. FUR's politics made it inevitable. Every attempt by a CT to break free was promptly jumped on by one or other of the parties and immediately neutralised.

FUR's main voice (and not only theirs) was silenced when the RR transmitters were blown up. On the following morning (November 8) the PRP called for armed insurrection as the only solution to the crisis: "The PRP defends armed insurrection . . . The objective conditions for a victorious armed uprising exist today in Portugal. Knowing the devotion to the revolutionary process of a great many officers of the Army and Navy, and knowing also the positions which they hold at the level of unit commands, it is easy to think of a scheme based on a sortie by these troops, in an operation of the type of April 25th."[8]

The ambiguities of the PRP position were now being exposed with a vengeance. They were still not facing up to the fact that the army was a

8   *O Século*, November 11, 1975.

class army. They still talked of a "split" within it, of "using" certain units. Their "revolutionary brigades" had already gone underground (a decision which "perturbed" Otelo who said he was not consulted) when, on October 23, the Sixth Government had made it illegal for civilians to bear arms. The PRP explained (*A Capital*, November 10): "As all history shows, the bourgeoisie promotes civil war to defend its interests. Happily in Portugal the right wing does not have an army. They rely on mercenaries with bases in Spain, or on the armies of the U.S. and NATO." They were, of course, totally wrong in this assessment. The right wing (i.e., capitalism) had an army in Portugal. It was the officer corps now dominating the higher bodies of the MFA. The PRP produced thousands of posters ("Organise, Arm, Advance—for Popular Power") which they plastered all around the working-class districts of Lisbon. Posters were, however, to prove no substitute for the creation of a workers' militia, or for propaganda consciously aimed at the disintegration of the MFA.

The PS-PPD was advancing, though they were being stopped by street mobilisations at every step. They began to purge the PCP from the ministries. The PCP's response was a belated turn to the grass roots. On November 13, the building unions called a strike. Some thirty thousand workers from all over the country marched on São Bento, trapping the ministers inside. "Mr. Minister, go work on the sites," one of their posters said. The Minister of Labour ordered his ministry to be closed for fear the workers might wreck it. "What a sad figure this Minister cuts," a leaflet said, "who shuts his door on the workers. Go pack your bags and off with you to the *Grémio*.[9] Don't worry, Mr. Minister. Workers who have always built such buildings are not going to destroy them now. What we want is an end to miserable wages, to exploitation."

The building workers' strike was supported by the PCP, Intersindical and all the left groups, except the most orthodox Maoist ones. Agricultural workers from Alentejo and militants from the Lisbon industrial belt showed practical solidarity. The deputies were trapped inside the building, without food. An Air Force helicopter hovered overhead "to save them from starvation" (as one leaflet put it later in the evening, after a PPD deputy had fainted—either from hunger or from fear). The workers remained massed outside the building. COPCON troops, summoned by the government to rescue it, refused to intervene. The workers and soldiers lit fires, sang songs, got drunk, slept, and waited. The building workers

---

9   The Grémio was the bosses' organisation during Salazarism.

had four demands: (a) nationalisation of the main sites; (b) discussion of a new collective contract; (c) an enquiry into the activities of the Minister of Labour; and (d) higher wages. At 5 a.m. the Prime Minister rejected the first three demands but granted the fourth.

The workers would not accept this "compromise." They issued an ultimatum, expiring at 10 p.m. The Prime Minister said it was difficult to hold a meeting of all the deputies. Why, some were not even there! To this the workers replied that they would "go and fetch them." President Costa Gomes issued five "declarations to the nation" during the day, calling for calm . . . and increased productivity. The workers refused to budge. When the Prime Minister told them that he wanted to attend an important meeting in Belém they told him where he could "stuff his important meeting." Finally, at 1 a.m. on November 14, the Prime Minister caved in. All the demands were conceded.

The same day a demonstration in Porto supported by PS–PPD–CDS burned an Intersindical office. A giant PCP demo ("unitary," "nonparty") on November 15 showed that the PCP was still a force to be reckoned with. Otelo, who did not appear at the meeting, sent a message which revealed the changed balance of forces. Parodying the well-known "Soldier, friend, the people are with you," the message read out over powerful loudspeakers said: "People, friends, Otelo is with you."

Three days later, on November 18, the newspapers O Século and Diário de Notícias again warned of a right-wing coup. On the 19th, headlines in both A Luta and Jornal Novo condemned the influence of PCP–FUR in the armed forces.

For bourgeois democracy it was an impossible situation. The government had become a laughing stock. On November 17, Pinheiro de Azevedo had even suggested a suspension of its activities, though this wasn't publicly announced until November 20. In the immortal words of Brecht, they would have loved to "dissolve the people and elect another one." On November 21, the Sixth Government went "on strike," threatening to move to Porto, where it may or may not have found more support. The Prime Minister's preoccupations were more or less those of "The Nine," spelt out in the "Plan of the Colonels." The PS and PPD were now openly calling for Otelo's resignation, because he had refused to order troops to act against the building workers on November 13. They were also after Fabião's blood. On November 19, the Constituent Assembly was packed with delegates discussing the situation. A demonstration (PRP–MES–UDP) in the public gallery shouted "Reactionaries out of the

Assembly, now." The PCP–MDP delegates present joined in the shouting, directed against the CDS–PPD. Jaime Neves, leader of the commandos, spoke bluntly to Costa Gomes and threatened to "tidy all this mess up himself," if something wasn't done soon. "The Cork," as usual, bobbed this way and that on the troubled waters. But effectively the President was being faced with a palace coup, led by "The Nine" and endorsed by the extreme Right.

With the government "on strike" the ground was free for a takeover. The situation could not last. Something had to give. There were meetings everywhere: in the upper echelons of the parties, of the "fronts," of the ministries, of the unions, of the local Juntas. In the cafés. And in the barracks.

Let us pause for a moment and look at the main contending forces. The Sixth Government, supported by the PS–PPD, wanted a very bourgeois kind of socialism, a "socialism" emanating from parliamentary institutions, consisting of a mixed economy of European type, liberally laced with private enterprise, and underwritten by a reliable army and an efficient police force. They saw themselves at the head of the state machine which would administer all this. The PCP was more "radical" in the sense of wanting the central power to control larger sectors of the economy. They also wanted the unions ("their" unions) to be an established estate of the realm. The other state capitalist forces were prepared to go "the whole way." What divided them was how much state intervention they would achieve (and how soon), and how much their own political tendency could or should control the institutions of the existing society, or of any new society in the making.

With so many potential governments lining up in parallel the overall situation was confusing in the extreme. One lived in a half-world, where the enemy came in all shades. People were cruelly forced to make false choices: defend this or condemn that. The choices remained confined to the political sphere, despite the widespread nonparty feeling which had come to the fore during recent months. Isolation was thus more abject, despite the fact that many extreme-leftists called this the most "revolutionary" period.

My ex-neighbour (I'd since moved into a larger apartment shared with three other people) chided the local men for supporting the PCP. Then, two sentences later, she would express fear that the CDS might smash it. She had got hold of a copy of the UDP *Voz do Povo* and said she liked it. "I'm a communist. But I just don't understand all these things about parties." The people, she said, had to unite to overcome all this confusion, to get beyond the groups. The problem was how?

For her the Portuguese revolt had started in hope as a way out of despair, but it was coming back to her as just that. She was on her pills again, like before April 25. Only now the irreversible step had been taken. She was politically aware and her awareness was mixed with extreme emotion. "The fascists are taking over again." She spat the words out with pure hatred. The feeling was widespread, even if ill-founded. It was as though she refused to admit she could be demoralised, as though somehow, in the maze of leftist ideology, demoralisation was just not on because it conflicted with the socialist-realist, machine gun-toting image confronting one at every corner. I too was vulnerable. I didn't want to see everything crushed in the interpolitical conflict. I couldn't admit certain things to myself—or I admitted them secretly and wouldn't admit them to others, which was even worse. Yet, paradoxically, there was peace of mind as long as the crisis lasted. Events quickly followed one another and it was impossible to figure everything out in an instant. It was like awakening after a cluster of dreams and having to sort out what was real and what wasn't.

People reacted differently to all this. In many tascas political discussion was bypassed on a grand scale, lest the fabric of everyday survival, woven over many years, be torn by loud ideological discussion. Argument became focused on such issues as where exactly the Ota base was, or on whether the neighbour down the road was a RAL-1 or a PM. It was safer to talk about murders, to become involved in sensational stories. I remember going to a café in October, where I had known some people. The only discussion I ended up having was about a vampire inspired neurotic who had killed five people in Germany. The story had been published on the front page of *Diário de Notícias*. Later PCP and PS militants spoke to me in private. The people I'd come to see either ignored me or showed (with their downcast eyes and forced interest in their dominoes) that they felt terrible. I left, feeling terrible.

On the other hand, the public bars of Lisbon were full of state capitalist elements. The "Lisbon Commune" was founded on the professional classes. It was dominated by that section of unproductive wage-labourers who are particularly prone to Leninist and ultra-Leninist perspectives: groups of intellectuals, lower functionaries in the state apparatus, ex-workers such as trade union officials, all setting themselves up as the guardians of "working-class science." Mário Soares and Cunhal were falsely said to be dining out in the chic restaurants, where Caetano's old deputies had dined before. Lisbon is a relatively small city: the techno-cratic class, politically powerful but numerically few were well known to one another, despite their differences. They acted as if they had the unique model of revolution and as if the rest (the "inferior" revolution-aries) had to follow suit or be denied salvation. The proletariat could be saved; they seemed to be saying, but only through their superior level of consciousness and their "more significant" interpersonal relationships. There seemed to be a Leninism of everyday life, relegating those who weren't of this or that political persuasion to a very primitive emotional consciousness.

The Left only hoped to push the PCP further along the state capital-ist road. No organised group criticised Capital per se, its hierarchies, its priorities, its social relations, its essence, on any mass basis. No significant group systematically or explicitly criticised the Left as the midwives of state capitalism. The various Inter-Empresas lined up behind the various parties which dominated them. They waited, by and large indifferent to the party political power struggle over the type of regime to be brought about.

XIV NOVEMBER 25

After *Rádio Renascença* had been blown up by a paratrooper unit on November 7, Vasco Lourenço went to Tancos Base. On behalf of the Council, he explained the decision to a plenário called by the officers. A few soldiers turned up, told him what they thought of him, and left to attend a counterplenário called by the sergeants. On the following day, 123 officers from the base resigned their commissions. On November 19, Commander Morais e Silva took drastic action: he ordered some 1,200 soldiers to take immediate leave, and to evacuate the base. The paras could not accept this decision. They "fired" their commanding officer and placed themselves under the authority of COPCON. "We offer you 20,000 shots per minute," one of the sergeants said.

On the base no one quite knew what was happening. The Right were on the offensive in a big way. Or was it a camouflaged PCP offensive? People phoned one another to report troop movements in various parts of the country and to ask if there were soldiers in the streets of Lisbon. Rumours reverberated. It was hard to distinguish between truths manipulated by party interests and lies manufactured to protect them. One story was that there was a plan to: a) seal off Lisbon (where most of the left-wing troops were stationed); b) gain control of the North; c) cut off all electricity and gas should Lisbon then still hold out.[1] The group around "The Nine" were tightening up their organisation. No one was sure if the initiative was really theirs or whether they were a front for other forces. "Portugal will not be the Chile of Europe" was a common PRP-MES slogan at this time.

On November 20, a meeting of PS-PPD delegates in Porto discussed moving the Constituent Assembly to the North, and later the government too. A large PCP-FUR demonstration calling for a "revolutionary government" went to Belém—of all places—to ask for it. The inevitable Costa Gomes appeared at the window. As usual he was able to float above

---

1   *Tempo Novo*, November 27, 1975.

the crowds who, in a sense, were against him. He thanked them for their support. He warned them of the dangers of civil war. Later in the evening a manifesto of the "Inter-Comissões of Soldiers and Sailors" was read. This federation, born a few days earlier, had met in Obidos to discuss "concrete issues relating to soldiers." It was really the (UDP-PRP) SUVs, reorganising and attempting to take a lead. The manifesto called for a wage of 2,500 escudos a month (instead of 250) and for free transport. Another manifesto—signed this time—was read from a "Group of Progressive Officers." It was a rehash of the August COPCON document, with one important difference: it called for the arming of the working class.

On the same day officers at Beirolas barracks promised to distribute guns to the workers ("enough to arm a demonstration"). The Army brass (whether they supported the Frente Militar Unida, COPCON, "The Nine," the few remaining Gonçalvists, the PS, the PPD, or the PCP) were in uproar and panic. "The Nine" (supported by the whole right wing) decided to remain firm. It was like in a Western. "Whoever moves first will eat it," as the Portuguese put it. No one wanted to advance . . . or to retreat. Most of the rumours of coups and countercoups were just bluff, aimed at gaining the upper hand. Most, but not all.

On November 21, the RAL-1s held their morning drill as usual. This time it was a drill with a difference, it was televised. General Fabião was present. So were representatives from many local CTs and CMs. "We soldiers swear to be loyal to the Motherland and to struggle for its liberty and independence. We swear to be always, always, on the side of the people, at the service of the working class, of the peasants, of the working people. We swear to struggle with all our strength, voluntarily accepting revolutionary discipline, against fascism, against imperialism, for democracy, for people's power, or the victory of the socialist revolution." A worker who spoke at the assembly said he was glad "the soldiers would no longer accept blind discipline." But he was being taken in by the folklore of the event. It was a horrible sight to watch on TV: the new "progressive" officers and generals standing at ease while the soldiers dutifully and obediently recited the prescribed words. To hell with military discipline, "left" or "right."

It was a show, of course, carried out by PCP-Gonçalvist forces seeking to take over from (or with, they weren't fussy) the Sixth Government. But "The Nine" were no fools. On the following day they decided that Otelo would have to go. They called on Vasco Lourenço (one of their own group) to take his place. Lourenço accepted, on condition Otelo did too. Many COPCON officers refused to accept all this. Inter-Comissões pledged support for Otelo. The RAL-1 men likewise refused to accept the proposed change, as did most of the officers of the Lisbon command. Otelo agreed to retain his post after a meeting, in Alto do Duque, of key officers of the Lisbon region.

The commandos were not only against Otelo. They also disliked the nomination of Vasco Lourenço. "There are many competent colonels around who could do the job as well," said Jaime Neves. The Artillery in Cascais, who had arrested MES militants some days earlier for paint- ing a great mural outside their barracks, were also against Lourenço. Pires Veloso hadn't made up his mind. He sent a message to be read in all Northern regiments, at the flag saluting ceremony, urging "voluntary and total acceptance and subordination to military duties, to discipline, and to respect for the hierarchy."

On Sunday, November 23, the PS called a large demonstration which criticised Otelo and Costa Gomes. Soares came out in support of Vasco Lourenço. He also supported Pires Veloso. Again the ominous chant of "discipline, discipline" was heard. It had been a hot weekend, in every sense of the word. PPD and PS were whipping it up against what they called the "Lisbon Commune." The PCP, politically promiscuous as usual, was wooing everyone simultaneously. They realised that Lisbon and the Alentejo, alone, could only last a few days against the Right.

For most people in the capital, however, things continued as usual. There were the customary traffic jams, the bus queues to work, the bus queues back from work, the buying of groceries, the visits to relatives. Workers in the cooperatives or in the bigger firms were perhaps more aware of the general crisis.

The weekend resolved nothing. The 1,500 paratroopers, all officially on leave, remained firmly implanted at Tancos, 130 km from Lisbon. Fooled on September 28 and on March 11, manipulated into the bombing of RR, they were now revolting against their "Nazi commanders." A member of their committee told *República* (November 22): "There are vast differences between us: in the messes, in the food, even in the cutlery, not to mention the cost of living allowances which the officers receive . . . The rank-and-file committee works in conjunction with the sergeants' com- mittee. There's no party manipulation. Or, if you like, the only manipula- tion is from the PS who supports the officers. Solidarity is increasing day by day. We have the support of many CTs in the area."

The CTs of the Lisbon industrial belt called a two-hour stoppage for Monday, November 24, to discuss the situation. Paratroopers who had arrived from Angola on the Sunday, and who had been stationed at the Air Force base at Ota, pledged support for the paras in Tancos. In Tancos itself civilians had elected a committee to look after the kitchens. Air Force Base 3, through their SUV committee, criticised their commanding officer and pledged support to Tancos and to their own second-in-command. Otelo made a speech on TV, criticising the "anti-working class" nature of the Sixth Government.

At a demonstration on November 23, Soares had said that the PS were not afraid of civil war and that "they too had guns." This was tantamount to inciting "The Nine" not to give an inch. "There is no left alternative to the Sixth Government," he said, berating the PCP for the present crisis and denouncing those "soldiers who organise within the armed forces and serve as an instrument of the PCP to impose its dictatorship." He had singled out Dinis de Almeida, of the RAL-1s, the most heavily armed group in the entire Lisbon area.

Later that evening, in Rio Maior, a meeting of CAP (Confederation of Portuguese Farmers) decided that the situation was intolerable. The group had organised a demonstration against the PCP in Santarém on November 7 and had criticised the "wild occupations" taking place all over the country. It was comprised of ex-latifundiários and their support-ers. At the meeting there was talk of a "left-wing" coup by the RAL-1s. The solidly conservative farmers decided to "cut the country in half." And they meant it. They had been addressed some weeks earlier by Galváo de Melo, of the CDS, who had spoken of the necessity "to drive the com-munists into the sea and drown them." This was now the moment of truth, the cut-off point between Southern revolutionary folklore and the "reactionary" North. Members of CAP from all over the country—includ-ing restored owners from Alentejo and land-renting landlords from the North—pledged themselves to cut down trees and block airports and railways between the North and South. The meeting had originally been called to mobilise support against Agrarian Reform. Its timing turned out to be a lucky coincidence for the Right.

At 4 a.m., on November 25, commandos took up positions outside the palace of Belém. There was nothing strange in this, as military units were increasingly taking "the law" into their own hands. At about this time a group of CAP members were leaving the palace, their demands "having been satisfied." They said they would take down the barricades. COPCON alerted its members. By 5 a.m. COPCON guards had been set up in *Emissora Nacional* Radio station and RTP TV station. Rumours of a right-wing coup spread like wildfire over the telephones. The soldiers (paras) occupied their bases at Monte Real and Montijo, as well as in Monsanto, to defend themselves against any reactionary manoeuvres, and to support their comrades in Tancos.

The Council of the Revolution had not as yet confirmed the demotion of Otelo. In the "official" version of events COPCON officers, waiting in nearby Alto do Duque, were accused of having given the order to occupy the bases. But feeling in the bases had been brewing for some days, and it was probably a series of coincidences which led to them being occupied. At 5:30 a.m. forces from the Lisbon Military School (EPAM) took over the TV transmitter outside Lisbon.

The morning news on Rádio Clube Português stated that Vasco Lourenço had been nominated Military Commander of the Lisbon Region, without Otelo's endorsement. The broadcast called on all PCP and MDP militants to report to their local headquarters. It also reported a PRP-MES manifesto supporting the occupation of the Tancos base. The manifestos of Inter-Comissões (of Soldiers and Sailors) and of the "group of progressive officers" were read out, again and again. When news leaked that the TV broadcasting station in Monsanto had been occupied, some workers began to arm themselves.

The radio reports that Northern troops as a whole are behind Pires Veloso and the Council. At 3 p.m. a telex from the Council prohibits all further military statements except those emanating from its own offices. At 4 p.m. a "state of emergency" is declared. Ramalho Eanes proceeds to Commando Headquarters in Amadora and announces he is taking over all military operations on behalf of "The Nine." Throughout Lisbon rumours abound of a coup "à la Pinochet." Troops from the Military school take up positions on the roofs of certain buildings such as General Electric. A note from the Chief of the Armed Forces says that "the pretext of a rebellion (by the paras) is a struggle against Morais e Silva and Pinho Freire" but that this is "obviously not the real objective of the manipulation to which they are being subjected."

Captain Clemente, who had organised the occupation of the TV transmitter, had spoken to potential viewers in the middle of the afternoon. But as the TV had never functioned before at this hour very few people can have heard his message. Over the RCP radio, Intersindical called for mobilisation. At 4:30 p.m. a few workers set up barricades in Lisbon, using buses. At 5:30 p.m. RCP called on the "popular masses" for support. But people were otherwise engaged. At 6 p.m. a few groups of twenty to thirty workers from various factories tried to block the path of the commandos in Monsanto. A similar barricade was set up at Rua Castilho, again by a small group of workers. Most of their mates were unaware of what was happening. They were in their factories, without radios. And most of those who knew did nothing.

At 7 p.m. Captain Clemente read two communiqués from the Union of Metalworkers calling for a "general strike" and "condemning the State of Emergency" and the curfew. At 9 a.m. news broke that Otelo was being held prisoner in Belém. "To prove that he was free," Otelo made a speech from a Belém window to three to four hundred people below. The commandos took over the TV transmitter near Lisbon, dislodging without bloodshed the leftist troops that had occupied it that morning. It was obvious that the paras were losing. Only Rádio Clube Português remained as a source of information. A building worker (speaking on behalf of his union) urged all workers to turn up at their union offices with heavy machinery. "The revolution is in danger," he said. The appeal was virtually ignored. Militancy was not suddenly improvised after months of systematic demobilisation. Direct action, long denounced as "leftist adventurism," could not be abruptly be switched on like water from a tap.

At 10 p.m., the State of Emergency was promoted to a State of Siege. At 1 a.m. (on November 26) the barricades of Rua Castilho, set up by workers from E.C. Esteves (PCP) were peacefully dismantled, most of the workers manning them having retired to bed. The streets of Lisbon were quiet, peopled only by a few drunks and haunted by a few revolutionary spirits, wandering aimlessly around. The "Lisbon Commune" was a ghost town.

The bubble had burst. By 3 a.m., "The Nine" and the right wing were in firm control of the situation (through the Frente Militar Unida and the commandos). Near Belém, a few revolutionary poltergeists were shot at by commandos. Three were wounded. A friend who phoned me at 5 a.m. from a house nearby said the Military Police were still holding out. She apologised for phoning at that hour, "not knowing whether it was early or late." At 7 a.m., a call from Belém to the Military Police told them they had until 8 a.m. to surrender. Majors Campos e Andrade, Tomé, and Cuco Rosa called a plenário, which decided to hold out. Campos e Andrade then decided to give himself up, anyway, but before he could do so the commandos arrived. Shots were fired over the barracks. Two Military Police and one commando were killed. Campos e Andrade phoned Costa

Gomes, asking for a cease-fire but to no avail. Major Tomé called on his troops to stop firing "to avoid further bloodshed." The three majors were then arrested.

By 3 p.m. all the Military Police were sent home on leave. It was a sad scene: "the armed vanguard of the revolution" lugging their bags past a group of 300 startled onlookers.

In other parts of the country, in the South in particular, the situation had been slightly different. In Alcácer, agricultural workers had demonstrated in front of the union, on April 24, asking what was going on. The union said they had received no orders: everyone should therefore go home. The workers were undecided. A union official climbed onto a truck and declared the hour to be "serious." But it was, he felt, better for everyone to disperse and await instructions. Some two thousand workers were involved. On April 25 and 26 they began to realise that the union didn't know—or didn't want to know. "Something is happening in Setúbal," someone said. Many workers wanted to go there. The PCP and the unions— very quickly this time—set up barricades to stop the workers from leaving Alcácer. The situation, they were told, was under control. There were only a few leftists in Setúbal, anyway.

In Vendas Novas, on November 25, workers from some thirty co-operatives joined up and decided to go to the union building. Again the union told them to go home. They protested and were then told to go to the barracks in Vendas Novas—"to defend the troops." PRP militants told them that a certain Captain R had promised guns, and that they should wait. The PRP guns were on the way, they said. The workers, distrusting the PRP, decided to go to the Agrarian Reform centre for guns. The bewildered workers told them they had none. The workers didn't believe them. The younger men went back to the barracks to await their guns, but they never got them.

In Évora the situation was one of utter confusion. No one knew what to do. Everyone waited. The radio and press having been suspended the local population was at the mercy of rumours brought in by party militants. Anyone arriving was questioned at length. In other regions, the same confusion and ignorance prevailed.

Many militants went to Tancos. Meeting after meeting called for revolutionary discipline. Zeca Afonso, the singer, was there and sang revolutionary songs and everyone joined in. The atmosphere was frantic. It had been learnt that not only was Otelo to be dismissed, but that the base itself was to be closed down. The failure of COPCON to mobilise any kind of united action (and the success of "The Nine" and of their military Front) threw the left politicians into complete disarray.

Air Force planes buzzed over Lisbon on November 26, signalling their victory. Communiqués over the radio and the Porto TV told the same story. "At 1 p.m. the base area of Montijo surrendered." "Base area no. 3 (Tancos) is also being normalised." On November 27, in the working-class district of Forte de Almada, a Captain Luz was arrested. This was a PCP stronghold and although the PCP tried to demobilise a spontaneous demonstration, the workers went to the barracks en masse, seeking information.

Setúbal was perhaps the only area which went further. A "Struggle Committee" (made up of PRP-UDP militants) was activated. The town, at this time, was witnessing a fierce struggle by CMs against rents and the cost of living. On November 26, this Committee called on everyone to mass in front of Infantry base II. Guns were called for—and some were handed out secretly, to known militants. Planes buzzed over the Camara which the Committee had taken over as headquarters. The Committee abandoned the building and met in the offices of *O Setúbalense* (the local paper). A special edition was prepared. *O Setúbalense* was the only daily published in the South at this time. It gave information on Tancos and the other para bases, and called for popular mobilisation against the commandos. On November 27, all the workers on the newspaper were arrested. There was no militia to defend them.

At 10 a.m. on the twenty-seventh, in the Lisnave shipyards, the workers met to discuss the situation, as they did in many other factories. A deputation from Setenave, the sister company, turned up. Soldiers from nearby Forte de Almada were also present. The PCP argued against any show of force by the workers. The PRP-UDP workers argued that "something had to be done." A "Committee of Struggle" was set up by 40 workers (out of 8,400). It called for a strike. The majority of workers totally ignored the call. Troops were moved down from the North. One by one the dubious units were neutralised. Meanwhile, "The Nine" (to justify themselves) began to invent a coup by the Left which they, the real revolutionaries, were allegedly dismantling. "The Nine" were clearly dominating the crisis. Hundreds gathered outside the RAL-1 barracks, asking for information. The guards at the gates fed garbled messages to the crowds, who carried them to other units in still more garbled form. Wall newspapers went up outside party offices and on street corners. The MRPP supported the government and attacked "the social-fascist coup." At the end of the day, Otelo and Fabião had officially resigned from the Council.

The PRP had been active in Setúbal, the UDP in Lisbon. CTs from twenty to thirty factories gathered in Baixa da Banheira, just across the river. The gathering constituted itself the "Federation of Organs of Popular Unity." They published a broadsheet on November 29 called *Estado de Sítio* (State of Siege). While the Setúbal meeting on November 26 (given the tense and confused situation) brought together many genuine workers and took place in a completely nonparty atmosphere, the UDP meeting proved different. The broadsheet of November 29 asked: "And now? Are we to stay indifferent with our arms crossed?" and proceeded to call for a plenário in Baixa da Banheira on November 30 "where all CTs and CMs and other base organisations should meet." It brought a new UDP front organisation into existence and no more.

By Wednesday, November 27, most of the country was back to normal. The Northern newspapers enjoyed a miniboom. Certain Gonçalvist officers fled, others were arrested. Workers, too, were arrested: those who had set up the barricades as well as workers from one or two companies (for instance J. Pimenta) who had sent out scouts on the night of the 26th to see what was happening.

On November 28, the paras tried to negotiate an agreement with the Council. Rumours had it that they were to be bombed out of the last of their occupied bases. A plenário decided that it was futile to struggle on, and that only senseless bloodshed would result. On leaving the barracks certain paratroopers were in tears. They said they had been "betrayed yet again." The scene was pitiful. An official communiqué rubbed home the message: "The spirit that made April 25th was a nonparty spirit unfor-tunately certain soldiers have allowed themselves to be manipulated, accepting relationships with the parties . . . They sought their political survival under the false banner of a self-proclaimed progressivism which the situation of the coup has unmasked . . ." The communiqué called for the arrest of Captain Clemente and of Varela Gomes (ex-Fifth Division officers). On the same day Vasco Lourenço took charge as Chief of the Lisbon Military Area.

XV A BALANCE SHEET

The almost spectacular indifference with which most workers reacted to the events of November 25 is not difficult to understand. Neither The Nine/FMU nor the PCP/FUR had anything relevant to offer in relation to their fundamental needs, to their real life. To choose the one rather than the other was to choose one boss in preference to another. In many ways the forces which came out on top on November 25 were the ones which appeared to offer the easiest way out, for to carry through the projects of FUR or COPCON would have brought the wrath of Europe and America down on the workers' heads; it was impossible to go it alone.

Sometime during the afternoon of April 25, the Central Committee of the PCP had drawn certain conclusions. They had two choices: a) To support the paras and call for street mobilisation. This, most probably, would have led to a "Lisbon and Alentejo Commune," rejected by the rest of the country but which might just have survived a few weeks. Such an "adventure," they must have calculated, could easily fail, lead to blood-shed and would have lost them the entire leadership of the crisis. b) To hold back, to compromise with "The Nine" (through Costa Gomes) and to seek to reap what benefits they could from this. Given the nature of the Party, the second strategy was the less dangerous. Although they would lose their power in the ministries, they would retain considerable control over infrastructures like the unions, the CMs, the CTs, the cooperatives, and hopefully some of the media.

In any event, the turnout on November 25 had been poor. The PCP was faced with the prospect of losing everything. It decided to throw to the wolves the officers it had used in the weeks prior to November 25. In return, it would keep its place in the government. "The Nine" knew they couldn't control the workers on their own. They needed the PCP. Brigadier Charais said as much in a radio interview on November 29.

As in all Portuguese crises to date the outcome was an extension of state control: the remaining capital of eight newspapers and of all radio stations was nationalised. But it wasn't so much nationalisation that was on the mind of "The Nine": it was control of the direction that the vast section of the economy already in the hands of the state (65 percent according to official statistics, though other reports—that of the Banco Pinto Magalhães for instance—put the figure as high as 74 percent). Five morning and three evening papers were given new managements. Information became a major state prerogative. *O Século, Diário de Notícias, A Capital, Jornal de Notícias, Diáro de Lisboa, Diário Popular, Jornal do Comércio,* and *Comércio do Porto* as well as a variety of state-owned magazines and radio stations received major "overhauls." The PCP lost most of its positions in the media.

The "coup" of November 25 wasn't "à la Pinochet" as PRP (and others) had forecast, though I must admit that I was afraid of something very bad happening that night, as were a lot of my friends. I got a few calls from international friends worried about me. I explained it was all okay. But it could easily have gone wrong, some stubborn fool meeting another.

The political parties, perhaps to their own surprise, survived November 25. Those inheriting the newly strengthened state realised that political parties (left or right) were a necessary ingredient of the democratic parliamentary camouflage. All the parties (PPD, PS, PCP, CDS FUR, UDP, PCP-ml, and MRPP) were invited "for talks" at Belém on Sunday, November 30.

The autonomous workers' groups (i.e., those outside party, or "non-party" party fronts) received most of the stick. A search for weapons was started. The National Republican Guard (now rearmed) "investigated" over forty cooperatives and autonomous proletarian organisations. The local Infantry School and National Republican Guard threw a cordon around the cooperative at Aveiras de Cima, in Ribatejo. The workers were herded out into the cold night, in their bedclothes. "Where are the guns?" No one answered. The National Republican Guard began to search, finding one G3. No one owned up. There were threats of arrests. A worker owned up for the rest; two men were arrested all the same. "All living together, eh? Sleeping together, too?" a National Republican Guard officer smirked. No one answered. Some factories were likewise searched as were the Popular Clinics of Santa Cruz and Cova de Piedade.

The PRP headquarters were raided, but then a raid there was almost *de rigueur* in view of their boasts about weapons. None were found. Had they been distributed? Were they hidden elsewhere (for an even bigger "emergency")? Had they ever existed? Captain Fernandes (who had certainly distributed 1,500 G3 automatic rifles and had then sensibly disappeared) was declared a deserter and an order for his arrest sent out. These searches, aimed at bringing the organisations into line, were to continue right up to March 1976.

The main repercussion of November 25 was a strengthening of the state, allowing it a more coherent and united approach to control and "planning." This required the modification of other projects of state control. This was achieved rather drastically, through a series of purges in various ministries—in particular the Ministries of the Economy, Internal Affairs, and Agriculture and Fisheries. More specifically it required firmer control over the workers' organisations and over the Army.

The differences between the two technocratic projects ("The Nine"-PS and PCP-FUR) can be looked at from an economic point of view, though obviously there were wider ramifications. The proposed "solutions" differed in the pace of the nationalisations envisaged and in the sectors to be nationalised and what future use they could be put to. What constituted the "commanding heights" of the economy depended on the general direction chosen for the "development of the productive forces" and this in turn was related to international agreement between various states. "The Nine" never questioned the principle of nationalisation: the argument was about the areas or sectors considered most in need of development. It was a question of the role of the state and control of these sectors. For the PS and PPD the future was European Parliamentary Democracy. For others (like Melo Antunes, for instance) it was the Third World. A few doubtless dreamed of endless trade with Albania and China. No one was asking at what cost—or at whose cost—the new production would be established. There was no basic awareness of the law of value—hence an ambiguity about the whole question of production and about the proletariat itself.

These technocrats (from the PS, through the military "Left," to the so-called extreme left groups) shared the same general historical perspectives: to subordinate the economic to the political and the sweat of production (done by the workers) to calculations about distribution (done by the technocrats). The proletariat, as Marx had said, had no ideals to defend. It was a body on which ideals would have to be fitted. Capitalists and state-capitalists alike were in business for just that. For the mass of maimed individuals salvation was a choice between one vanguard and another (each pretending it wasn't a vanguard). The superrevolutionary vanguards are never like ordinary people. That's why we're supposed to look up to them, and never voice what our alienation demands. For the revolutionary misfits (that is, the proletariat), decisions about life were being taken by others. Tomorrow, as the anthem of international socialism put it, the International "would be the human race." But today, sadly, demands and perspectives were just to be centred on smaller issues like "national independence."

Nor did it herald the immediate return of capital into private hands as all the foreign press (including the *Financial Times* and *Le Monde*) said it would.[1] It represented a step, a pause, an attempt by the state to catch up with itself, to draw its breath and to generate policies from above and to put its house in order. As a first step all military communiqués other than those emanating from the Military Chief of Staff and the "Revolutionary Council" were forbidden. A decision was taken to reduce the armed forces to twelve thousand men by 1978. Many conscripts, due to be called were excused. But the army provided employment for thousands of young then and there would be difficulties. In the meantime the Assemblies in the barracks were abolished. Traditional military discipline was restored.

Plans for the "censorship of pornography" were worked out (the military always have an obsession about this matter). All further occupations of land were prohibited by the Minister of Agriculture. Only four occupations took place between November 1975 and February 1976, compared to the four hundred between September and November 1975. Some seven hundred thousand hectares had still to be reallocated if the "law on Agrarian Reform" was to be implemented, but the state clearly wanted to assimilate what had already been taken over before any new steps were taken.

All this, of course, didn't satisfy the extreme Right, who saw Melo Antunes as a "dyed-in-the-wool" communist. The forces of the extreme Right continued to organise and to dream of a return to the "good old days." Bombings continued in the North, in Braga, in Póvoa de Varzim, etc. The UDP and the unions were the chief targets. The forces which had been active on September 28 and March 11 were again on the offensive. There was a lot of talk of a "return of the bosses" from Brazil and the U.S. But the new state was not prepared to give them back what it had gained.

---

1   Events would overshadow all of this and laissez-faire capitalism was to find new ways to expand. Although it was difficult, at this time, to foresee the collapse of the Soviet Union Bloc and the rise of neoliberalism, or what Naomi Klein has termed "the shock doctrine," leading to one of the longest periods of capitalist successes in history, the experience, I believe, still has lessons for us all.

In certain instances, certain bosses were allowed back . . . as managers. By mid-January 1976, some 128 "requests" by ex-bosses had been received. Tellingly, it was the Ministry of Labour whose task it was to unravel all this. The Ministry of Agriculture issued instructions giving March 1, 1976, as the closing date for compensation claims by ex-landowners. By March, only nineteen cases of "reoccupation" had been registered and some ten cases of "reprivatisation" (i.e., return to private ownership). The latter cases (all in the Northern textile industry) had been called for by the workers themselves and frequently where workers had called for support for the old boss this was refused by the state authorities.

What had happened on November 25 was that one of the bureaucratic-military groups, the military wing of the PS/Nine had managed to impose its will on the others. But there were enormous differences between the old PIDE and the new state: the new regime regarded the opposition parties as essential and concentrated its attacks on the base groups. During the first waves of reprisals, the parties moved to defend themselves first and foremost. Their first reflex was to tighten up their own apparatus. But really they had little to fear: they were essential to the new schema.

The government moved more cautiously in relation to the working class in general. They were still a force to be reckoned with. They were confronted with some eight hundred industrial cooperatives and with some two hundred enterprises under workers' control, not to mention the thousands of cases of "workers' vigilance" (a term coined by a Lisnave worker to describe the situation in that firm). In addition there were over six hundred agricultural cooperatives (most of them legalised by May 1976). This meant that over one-fifth of all agricultural land in Portugal (one million hectares out of 4,974,158) was under some form of collective control. House occupations, which had reached thirty-five thousand before November 25, were maintained. Squatters were not prepared to give up their rights just because the Left had lost a few ministries.

November 25 was, however, to affect the workers in a very direct way. On the grand scale, even if it wasn't immediately obvious, it was to be the culmination of the revolutionary experiment that had been the experience of the previous eighteen months. But on the everyday life scale it was also to have immediate effects. Prices had been frozen after March 11 "for the remainder of the year." They were now reset and this meant they now incorporated all the hidden, state-supported inflation that had occurred in the intervening nine months. In January 1976, there was an all-round 40 percent increase in food prices. People complained and there were cases of refusal to pay. But no organised opposition developed. The workers tried to increase their pay packets, to get the extra month's wage which most had "won" over the previous year, but which many private and state enterprises were refusing to pay. In 1976, some 380 factories went on strike during February and March and thousands passed protest motions against the new policies. The bosses had found a new confidence and the state was gradually taking things under its wings.

With a million hectares under occupation, the workers prepared for their first "collective" harvest. What the new government planned was to "commercialise" these cooperatives, forcing them to sell their olive oil, wine, and cereals to state-controlled institutions (the Wine-producers Association, the Institute of Cereals, etc.) who would arrange for their further distribution. Failing this, credits would not be allocated.

By prohibiting all further occupations the state was creating a certain division among the agricultural workers, hoping thereby to control them better. Many further occupations were attempted (like at Vale de Sobrados near Évora) but the local National Republican Guard were immediately called and the workers evicted.

In places workers attempted to set up parallel economic structures. Direct selling from cooperatives to Neighbourhood Committees was organised on a wide scale in the Centre and South and proved very popular, given the increase in the cost of living. Cabbages costing fifteen escudos in the supermarket were sold for four escudos. Wine and olive oil were also sold at much lower prices.

The now fully nationalised radio and TV were amalgamated. The new company would avoid the confrontation of political views heard before November 25. The nationalised papers were given a new set of editors, mainly PS-oriented though including some "independents" close to the PPD. It was horrible. "The radio now spoke for the people," the people were told, "for the real people of Portugal who were tired of songs of revolt." The authorities seemed to think the people would prefer the soft-cushioned, social-democratic music of American ice-cream parlours. Self-discipline (in their mouths a euphemism for self-repression) was urged on everyone, daily.

Second-rate poets, novelists, and professional lawyers took over the editorial desks in magazine and newspaper offices. The weekly *Vida Mundial* and *A Capital*, which had been reasonably objective, were entrusted to the timid imagination of small minds. News consisted of information about what technocrats were thinking, or doing, or thinking of doing. Whereas before November 25 all news had been related to Portugal, it was now the opposite. International events, earthquakes, official visits, the Lebanese war all received major coverage. Comments about local affairs consisted of tirades against anarcho-populism, "Copconism," and the burning down of the Spanish Embassy. Those who contested—and even those who questioned—were denounced to a chorus of cries of "discipline, discipline." Economic collapse was predicted a hundred times a day and the workers held up as scapegoats. The workers, it appeared, were all being manipulated. Except those, of course, who had followed the parties "victorious" on November 25. Everyday life was trodden to death with half-truths culled from the masochist repertoire of petty officials. One wanted to scream at them, at their "freedom"—to hurl at them Mallarme's quietly desperate "the flesh is sad, alas, and I've read all the books." Had they an inkling of the torment they were causing, of the pit into which they were pushing their listeners? What did they know of the yearnings which, in the hectic pre-November days, had provided such a strange peace of mind? Did anyone tell them that pills and alcohol were repressed forms of class struggle? Could they feel the real immiseration of the proletariat which in their mouths immediately became empty rhetoric?

These new rulers, great antifascists all, were out to destroy both imagination and any semblance of life. These morons, with their ideas of "pluralism" had a vision of socialism so lifeless that, as Lukacs put it, it "crippled to the point of abnormality." Moralism and mediocrity buttressed one another. All this pettiness in the name of order, "sanity" . . . productivity.

But if all this didn't satisfy the workers, it didn't satisfy the extreme Right either. With international help they launched a series of new papers attacking the Left: *O País*, *Rua*, *Rossio*, *Retornado*, and *O Dia*. The PCP, having lost its dominant influence in *Diário de Notícias* (now the propaganda organ of an aggressively insipid PS) set up its own daily newspaper: *O Diário*. The Left, having lost *República* because of financial difficulties, set up weeklies such as *Gazeta da Semana* and *Página Um*. The former was edited by an ex-MES militant who had resigned from the Fifth Government; the latter was in the hands of the PRP.

Rádio Renascença was handed back to the Church. Even Otelo began to wonder if his decision to back the workers had been the right one, strategically. The Church had proved so strong. Masses were again heard over the radio on Sundays, after six months of sublime silence. Mysticism was peddled everywhere.

On March 8, *Diário Popular* reported that 1,040 PIDEs had been freed since November 25, leaving only 300 in prison. The latter were to be released later. Of those freed, 600 were under semi-house arrest. This didn't stop them from moving freely around the country, attending meetings and conducting political propaganda. Until April 1976, not a single case had been brought against the PIDEs. Up to May 1976, two years after the coup, only 108 cases were being "processed."

The cooperative movement was to be reorganised and new laws were drafted to control them. The Cooperatives were in any case not born as a revolutionary challenge to capitalism but as a state capitalist attempt to control the occupations and to guide it into channels which the established institutions could dominate. The workers occupied land, houses, and factories. The state then came along with promises to "legalise" some of their achievements. The workers, in order to survive, were forced to accept these recuperated results of their own self-activity.

It is obvious that nationalization (or stratification, as it should preferably be called) has nothing to do with socialism: it is merely a means of ensuring the smooth functioning of vital sectors of the economy such as transport, power, the distribution of raw materials, thereby making possible both state planning and an overall development of the productive forces. But whether these benefit the workers or not depends on how the fundamental decisions have been taken—and by whom—in the last resort on who holds power.

The Portuguese experience is modern in every sense. So is the Portuguese revolutionary movement. It lasted some eighteen months altogether but in that time it went through everything that a modern class society could throw at it. It was modern not just in the attitudes of the workers and in the nature of their demands but also in the pattern of state-capitalist counterattack which the working-class practices unleashed. It is a movement which has transcended the sterile arguments between the Leninists and left communists which had raged for over fifty years before it. The advocates of the Vanguard Party were forced to disclaim the very core of their beliefs and to say that they are not parties. Council forms were fetishised and put on show, even if they have no socialist content. And people who call themselves materialists (even historical or dialectical materialists) refuse to see the material reality that stares them in the face.

The Portuguese experience between 1974 and 1976 shows that revolutionary activity does not develop as the result of strategies devised by system analysts or bourgeois planners, masquerading as revolutionary generals like Otelo or Costa Gomes. It emerges in the course of the struggle itself and its most advanced forms are expressed by those for whom it is a necessity to struggle. Hundreds of thousands of workers entered the struggle in Portugal. But the enemy constantly appeared before them in unexpected garb: that of their own organisations. Every time they set up an organisation they found it manipulated by so-called vanguards or leaders who were not of their own and who understood little about why they were struggling. Even the groups who paid lip-service to a critique of state capitalism did so because of their weakness. They were forced to support the base organisations for the time being.

The revolutionaries—on a massive scale—were found to be part of the problem, not part of the solution. In this the Portuguese experience may prove to be a prefiguration of revolutions to come. The lessons should be pondered while there is yet time. The alternative is clear. It was put concisely many years ago: "the liberation of the workers is the task of the workers themselves.

AFTERWORD

Maurice Brinton[1]

This is an uncooked slice of history. It is the story of what happened in Portugal between April 25, 1974, and November 25, 1975, as seen and felt by a deeply committed participant. It depicts the hopes, the tremendous enthusiasm, the boundless energy, the total commitment, the released power, even the revolutionary innocence of thousands of ordinary people taking a hand in the remoulding of their lives. And it does so against the background of an economic and social reality which placed limits on what could be done. This tension dominates the whole narrative.

Phil's book is not only a perceptive account of real events. It is an attempt at a new type of historiography. The official statements of the MFA and of the political parties, and the pronouncements of politicians, are relegated to appendices.[2] The text proper explodes with life, the life of people seeking—in many contradictory ways—to write a chapter of their own history.

Characters and events literally hustle one another off the pages. Images remain, pell-mell, like an afterglow. The intoxication and euphoria

---

1 Maurice Brinton was the pen name of Chris Pallis (1923–2005), who wrote and translated for the British libertarian socialist group Solidarity from 1960 until the early 1980s. Born in India in 1923 to a wealthy Anglo-Greek family which settled in Switzerland, he became fluent in English, Greek, and French. He went to Oxford in 1941 to study medicine and joined the Communist Party of Great Britain but was almost immediately expelled on account of his criticism of its policy on the Second World War. He moved on to Trotskyism and supported the Revolutionary Communist Party until 1946 but then dropped out of politics for a decade while he pursued his medical career. In 1957, he rejoined a Trotskyist group, the Club, which in 1959 became the Socialist Labour League but was expelled in 1960 and with a group of other ex-members of the SLL immediately set up Solidarity, highly influenced by the work of Cornelius Castoriadis, the main thinker of the French group Socialisme ou Barbarie. He wrote two short books, *The Bolsheviks and Workers' Control*, 1970, on the aftermath of the Bolshevik Revolution, and *The Irrational in Politics*, 1974, on sexual politics.
2 The original edition of this book had twenty-six appendices, mainly political manifestos. These have been omitted from this edition as they are freely available elsewhere.

of the first few weeks. Politics in the first person. The crowds in the streets. Civilians clambering over tanks and armoured cars. The atmosphere of the great days: May Day and September 28, 1974; March 11, 1975. Strikes and occupations. The declarations of people in bitter struggle which, in their concern for fundamentals, seemed to echo the thunder of the *Communist Manifesto*. Lisbon dockers, talking of a "total remodelling of society," of a struggle which would have to be waged "outside the unions," given the total involvement of such bodies in the iniquities of the previous regime. The sheer poetry of some landholders' documents, asking what will happen "now the sowing time is over and the olives have been picked." The tenants' committees. The nonmanipulable struggle of those at the very bottom of the social ladder, the shanty town dwellers, for whom nobody had the audacity to claim they were speaking. Taxi drivers wanting the Institute for the Reorganisation of Agriculture to take over . . . their taxis. The Revolution creating its own surrealist precedents. The Second Congress of Councils, in the Technological Institute in Lisbon, complete with latter-day Leninists dreaming of Smolny and Putilov, amid the paraphernalia of modern television. Revolutionary tourists and their hang-ups. Soldiers inviting civilians into the Artillery Regiment of Serra do Pilar barracks for a week-long festival, sing-song and orgy . . . of political discussion. The seemingly endless birth-pangs which only produced a still-born infant. The surfeit of revolutionary rhetoric and the return to reality. The problems and anxieties, the achievements and the failures. The joy and the sadness. The longings and the frustrations. And, throughout, the concern (in the words of Spinoza) "neither to laugh nor to weep, but to understand."

Why did the revolutionary process not develop further in Portugal? A meaningful social revolution comes about when a large number of people seek a total change in the conditions of their existence. Massive pressures had certainly built up within Salazarist Portugal. But the aims of those opposed to the old society were disparate. For varying reasons different groups wanted an end to the colonial wars, to the futility and frustrations of a long period of compulsory military service, to the censorship, and to the ubiquity of the hated PIDE. The consensus, however, hardly went any further.

Beyond this, the paths diverged. The forward-looking section of the Portuguese bourgeoisie had one objective—a liberal capitalist society, in which they would accumulate wealth in a "civilised" manner. "Antifascism" was the ideal cover for a crying need to modernist the bourgeois state. A liberal capitalist society provided a freer framework for the important business of making money. The "trouble" was that the working class too had aims of its own, less explicitly formulated perhaps, but in conflict with the above. Its very conditions of existence compelled it to struggle. The objectives of the PCP and of the various left groups amounted to various forms of state capitalism. At every stage their actions sought to canalise popular discontent into channels which enhanced either the power of the state, or the power of the political parties themselves. They manipulated the social disaffection to achieve a society in which they themselves would wield political power as the "legitimate representatives of the illiterate masses." This was the reality, perceived or not, behind all their rhetoric.

The working class, concentrated in the great conurbations of Lisbon, Setúbal and Porto, of Braga and Aveiro—but numerically weak and scattered elsewhere—met both successes and reverses in gaining specific objectives of its own. Initially, in the strike movement that preceded April 25 (and was to gain such impetus after that date) the working class succeeded for a while in imposing some redistribution in its own favour of the total social product. It created autonomous organisations, the Workers' Committees (CTs) and Federations of CTs (like Inter-Empresas). But no amount of wishful thinking—or of Bolshevik bravado—could circumvent the hard facts of social geography. There were vast areas of the country where a smallholding peasantry, intensely property-conscious, exerted an enormous weight. There was the legacy of intimidation, temporal and spiritual, by policemen and priests. And there were other facts of equal relevance. A social revolution is not just a reflex response to the iniquities and oppressions of an existing order. Such responses may bring a society crashing to its knees. They do not ensure that it is replaced by one that is qualitatively different. Such an outcome requires a vision, shared by a substantial number of people of a totally different way of life.

Did the working class of Portugal—or any substantial part of it—have such a vision? Who knows? There were certainly attempts to reduce wage differentials, to elaborate a pattern of distribution that would bypass traditional market mechanisms, to break down the barriers between intellectual and manual labour, to produce and live together according to different norms. But these were, more often than not, empirical adaptations to specific circumstances: the need to raise the miserable living standards of Cape Verdean building workers, to dispose of the products of some self-managed factory, to solve practical problems in some shanty town, or to administer some seized latifundio. More fundamental social objectives, such as the abolition of hierarchy, of wage labour and of commodity production were never really on the historical agenda.

The proletariat, both urban and rural, was one of the driving forces of the Portuguese upheaval. Of this, there can be no doubt. But its forward surge, in the months after April 1974, was eventually broken. Piecemeal, the ruling class succeeded in reestablishing their order, their discipline, their ownership of land, houses and plant, and—through a fine admixture of coercion and cooption—the productivity of "their" workers. The working-class advance was broken by a combination of factors of significance to all concerned in the dynamics of revolution.

Firstly, the upsurge did not take place in an economic or geographical vacuum. Portugal could not be isolated from the world market. It is a "poor" country. Large areas of its production are geared to world demand and it has to import many of its finished goods. None of the fundamental problems could be solved in the Portuguese arena alone. Portuguese capitalism was but a link in a vast international network: the onslaught against it was doomed to failure if confined to Portugal. The workers of Portugal remained isolated, deprived of their natural allies. During the crucial months the Spanish tinder failed to ignite.

Within this general context of economic dependence and revolutionary isolation there were many specific difficulties. There was fear, induced by realities of unemployment (some of it deliberately engineered by Portuguese capitalists). During 1974-75 some 10 percent of the working population was constantly out of work. Life was hard. After some initial gains wages were more or less frozen—throughout a period of intense inflation (up to 18 percent per annum). The gross national product fell by some 24 percent. There was then the painful awakening from certain illusions, the illusion for instance that the working class had "allies," as distinct from people who were prepared to "ride it" (as one would a horse) to the "revolution." The relevant implications began to dawn, namely that the workers could not leave it to others (such as "progressive" officers or student radicals) to solve their problems for them. They began taking the appropriate measure: the creation of autonomous organisations controlled from below. But then the old enemy reappeared in a new garb. Those who used words with the same ease as the peasant his scythe or the bricklayer his trowel began to organise, to dominate, to manipulate the plenários. There was a massive retreat from political activity, in disgust at the behaviour of the leftist sects. There was the feeling of despair and impotence in relation to the enormity of the tasks to be solved.

The Portuguese working class proved unable—at this moment in time—of further developing the autonomous forms of organisation needed, were they even to hold what had been gained. The Leninist groups here bear a tremendous, almost a historic responsibility. Instead of helping to develop and consolidate the new creations of the class, they did all in their power to make the movement conform to textbook models. They talked learnedly of Kerensky and Kornilov when people needed confidence in their own ability to organise textile production to process and distribute the season's cork, to find storage facilities for rural produce being sent directly to the towns. Their concerns were not felt to be genuine, and their relationship to the real movement was never sensed to be an honest one. For example those who spoke loudest about "arming the people" in fact ensured that available weapons went to their own particular groups. They identified themselves with the proletariat, but the proletariat refused to return the compliment.

Yet, when all is said and done, one further fact remains, enormous in its implications. In April 1975, the Portuguese people voted for the Constituent Assembly. A year later they elected an Assembly of the Republic. Even the smallest political groups participated, their message stridently proclaimed from every wall and roof top. As far as political propaganda and access to the media are concerned these were the two "freest" years in Portuguese history. The apparatus of repression was largely in disarray. The electoral campaigns were possibly more vigorous and more sustained, more varied and more vitriolic than at any other time, in any other bourgeois democracy. Parties legally put up posters advocating armed insurrection. In June 1976, a President was elected: Ramalho Eanes, the law-and-order candidate, campaigning against "states within the state," polled over 60 percent of the vote.

It is too easy to attribute this event solely to the factors we have mentioned, important though they be. The vote also represented a yearning for stability, for a breathing space, for a predictable pattern to everyday life, for the easier option of delegated authority. It was repudiation, hopefully temporary, of the din of discussion, of the pressure to participate, of the stress of responsibility, of the fatigue and frustration of an involvement that seemed to lead nowhere. It was the personal price one paid to escape the demand for permanent self-mobilisation, a demand dictated by the state of permanent stalemate in the political and social arena outside. It is a new pattern of bourgeois recuperation. Realists will recognise it as a hallmark of the vastness of the task ahead.

239

Several lessons can be drawn from the Portuguese experience, lessons which transcend the frontiers of Portugal. The foremost, I think, is that in future upheavals the traditional revolutionaries will prove part of the problem not part of the solution. The Portuguese events bring irrefutable testimony to this assertion. Past revolutions faced two main dangers. They could be annihilated by those whose privileges they threatened (Paris, 1871; Germany, 1918–19; Spain, 1936; Hungary, 1956). Or they could be destroyed from within, through bureaucratic degeneration (as happened to the Russian Revolution of 1917). A third alarming risk now looms on the horizon. It is the risk of genuinely radical upheavals being deviated into state capitalist channels. It is the danger that any new creation (in the realm of ideas, relationships or institutions) will immediately be pounced upon, penetrated, colonised, manipulated—and ultimately deformed—by hordes of power-hungry "professional revolutionaries," midwives of state capitalism, and all the more dangerous because draped in the red flag.

These people bring with them attitudes and patterns deeply (if not always consciously) moulded of behaviour by Lenin's notion that the workers, left to themselves, "can only develop a trade union consciousness." Their current organisation practices and their prescriptions for the future are bureaucratic to the core. Because of all the extraneous matter they drag in their historical wake and seek to inject into live situations (like some flies inject their larvae into living flesh) these "professional revolutionaries" (Stalinists, Maoists, Trotskyists and Leninists of various kinds) succeed, between them, in polluting the very concept of independent political action. Their preoccupation with leadership destroys initiative. Their concern for the correct line discourages experiment. Their obsession with the past is a blight on the future. They create around themselves a wasteland of cynicism and disgust, of smashed hopes and disillusion that buttresses the deepest dogma of bourgeois society, namely that ordinary people are incapable of solving their own problems, by themselves and for themselves. Otelo Saraiva de Carvalho was wrong when he endorsed the anarchist jest that *cozido* (a local dish of boiled meats and potatoes) was the only specifically Portuguese thing to be had. There was more. The Portuguese upheaval of 1974–75 coined a new word for the political lexicon, an adjective that denoted an aspiration: the word *apartidário*. The literal translation is "nonparty." But the term reflects the longing for genuine autonomy in struggle, for an activity that is not manipulated by some *cúpula* (political clique) or other.

Another lesson, intimately linked to the first, concerns the role of the MFA. People had many illusions about the MFA, illusions which were to be rudely shattered on November 25, 1975. The Left not only did nothing to dispel these illusions, it in fact constantly reinforced them. The army is a fundamental pillar of class rule and it is dangerous nonsense to believe that it can somehow be transformed into something else, into an instrument of social change for instance. To believe that this can be brought about through gaining the leadership of certain regiments or through the creation of rank-and-file committees in certain battalions is positively suicidal. In Portugal, the "putschist and militarist conception of the social revolution" was to have dire consequences for the working class.[3]

Leninist groups are permeated through and through with Jacobin (i.e., bourgeois) notions concerning the conquest of power. The citizen armies of the French Revolution may have toppled the old feudal structures, enabling the bourgeoisie to assume political power and the bourgeois mode of production (which existed before the revolution and was capable of autonomous development) to gain unfettered ascendancy. But the specialist revolution is something very different. The working class does not already have its own mode of production operating within bourgeois society. The revolution will be a protracted process of conscious social creation. Its concerns are as much the capture of the hearts and minds of ordinary people and the discarding of outmoded beliefs as the capture of some Winter Palace or the deposition of some feudal monarch. It neither begins nor ends with the military question. This is not to say that the ruling classes will peacefully surrender what they have. But this is another question.

The Leninist groups in Portugal, given their views, failed to conduct any systematic propaganda against the MFA *as such*.[4] They failed to denounce the totally mystifying concept of the "alliance" between the MFA and "the people." They equated political power with military power in the crudest possible way. Elements of the Portuguese experience fed this disastrous identification. After April 25, there was certainly an overlap between military and political apparatus. Moreover the lessening of autonomous working-class action—an ebbtide to which the Leninists had signally contributed—created an atmosphere in which their substitutionary attitudes

---

3   Charles Reeve, *L'expérience portugaise: la conception putschiste de la revolution sociale* (Paris: Spartacus, 1976), 25. I have borrowed heavily from this excellent short text.
4   The MRPP was an exception, but its later attitudes to the coup of November 25 and to Eanes finally deprived it of all credibility.

241

could further flourish. The "revolutionaries" placed their faith—and even what cadres they could—in COPCON. They boasted with a wink, of their contacts in the upper echelons of this body. In their hands the social struggle became reduced to a question of intrigues, of tactical alliances and manoeuvres: of giving critical support to one lot of officers against another, to one military clique against another. Groups on the "extreme Left" described the MFA as the "guarantor of the Revolution." In the words of Cohn-Bendit, "they spoke of power just like everyone else does. There was nothing emptier than their description of it . . . They don't ask what does the conquest of social power mean? No, they don't go beyond the question of centralised, politico-military power." Social power was something more difficult to grasp, and far more difficult to achieve; "It was the reality of work relations, with hierarchy, in people's heads."

The debacle of November 25 (described with feeling and wit in Phil's narrative) left a trail of confusion and disarray. If anything is to be learned from it we must speak bluntly: to accept the primacy of the Army (i.e., of an institution moulded by capitalism and permeated by capitalist values) in the Portuguese situation was doubly nefarious. It fostered reliance on others, which was bad enough. But more specifically it fostered reliance on a body which, when the crunch came, would turn out to be *on the other side*. Constantly to emphasise the preponderant role of the Army was tantamount to injecting deeply bourgeois ideas (submission to leaders, the centralization of power into very few hands, the abdication of the right to determine objectives or to participate in decision-making) into what was undoubtedly a movement for social change. The damage proved incalculable. Strange partners peddled this mystification. The PCP did all in its power to boost the MFA as a "guarantor of democracy." It proclaimed that "no country, not even the oldest democratic countries, allows open calls to desertion and agitation in the armed forces. It exerted pressure on deserters and those avoiding call-up "to do their military service, like all other young Portuguese." Meanwhile, the leftist groups, with their "contacts" and "areas of influence" in the middle echelons of the MFA, covered up for the early strikebreaking role of the Army.

Some people still talk about "Portuguese particularism," about the "specificity of the Portuguese situation," about Portugal being "different." They still described the MFA as having been "the motor of the revolution." To do this they stress the role of the Unit Assemblies (ADUS) and of rank-and-file organisations such as SUV (Soldiers United Will Win). This mythology must be exploded before it gains a foothold.

The ADUS were created from above, in 1974, as "structures for rank-and-file participation." They were to be based on a new "revolutionary" discipline, "agreed and not imposed," and on a "hierarchy of aptitudes." Their concerns, however, never extended beyond the walls of the barracks. Their real implantation. varied from region to region. The role of the MFA officers remained preponderant within them. Communication between ADUS remained in the hands of such officers. Even at a General Assembly of one of the "red" regiments of the Lisbon area, in December 1974, it was stressed that the function of the assembly was "consultative, a function of education and information." The Fifth Division, in which there was deep PCP penetration, did all it could to promote the ADUS. Its influence within the MFA reached its peak at the time of the Fifth Provisional Government of Vasco Gonçalves. But this influence (which sought to make of the Fifth Division a political education centre for the armed forces as a whole) was not associated with any real shift of power towards the base. Attempts to increase the area of authority of the ADUS provoked an indignant statement by the Cabinet for the Dynamisation of the Army (linked to the Fifth Division). "The ADUS," it was stressed, "are organs for advising and supporting the Command . . . In no way do the question the authority of the Command in the realm of decisions."

At this point a "left" critique of the military policies of the PCP had gained a certain hearing. It originated around officers close to the PRP (and to COPCON) who saw in the way the PCP was alienating support an opening for their own implantation into the military apparatus, and hence into the apparatus of the state. This tendency sought a base in the social movement outside the army. The COPCON documents of early summer 1975 reflect these aspirations.

But the virtual eviction of the PCP from the government a few weeks later (and the victory of "The Nine" over the Gonçalvists in the military apparatus) was to lead to a PCP volte-face. It began endorsing the "radical" COPCON proposals it had previously denounced. At last, some leftists saw a chance to consummate the lust of a lifetime, to have a united front with the PCP. It was against this background that the semiclandestine SUV groups began to emerge, "real" rank-and-file groups, "committed to the class struggle," highly critical of the "antidemocratic structures of the ADUS." But the SUV were themselves being manipulated by leftist groups in search of new tactics for the capture of state power. Their call was "reactionaries out of the barracks!" This could only imply one thing: "Barracks, yes, but commanded by leftist officers."

The moment of truth arrived. On November 25, fewer than two hundred commandos "overcame" several "red" regiments armed to the teeth. Among the regiments that "surrendered" were those that had been most loudly proclaiming that "their leaders were not only behind them but in front of them, that they were revolutionaries." The whole elaborate and mystifying set-up collapsed: ADUS, Soldiers Commissions, Vigilance Committees, SUV. All this showed itself for what it was: precisely nothing; isolated, divided, without links with one another, without information, and above all without initiative, the rank-and-file soldiers were in a state of total dependence on the military hierarchy, on the "progressive" officers. They followed faithfully and confidently; orders to arm, orders to disarm, orders to defend themselves, orders to stop defending themselves, orders to remain within the barracks, orders to move out of them. Meanwhile the "progressive" officers, caught up in political manoeuvres, tempted by political deals, one eye on possible "compromises" cooked up in the Presidential Palace, either abandoned the barracks or got themselves arrested . . . "to avoid bloodshed." The rank-and-file soldiers were handed over in a triple shackle, political, ideological and organisational. The veil was ripped asunder. The "military policy" of all the leftist groups was revealed for what it was: a pathetic faith in what the attitude of the "progressive officers" would be when confronted with a choice.

One of the RAL-1 soldiers put it very simply: "On November 25, we suddenly had the impression that there was no command, nothing! Progressively we felt we were entirely alone." After months on a Leninist diet, to be suddenly without "left" leaders spelled starvation. After a year of agitation in the army, the rank-and-file groups never played any important role. They never achieved the least control over the functioning of the military machine. On the contrary, they ended up reinforcing the lack of initiative of the soldiers, their belief in the "good army" the army of "progressive officers."

It takes no great effort to see the similarity between the military "policies" of the Left in Portugal and their attitudes to such matters as Parliament and the trade unions elsewhere. In each instance they propose to the revolutionary movement to fight on the territory—and with the weapons of the class enemy. And then they seem surprised that they are defeated—or that, if "victorious," the fruits of their victory proved rather different from what they had expected. A final by-product of the Portuguese events—bizarre this time, rather than sinister—was the appearance of a new political hybrid: the social democratic Maoist. Throughout the Portuguese upheaval their hatred of the "social-fascists" of the PCP drove the MRPP into some very strange political alliances. They welcomed the bombings of the PCP headquarters in the summer of 1975 as evidence of "popular justice against the revisionists." In the trade union field they concluded a whole series of electoral alliances with the PS and PPD—and even with the CDS—aimed at diminishing the influence of the PCP. They reproached the victorious officers of November 25 with being too indulgent in relation to "the principal enemy: social-fascism." In fact, they welcomed the coup. "The situation is excellent," they claimed in December 1975, "Revisionism is being increasingly unmasked." In the presidential elections of June 1976, the MRPP even urged their supporters to vote for Eanes, the PS-backed law-and-order candidate. The telling critiques which the MRPP made of the PRP-BR, whose setting up of "workers' councils" the MRPP correctly described as "providing a mass basis for COPCON"—will soon be forgotten when the MRPP itself is seen to have provided a similar basis for the PS or for "The Nine." But then, for all its verbal leftism and denunciations of the MFA, does not the MRPP itself propose "a democratic and popular revolution made not only by workers and peasants but by other revolutionary sectors of society, such as small and medium shopkeepers, small and medium farmers, small and medium industrialists, etc."

The book deals clearly, concretely and honestly with the problems and limitations of self-management, attempted in a capitalist context. To take over a factory or farm abandoned by their owners is a natural enough reaction of workers seeking to maintain a living in an environment they know. But the capitalist market immediately obtrudes. Outlets have to be found for the goods produced. The relation of the "self-managed" enterprise to the outside world remains all-pervading. Disposing of stocks—or even of capital equipment—to pay oneself wages is no lasting solution. The "need" to sell one's labour power—with all that this entails—persists, unrelenting. In Portugal the price paid for the enhanced internal democracy of certain workshops or farms was often a lengthening of the working day, or an intensification of the labour process to "allow" the self-managed unit to remain economically "viable." In this sense islands of self-management became islands of capitalist recuperation. In Guimaraes I saw a self-managed textile factory, its walls plastered with extracts from Marx's *Economic and Philosophical Manuscripts*. The workers don't need to be told that this is self-managed alienation. They live it daily, in their flesh. But what is the real, practical, immediate alternative? Is it communist production? Is it the scrap-heap capitalist unemployment?

Or is it something else, something variable, something created anew, every day, in a thousand different workplaces, moulded by the differing relation of forces there? No generalization can cover all that was created, the full variety of the experience or the bitterness engendered by failure. Whatever the concrete forms evolved the essential, as always, is to avoid telling lies, to avoid mystifying both oneself and others.

All this of course has little to do with the cardinal relationship of self-management to socialism. Some speak today as if the Portuguese experience in some sense invalidated this relationship, as if it proved that self-management had nothing to do with socialism, as if all talk of self-management was the ultimate recuperative plot of Machiavellian capitalism. The confusion—where it is not deliberate and therefore dishonest—shows a pathetic conceptual poverty. That, under capitalism, self-management may become a potent means of capitalist recuperation is undoubted. But what has this to do with the question of whether self-management is the essential institutional (not economic, but institutional) framework of socialist society?

One can certainly conceive of self-management without socialism. But can one imagine any socialism worth living under without self-managed individuals, collectivities and institutions? Those who can visualise such a society should let us share their vision. But they should seek to make it as explicit as possible. *Who*, if not those directly involved, would have the greatest say in the fundamental decisions? And how would such a non-self-managed "socialist" society differ from all the monstrous societies we see around us today, societies in which minorities take all the fundamental decisions and—through their access to information and power—perpetuate their own privileges.

To an outsider, there was much that was very specifically Portuguese in the Portuguese upsurge. The will to dare the unknown, to disregard the advice of "experts," to take history and reality by the scruff of the neck—all that is summed up in the term *Sebastianismo*—was very evident in the early months.[5] Without batting an eyelid at the enormity of what they

---

5   In June 1578 Dom Sebastião, a twenty-four-year-old monarch, sailed out of the Tagus to conquer Morocco from Moulay Abdel Malik. It was an insane enterprise, carried out against the advice of all his councillors. Dom Sebastião's forces were annihilated in the Battle of Alcácer-Quibir in North Africa. The young king's body was never recovered and this gave rise to the belief that he would return some day to save Portugal. Throughout the Spanish occupation that followed, one false Dom Sebastião after another kept appearing, rekindling hopes of an eventual, messianic liberation.

were attempting, young revolutionaries (and older ones) talked seriously of a direct transition from fascism to libertarian communism. They acted as if a belief in miracles could drive people to attempt—and, who knows, perhaps even to achieve—the "impossible."

Like all radical endeavours in history the upsurge was a joyful affair, at least to start with. An immensely popular song, after April 25, was entitled "Gaivota" ("The Seagull"). Poster wit, although perhaps never achieving the insights of May 1968 in France, nevertheless developed into a telling instrument of social critique. The anarchists ensured that it was used as often against the so-called left as against more obvious targets. With the joy went a very Portuguese toughness.

The fado persisted, not as an embodiment of despair and resignation (as claimed by the superficial sociologists) but as a down-to-earth and uncompromising statement of the life of the poor. I recall a letter Phil once wrote me. He was entering the Alentejo: "The tiny hills begin to roll across the flat countryside. Crouched eucalyptus trees hide in the barren dales. Here is a land of tradition, of rich struggles against elements and of wine, olives and music, of landowners alike, a land of everyday survival, difficult to penetrate except by those who care for it. It is as if the stunted growth of the trees said all that needed to be said about hardship, abandonment, work—about the constant fight against a poor and unyielding soil on which lived giant women and monstrous men. But however ungrateful the land, the spirit was never crippled."

Although not songs of revolt, the fados testify to this indestructibility of the oppressed, to this deep unity of man and nature. Romany roots endow some songs with a fierce pride, with a scorn for what "the bourgeois" will think or say, enabling them boldly to deal with such themes as women's right to sexual pleasure. No sentimentality, no soothing syrup. Love may mean pain, but is worth it. No neurotic trendiness. Just things as they are. Is not this the raw material of which revolution will be made?

Other features too had their roots in history. As their documents show, the MFA was probably one of the most articulate and prolific groups of soldiers the world has ever produced. In this they reflected the *intellectualismo* of the Portuguese elite. Intellectuality would be an inadequate translation. The term—as I was repeatedly told in Portugal—really denotes something else, concern with speaking rather than with doing, and with the surface rather than with the core of things. Its loci are the cafés, not the cloisters of Coimbra. Eça de Queirós, the Aveiro novelist of the end of the last century, grasped this and made of it the kernel of some of his most scathing satires. His second *Farpa*, published in 1871, could have been written in the summer of 1975, a lampoon of later Leninist sects rather than of the bourgeois parties of his day:

> There are four political parties in Portugal: the Historical Party, the Regenerating Party, the Reformist Party and the Constitutional Party. There are, of course, others, more anonymous, only known to a few families. The four official parties, with newspapers and headquarters, are in perpetual and irreconcilable antagonism, always fighting amongst themselves in their leading articles. They have tried to restore peace, to unify. Impossible! The only thing they have in common is the ground of the Chiado on which they all tread, and the Arcade which shelters them . . . All four are Catholic. All four are centralizing. All four have the same yearning for order. All four want progress and cite the case of Belgium. The conflagration is immense.

Forty years before the French Revolution, Sebastião José de Carvalho e Melo, First Marquis of Pombal, had declared war on clerical reaction and obscurantism, disbanded monasteries and convents and expelled the Jesuits from Portugal. The revolution of 1910 gave a new impetus to his ideas. But the Salazar regime made peace with the Church and the Jesuits crept back. One morning, not long after Salazar had effected this reconciliation, people passing Pombal's huge statue at the top of Lisbon's Avenida da Liberdade, were delighted to read, in enormous letters of black pitch—all shiny on the white marble—the following inscription:

> Come down, Marquis
> Because they're back again! [6]

Today the old faces are creeping out once more. The gains of the early months are being whittled away piecemeal. The owners are reappearing—sometimes as managers. One would like to urge the spirit of 1974–75 to descend from its reified pedestal and help sweep the rubbish away. Who knows when it will move again? For the moment things are fairly quiet. But even the widespread disillusion has a certain Portuguese tinge to it. The early prevocational innocence may have been lost. But the faintly amused nostalgia the Portuguese call *saudade* prevents sad sophistication degenerating into pure cynicism.

---

6   Quoted in Fryer and McGowen Piheiro, *Oldest Ally* (London: 1961).

An impossible revolution? Yes, some will argue. Impossible within the confines of Portugal. Impossible because no island of libertarian communism can exist in a sea of capitalist production and of capitalist consciousness. Impossible because the upsurge was rooted—as in concrete—in the underdevelopment of Portuguese society as a whole. Impossible, given the social composition of modern Portugal, the weight of the Northern, smallholding peasantry, the influence of the Church, the erosive and demobilizing effects of chronic poverty and unemployment. Impossible, finally, it is claimed, because state capitalism, not socialism, was "objectively" on the historical agenda, and because of the state-capitalist mentality of the "socialist" revolutionaries.

But men and women have always dreamed "impossible" dreams. They have repeatedly sought to "storm heaven" in the search for what they felt to be right. Again and again they have struggled for objectives difficult to attain, but which they sensed to embody their needs and desires. It is this capacity which makes of human beings the potential subjects of history, instead of its perpetual objects. This is why a study of the Portuguese events of 1974–75 is relevant to modern revolutionaries.

How should revolutionary libertarians have reacted to the Portuguese events? To have sat at home, dismissing the revolution as "impossible," was out of the question. Should they, to paraphrase Lenin, have started struggling before anyone else, and not ceased struggling until after everyone else had? "Struggling" can be as meaningful—or meaningless—as any other activity. It depends on the ends being fought for, and on the means being used. The revolutionary libertarian seeks to convince working people of their ability to organise and manage their own affairs, to foster a critical spirit towards external groups claiming to be on their side (including his or her own) and to expose the illusions spread by such (mainly Leninist) groups. This is a constant, everyday task which the libertarian revolutionary sees as his or her main concern. Perhaps in Portugal the opportunity for revolution has receded for the time being, but this role of the revolutionary never ceases (and has certainly not ceased in Portugal). Soon, in Spain, the Stalinists will be dusting down the living corpse of La Passionaria—a far more potent symbol of resistance than Álvaro Cunhal. The Illusionists will be at work again, having learned nothing from the experience of Portugal, and living on the battle cries of 1936.

Words such as "possible" and "impossible" have an historical dimension as well as an immediate one. What is impossible today may become feasible tomorrow. Moreover it may become feasible *because* of today's unsuccessful endeavours. To declare a revolution "impossible" is to pass a verdict on a process, as if it were an isolated event. It is to deny to those indicted the right to be judged by posterity. There are fruitful defeats in history as well as sterile victories. The Paris Commune defeat of 1871 was in the minds of the Russian revolutionaries of 1917. The events of Kronstadt (1921) or of Hungary (1956) still evoke echoes. They helped mould revolutionary libertarian attitudes that are very much part of current thinking. But there is more. Preconceived ideas are not just ideological straitjackets. To declare a revolution "impossible" may, under certain circumstances, contribute to obstructing it. The masses in action are always more revolutionary than the most revolutionary of the revolutionary organisations. The reasons are obvious. The revolutionary organisations are wedded to past models (usually 1917). The masses want to create the future.

Some people see history as a railway line, leading to a predetermined goal. They see the action of classes as just generating the steam which will enable men, or great parties ("the drivers of the locomotive of history," to use Stalin's monstrous phrase) to take charge of events. This is a prescription for bureaucratic practices, for it legitimises the power (both today and tomorrow) of those who think they know the track—and of those who think they can handle the engine.

No goal (certainly no political goal) can be defined as clearly as this. Material conditions (including cultural conditions) influence what is feasible and what is not. But they do not determine it, in any univocal sense. There is seldom, if ever, only one way of solving the problems created by a given pattern of economic or social organisation. History shows how quite different forms of living, and quite different constellations of belief, proved possible on the basis of fairly similar technological infrastructures. "Be realistic, demand the impossible," the walls of Paris proclaimed in May 1968. The words had a significance that went far deeper than their ability to startle. The first echoes were heard in Portugal. Where life pulsates, there is expectation. Sooner or later struggle breaks down the obstacles to the fulfilment of one's needs. Who knows where, and in what form, the subterranean stream of human hope will next surge to the surface?

CHRONOLOGY

1926	**May**. Right-wing military uprising begins in Braga. Gains support of large sections of the armed forces.
1927	**February**. Abortive countercoup in Porto: 120 killed and 700 injured. Supported by anarcho-syndicalists of A Batalha and the CGT.
1928	**March**. Sole candidate Carmona overwhelmingly elected President. Continues in office till his death in 1951.
	April. Salazar appointed Finance Minister.
1931	**April**. General strike. Left-wing military revolt in Madeira. Both crushed.
1932	**July**. Salazar becomes Prime Minister.
1933	**March**. Proclamation of Estado Novo (Corporative Constitution).
	September. National Statute of Labour proclaimed, creating "syndicates" based on Italian (fascist) model.
1934	**January**. PCP and CGT (anarcho-syndicalist) call general strike that leads to insurrection throughout the country. Soviet proclaimed in Marinha Grande.
1936	**September**. Crews of three ships, sent by Salazar to aid Franco's troops, mutiny. Creation of paramilitary Portuguese Legion.
	October. Creation of fascist youth movement (Moçidade Portuguesa).
1937	**July**. Anarchist attempt on life of Salazar. Underground Popular Front formed, uniting various reformist parties (including PCP).
1940	**July**. Exhibition in Lisbon of "The Portuguese World" (a living museum of slavery and colonial booty).
1941	Reorganisation of PCP under Álvaro Cunhal.

1944   **August**. Large strike movements in the South. Demonstrations in Lisbon. Many arrests.

1945   **May**. Official half-day mourning for Hitler. Demonstrations in support of allied troops. Salazar promises elections "as free as in free England." **October**. Creation of MUD (Democratic Unity Movement).

1946   **October**. Abortive revolt in the North: 91 soldiers arrested.

1947   **April**. Abortive revolt by Army officers. Sabotage of military planes. Palma Inaçio (future leader of LUAR) involved. General strike in Lisbon.

1950   **May**. Álvaro Cunhal sentenced and imprisoned. Escapes in January 1960.

1954–55   Dispute with India over Goa.

1958   **June**. First contested presidential election under Salazar regime. Two opposition candidates: Arlindo Vincente (PCP) and General Humberto Delgado (dubbed "General Coca Cola" by the PCP, who at first refuse to have anything to do with him). PCP finally support Delgado, after great demonstrations in his favour all over the country. Américo Tomás, the "official" candidate declared elected.

1959   Abortive revolt in Lisbon. Thousands arrested.

1961   **January**. Henrique Galvão and a mixed group of Spanish and Portuguese (Revolutionary Command for Iberiai Liberation) seize the Santa Maria in the Caribbean. Santa Maria chased on the high seas by eight American, two British, four Dutch, and eleven Portuguese ships. Finally docks at Recife, Brazil. **February**. MPLA launches nationalist revolt in Angola. "Universal suffrage" withdrawn in Portugal. **November**. First known case of sky-jacking. Palma Inaçio seizes a TAP plane and bombards Lisbon and Porto with leaflets. Granted political asylum in Tangiers. **December**. Abortive revolt in Beja led by Delgado supporters.

1962	FPLN (Patriotic Front of National Liberation) formed, with PCP participation. Head office in Algeria. Broadcasts regularly to Portugal (The Voice of Freedom). Nationalist revolt in Mozambique. Massive antiwar demonstration in Lisbon in defiance of law banning demonstrations.
1964	Split in PCP between Russian and Chinese factions after "Hundred Flowers" movement in China. Marxist-Leninist Committees (CMLP) and Armed Portuguese Front (FAP) formed. Castroist ideas permeate FAP.
1967	LUAR formed by Palma Inaçio. Bank robbery in Figueira da Foz.
1968	Attempt by LUAR to storm the town of Covilhá. Many militants arrested, including Palma Inaçio who escapes after his trial. A price is put on his head. He is captured in Spain. Mario Soares deported. In a wave of strikes, 5,000 Lisnave workers occupy shipyards. Occupation of some factories broken by GNR. So-called liberalisation period of Marcelo Caetano: CEUD (Electoral Committees for Democratic Unity) formed without PCP. Later merge with CDE (Committees for Democratic Elections) in which PCP is represented. Formation of Intersindical.
1970	MRPP (Movement for the Reorganisation of the Proletarian Party) formed by Maoist tendencies. Active in universities and some factories. Front organisations like RPAC (Popular Anti-Colonial Resistance) formed within the armed forces. Strike by transport workers, who refuse to collect fares. Formation of SEDES, a liberal-capitalist technocratic group.
1971	PCP expelled from FPLN. First actions of Revolutionary Brigades (BR). NATO communications centre, outside Lisbon, blown up. ARA (armed wing of PCP) blows up plane hangar and attempts to attack a PIDE office.
1972	**November**. Ribeiro Santos (MRPP student) murdered by PIDE.

1973	Formation of PRP. Unites with BR. Split in FPLN. Portuguese Socialist Party (PS) reconstituted. A wave of strikes for higher wages in textile and electron‑ics industries. Strike at TAP (Portuguese Airlines) during which strikers are trapped in hangar and three workers are shot by PIDE. Office workers support strikers. CDE fights elections for one month and withdraws at the last minute. Many candidates arrested. Meeting of the clandestine "Movement of the Captains," Lisbon. Meeting in Obidos in December decides to carry out coup.
	December. Abortive revolt by right‑wing generals.
1974	**March**. Abortive revolt by units from Caldas da Rainha.
	April. Successful revolt by "Movement of the Captains," which becomes known as the MFA (Movement of the Armed Forces).

AFTER APRIL 25

May 1	Massive demonstrations all over the country,
May 8–20	Strike wave hits all sections of industry. Main demands are minimum monthly wage of 6,000 escudos and forty‑hour week.
May 16	Formation of First Provisional Government. At Ministerial level includes PS, PCP, MDP/CDE, PPD, and SEDES.
May 29	Timex workers launch appeal for "a day's wages for the workers on strike."
June 7	Saldanha Sanches (MRPP) imprisoned for calling on troops to desert. Demonstration for his release.
June 14	Riots by common law prisoners who want civil rights.
June 17	Postal strike (CTT) begins. Denounced by PCP. Army plans to occupy post offices. Two soldiers imprisoned for refusing to strike‑break.
July 8	Collapse of First Provisional Government of Palma Carlos.
July 17	Second Provisional Government includes PS, PPD, PCP, and SEDES. Vasco Gonçalves chosen as Prime Minister.

August 16	Riot police fire into crowds at demonstration of "Friends of Mozambique"; one dead, four wounded.
August 27	Government introduces antistrike law.
August 28	MFA officers threaten to arrest striking TAP workers.
September 10	Speech by Spínola against "anarchy." He calls on "silent majority" for their support.
September 12	Lisnave workers march into Lisbon in forbidden demonstration against antistrike law.
September 28–30	Barricades go up around Portugal to stop the right-wing "silent majority" demonstration. Spínola resigns. Costa Gomes becomes President. Third Provisional Government formed (PS, PCP, and PPD). Superior Council of the Revolution (Council of 20) replaces the Junta of National Salvation.
October	Chemical workers union comes out against PCP control of Intersindical. Strike wave hits many sectors of industry. Factories are occupied, products sold on the streets.
November 4	Meeting of CDS youth section broken up by MRPP demonstrators. Police fire into crowd; one dead, sixteen wounded.

1975

January 14	Large Intersindical demonstration in favour of mono-lithic union structure (*unicidade*).
January 25	Land occupations spread in Alentejo.
February 7	Demonstration by Federation of Workers' Committees (Inter-Empresas) against NATO visit and rising unemployment. Massive participation despite prohibition by government and attack by PCP.
March 11	Abortive right-wing coup by Spínolist officers, RAL-1 bombed. Collapse of Third Government. Fourth Provisional Government includes MDP-CDE and ex-MES, in coalition with PS, PCP, and PPD. Superior Council of the Revolution enlarged to 28. Decrees large-scale nationalisation of private monopolies.
April 19	PRP "launches" the Revolutionary Workers' Councils.
April 25	Elections to Constituent Assembly (38 percent PS, 26 percent PPD, 12.5 percent PCP).

May 10–15	Strike by 5,000 hotel and restaurant workers.
May 19	*República* occupied by its workers; PS condemns it.
May 20	*República* evacuated.
May 26	MFA Assembly pledges support for Vasco Gonçalves and discusses various documents on "popular power."
May 28	Some 400 Maoists (MRPP) arrested by COPCON.
June 2	First meeting of Constituent Assembly.
June 8	MFA General Assembly discusses "Guiding document on Popular Power."
June 16	COPCON allows *República* workers back into premises.
June 18	Demonstration against decision to hand RR back to Church.
June 21	MFA publish "Plan for Political Action."
July	Large demonstrations in the North, manipulated by the Church.
July 2–5	Strike wave hits main service industries: CTT, TLP, TAP. Chemical workers strike in the North. Hotel workers strike for a week.
July 4	Vast demonstrations in support of struggles at *República* and RR.
July 7–9	General Assembly of MFA (240) institutionalizes "pact" between the MFA and "the people."
July 11	PS withdraws from Coalition.
July 16	Tanks and armed soldiers support a demonstration in Lisbon called by Inter-Comissões (Federation of shanty town Neighbourhood Committees). PPD withdraws from Coalition. Collapse of Fourth Government.
July 18	PS supporters stopped from assembling in Lisbon.
July 21	Fifth Division reiterates its support for Vasco Gonçalves.
July 25	Costa Gomes warns that "revolution is taking place at too fast a pace."
July 27	MFA Assembly appoints "triumvirate": Costa Gomes, Gonçalves, Otelo.
August 7	"Document of The Nine."
August 8	Vasco Gonçalves forms "unitary" Fifth Provisional Government, supported by PCP and MDP.

August 13	COPCON document also attacks Fifth Government and calls for strengthening of organs of "popular power."
August 18	Almada speech by Vasco Gonçalves calling for "strong government"—to be carried out with "reduced forces" if necessary.
August 20	Massive demonstration in Lisbon in support of COPCON document.
August 25	PCP forms alliance with left-wing groups (FUR). Alliance collapses the following day.
September 6	MFA Assembly at Tancos forces resignation of Vasco Gonçalves.
September 8	SUV movement (Soldiers United Will Win) issues its first communiqué.
September 11	SUV demonstration in Lisbon.
September 13	Military Police demonstrate against being sent to Angola.
September 19	Sixth Provisional Government takes office. Includes PPD, PS, PCP.
September 20	Disabled ex-servicemen occupy bridge over Tagus (Lisbon).
September 26	Large SUV demonstration (Lisbon). Covilhá Congress of Factory Committees.
September 27	Spanish Consulate and Embassy burnt to ground (Lisbon).
September 29	Radio stations occupied by military. RR silenced.
October 1	PS calls for mobilisation against possible RAL-1 coup.
October 6–13	CICAP-RASP bases in Porto occupied.
October 22	Demonstrators reopen Rádio Renascença.
October 23	Revolutionary Brigades (BR) go underground.
November 7	RR blown up by unit of paratroopers.
November 9	Large PS-PPD demonstration in support of Sixth Government.
November 10	Officers resign from Tancos school.
November 13–14	Building workers besiege government in São Bento.
November 16	Enormous PCP demonstration in Lisbon attacks Sixth Government.
November 19	1,200 paratroopers suspended from Tancos occupy the base.

November 24	Otelo replaced as Lisbon Military Commander. Two-hour strike in Southern factories.
November 25	Commandos take up positions at Belem. "State of Siege" proclaimed. Over 200 arrests.
November 26	Commandos force surrender of Military Police (three of whom are killed). Otelo refuses post of Vice Commander of Lisbon Military Region (offered by Costa Gomes). COPCON abolished.
November 27	Nationalisation of remaining capital in newspapers and radio stations.

APPENDIX
TRANSCRIPT OF RÁDIO RENASCENÇA BROADCAST, OCTOBER 23, 1975

VOICE: It is now 30 minutes and 35 seconds after midnight. Transmitting is Rádio Renascença, occupied by its workers in the service of the working class, of the peasants, of all working people in general . . . (*music in background—growing louder*)
The events of March 7 in Setúbal was the subject of an official report.[1]

SONG: It was in the city of the Sado . . .

VOICE: A report which people disagreed with everywhere and which seems to have convinced no one. (*music continues*)

VOICE: We are going to hear Zeca Afonso describe certain events in a song. He wrote the music. The words are by neighbours and workers from Setúbal.

SONG: On the 7th day of March
On a Thursday began to be heard
Rumours which had it
That the PPD was the CIA.

Yellow leaflets distributed
Inviting all and sundry
Come ye all to a meeting
Of Social Democracy.

There were perhaps 400
Shouting from the depths of their lungs
"Down with capitalismo!
We don't want any more sharks!"

---

1   See p. 101 for a description of these events.

Inside were sixty guys
From the PPD who displayed
Clubs and firearms
And more, which we couldn't see.

At a prearranged signal
Many policemen arrived
Beat, ye policemen, beat
For the Totta Açores[2] will pay.

Friend, break down the door
They are going to kill the people
The beasts have opened fire
Outside we have to struggle.

The suffocating teargas
The shots which then rang out
Here come more squadrons of police
To protect the PPD.

João Manuel was killed
A man from the Algarve
Eighteen were already wounded
And the Naval Club was emptied.

Justice, in the night outside,
Called the people to the streets
Death to the murdering police
Friend, victory is yours.

On the 11th of the same month
At 11 o'clock in the morning
While Joao was lying
While Joao was dying.

On the other side of the river
The soldier Luís was also to die
Soldiers, sons of the people,
Let's go make our own country. (*fade out*)

---

2   A bank.

VOICE: Here is now a song which speaks of the anticommunism which has risen all over the country. (*music*) It is by Vieira da Silva and is called "The Wolves Are Here." (*music*)

SONG: Those who are here are the wolves
Those who are here are the hyenas
Liberals, capitalists, quarrelling over the country
The Legionários are your strength
(*The whole song is played*)

VOICE: We have just heard Vieira da Silva's song which spoke about anti-communism, (*music*) the anticommunism which many people would like to see as a permanent thing, (*music*) the anticommunism which disturbs many people (*pause*) because the people are not reactionary . . .

SONG: The bosses are the enemy of the working people . . .

VOICE: Yes the bosses are the reactionaries . . .

SONG: The bosses are the enemy . . .

VOICE: The bosses are the enemy of the working people . . . as we are told in a song (*music*) by a worker, Antero Correia.

SONG: The people are fed up with misery
The misery imposed upon them
The misery in which we spend our lives
The people have decided to end this
lai lai lai lai lai
lai lai lai lai lai.

The people decided to go on strike, to protest
To get better wages and good houses to live in
Good houses to live in
Because it is our right
And if they try to stop us
Then none will get away
Land, peace, and love
Popular Democracy.

VOICE: We have just heard Antero Correia, worker-singer in "The Bosses" composed by Tino Flores. (*new music starts*) Now, from Spain, we hear from FRAP (*music*) the Anti-Fascist and Patriotic Resistance Front. (*music*)

SONG: "It is in Spain that the people's guerilla war has begun" . . . (*song is completed*)

VOICE: Now for more revolutionary songs from Spain. Here is the voice of Pedro Faude, in "43 Years of Struggle for a Republic." (*song is sung*)

VOICE: Now from Cuba, this music from Carlos Pueblo y los tradicionales. It is a piece called "Hasta Siempre" in homage to Ernesto Che Guevara (*music and song follow*)

SONG: New song begins without introduction: "Come, workers, we have to struggle . . ." (*song finishes*)

VOICE: We have just heard Tino Flores in "Vamos Camaradas": Tino Flores has a very important message: organise the invincible people.

It is now eight minutes to one in the morning. At 1 a.m. we will have a news bulletin. From Italy, we now have this music from Lotta Continua. (*song follows, in Italian*)

VOICE: Yes, Lotta Continua: for communism, for liberty.

It is now four minutes to one. We just have time for two more songs from Cuba: "Pablo Milanes" and "Campesina." At one o'clock we'll have another news bulletin. (*Cuban songs played*)

VOICE: This is Rádio Renascença, occupied by its workers in the service of the working class, of the peasants, of all working people in general . . .

ABOUT PM PRESS

PM Press was founded at the end of 2007 by a small
collection of folks with decades of publishing, media, and
organizing experience. PM Press co-conspirators have
published and distributed hundreds of books, pamphlets,
CDs, and DVDs. Members of PM have founded enduring
book fairs, spearheaded victorious tenant organizing campaigns, and worked
closely with bookstores, academic conferences, and even rock bands to deliver
political and challenging ideas to all walks of life. We're old enough to know what
we're doing and young enough to know what's at stake.

We seek to create radical and stimulating fiction and non-fiction books, pamphlets,
t-shirts, visual and audio materials to entertain, educate and inspire you. We
aim to distribute these through every available channel with every available
technology — whether that means you are seeing anarchist classics at our bookfair
stalls; reading our latest vegan cookbook at the café; downloading geeky fiction
e-books; or digging new music and timely videos from our website.

PM Press is always on the lookout for talented and skilled volunteers, artists,
activists and writers to work with. If you have a great idea for a project or can
contribute in some way, please get in touch.

PM Press
PO Box 23912
Oakland, CA 94623
www.pmpress.org

FRIENDS OF PM PRESS

These are indisputably momentous times—the financial system is melting down globally and the Empire is stumbling. Now more than ever there is a vital need for radical ideas.

In the four years since its founding—and on a mere shoestring—PM Press has risen to the formidable challenge of publishing and distributing knowledge and entertainment for the struggles ahead. With over 175 releases to date, we have published an impressive and stimulating array of literature, art, music, politics, and culture. Using every available medium, we've succeeded in connecting those hungry for ideas and information to those putting them into practice.

Friends of PM allows you to directly help impact, amplify, and revitalize the discourse and actions of radical writers, filmmakers, and artists. It provides us with a stable foundation from which we can build upon our early successes and provides a much-needed subsidy for the materials that can't necessarily pay their own way. You can help make that happen—and receive every new title automatically delivered to your door once a month—by joining as a Friend of PM Press. And, we'll throw in a free T-shirt when you sign up.

Here are your options:

- **$25 a month** Get all books and pamphlets plus 50% discount on all webstore purchases

- **$40 a month** Get all PM Press releases (including CDs and DVDs) plus 50% discount on all webstore purchases

- **$100 a month** Superstar—Everything plus PM merchandise, free downloads, and 50% discount on all webstore purchases

For those who can't afford $25 or more a month, we're introducing **Sustainer Rates** at $15, $10 and $5. Sustainers get a free PM Press T-shirt and a 50% discount on all purchases from our website.

Your Visa or Mastercard will be billed once a month, until you tell us to stop. Or until our efforts succeed in bringing the revolution around. Or the financial meltdown of Capital makes plastic redundant. Whichever comes first.

All Power to the Councils!: A Documentary History of the German Revolution of 1918-1919

Edited and translated by Gabriel Kuhn

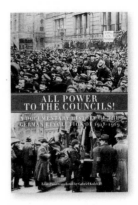

ISBN: 978-1-60486-111-2
$26.95   344 pages

The defeat in World War I and the subsequent end of the Kaiserreich threw Germany into turmoil. While the Social Democrats grabbed power, radicals across the country rallied to establish a socialist society under the slogan "All Power to the Councils!" The Spartacus League staged an uprising in Berlin, council republics were proclaimed in Bremen and Bavaria, and workers' revolts shook numerous German towns. The rebellions were crushed by the Social Democratic government with the help of right-wing militias like the notorious Free Corps. This paved the way to a dysfunctional Weimar Republic that witnessed the rise of the National Socialist movement.

The documentary history presented here collects manifestos, speeches, articles, and letters from the German Revolution, introduced and annotated by the editor. Many documents, like the anarchist Erich Mühsam's comprehensive account of the Bavarian Council Republic, are made available in English for the first time. The volume also includes appendixes portraying the Red Ruhr Army that repelled the reactionary Kapp Putsch in 1920, and the communist bandits that roamed Eastern Germany until 1921.

All Power to the Councils! provides a dynamic and vivid picture of a time with long-lasting effects for world history. A time that was both encouraging and tragic.

"The councils of the early 20th century, as they are presented in this volume, were autonomous organs of the working class beyond the traditional parties and unions. They had stepped out of the hidden world of small political groups and represented a mass movement fighting for an all-encompassing council system."
— Teo Panther, editor of *Alle Macht den Räten: Novemberrevolution 1918*

"The German Revolution of 1918-1919 and the following years mark an exceptional period in German history. This collection brings the radical aspirations of the time alive and contains many important lessons for contemporary scholars and activists alike."
— Markus Bauer, Free Workers' Union, FAU-IAA

"The struggles of the German working class in the early 20th century are perhaps some of the most bitter and misunderstood in European history, and it is time they were paid more attention."
— Richard Parry, author of *The Bonnot Gang*

The CNT in the Spanish Revolution Volume 1

José Peirats
with an introduction by Chris Ealham

ISBN: 978-1-60486-207-2
$28.00   432 pages

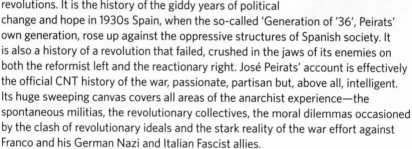

The CNT in the Spanish Revolution is the history of one of the most original and audacious, and arguably also the most far-reaching, of all the twentieth-century revolutions. It is the history of the giddy years of political change and hope in 1930s Spain, when the so-called 'Generation of '36', Peirats' own generation, rose up against the oppressive structures of Spanish society. It is also a history of a revolution that failed, crushed in the jaws of its enemies on both the reformist left and the reactionary right. José Peirats' account is effectively the official CNT history of the war, passionate, partisan but, above all, intelligent. Its huge sweeping canvas covers all areas of the anarchist experience—the spontaneous militias, the revolutionary collectives, the moral dilemmas occasioned by the clash of revolutionary ideals and the stark reality of the war effort against Franco and his German Nazi and Italian Fascist allies.

This new edition is carefully indexed in a way that converts the work into a usable tool for historians and makes it much easier for the general reader to dip in with greater purpose and pleasure.

"José Peirats' The CNT in the Spanish Revolution *is a landmark in the historiography of the Spanish Civil War . . . Originally published in Toulouse in the early 1950s, it was a rarity anxiously searched for by historians and others who gleefully pillaged its wealth of documentation. Even its republication in Paris in 1971 by the exiled Spanish publishing house, Ruedo Ibérico, though welcome, still left the book in the territory of specialists. For that reason alone, the present project to publish the entire work in English is to be applauded."*
—Professor Paul Preston, London School of Economics

" . . . this is a wonderful work and an essential resource for anyone interested in the history of the CNT and the Spanish revolution. Indeed, reading Peirats' work you see how much other historians (and other anarchists) have lifted from it in their books. It is great to finally have the work available in English."
—www.struggle.ws

"For those whose field of study is modern Spain, this is indeed an obligatory purchase. Given that this edition has been indexed and footnoted it may prove more useful to scholars than the original Spanish-language editions."
—Kate Sharpley Library

Anarchist Seeds beneath the Snow: Left-Libertarian Thought and British Writers from William Morris to Colin Ward

David Goodway

ISBN: 978-1-60486-221-8
$24.95   420 pages

From William Morris to Oscar Wilde to George Orwell, left-libertarian thought has long been an important but neglected part of British cultural and political history. In *Anarchist Seeds beneath the Snow*, David Goodway seeks to recover and revitalize that indigenous anarchist tradition. This book succeeds as simultaneously a cultural history of left-libertarian thought in Britain and a demonstration of the applicability of that history to current politics. Goodway argues that a recovered anarchist tradition could—and should—be a touchstone for contemporary political radicals. Moving seamlessly from Aldous Huxley and Colin Ward to the war in Iraq, this challenging volume will energize leftist movements throughout the world.

"Anarchist Seeds beneath the Snow *is an impressive achievement for its rigorous scholarship across a wide range of sources, for collating this diverse material in a cogent and systematic narrative-cum-argument, and for elucidating it with clarity and flair… It is a book that needed to be written and now deserves to be read.*"
— *Journal of William Morris Studies*

"*Goodway outlines with admirable clarity the many variations in anarchist thought. By extending outwards to left-libertarians he takes on even greater diversity.*"
— Sheila Rowbotham, *Red Pepper*

"*A splendid survey of 'left-libertarian thought' in this country, it has given me hours of delight and interest. Though it is very learned, it isn't dry. Goodway's friends in the awkward squad (especially William Blake) are both stimulating and comforting companions in today's political climate.*"
— A.N. Wilson, *Daily Telegraph*

"*The history of the British anarchist movement has been little studied or appreciated outside of the movement itself.* Anarchist Seeds beneath the Snow *should go a long way towards rectifying this blind spot in established labour and political history. His broad ranging erudition combined with a penetrating understanding of the subject matter has produced a fascinating, highly readable history.*"
— Joey Cain, edwardcarpenterforum.org

Asia's Unknown Uprisings
Volume 1: South Korean Social Movements in the 20th Century

George Katsiaficas

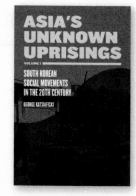

ISBN: 978-1-60486-457-1
$26.95   360 pages

Using social movements as a prism to illuminate the oft-hidden history of 20th century Korea, this book provides detailed analysis of major uprisings that have patterned that country's politics and society. From the 1894 Tonghak Uprising through the March 1, 1919, independence movement and anti-Japanese resistance, a direct line is traced to the popular opposition to U.S. division of Korea after World War Two. The overthrow of Syngman Rhee in 1960, resistance to Park Chung-hee, the 1980 Gwangju Uprising, as well as student, labor, and feminist movements are all recounted with attention to their economic and political contexts. South Korean opposition to neoliberalism is portrayed in detail, as is an analysis of neoliberalism's rise and effects. With a central focus on the Gwangju Uprising (that ultimately proved decisive in South Korea's democratization), the author uses Korean experiences as a baseboard to extrapolate into the possibilities of global social movements in the 21st century.

Previous English language sources have emphasized leaders—whether Korean, Japanese, or American. This book emphasizes grassroots crystallization of counter-elite dynamics and notes how the intelligence of ordinary people surpasses that of political and economic leaders holding the reins of power. It is the first volume in a two-part study that concludes by analyzing in rich detail uprisings in nine other places: the Philippines, Burma, Tibet, China, Taiwan, Bangladesh, Nepal, Thailand, and Indonesia. Richly illustrated, with tables, charts, graphs, index, and footnotes.

"George Katsiaficas has written a majestic account of political uprisings and social movements in Asia—an important contribution to the literature on both Asian studies and social change that is highly-recommended reading for anyone concerned with these fields of interest. The work is well-researched, clearly-argued, and beautifully written, accessible to both academic and general readers."
— Prof. Carl Boggs, author of *The Crimes of Empire* and *Imperial Delusions*

"This book makes a unique contribution to Korean Studies because of its social movements' prism. It will resonate well in Korea and will also serve as a good introduction to Korea for outsiders. By providing details on 20th century uprisings, Katsiaficas provides insights into the trajectory of social movements in the future."
— Na Kahn-chae, Director, May 18 Institute, Gwangju, South Korea

Capital and Its Discontents: Conversations with Radical Thinkers in a Time of Tumult

Sasha Lilley

ISBN: 978-1-60486-334-5
$20.00   320 pages

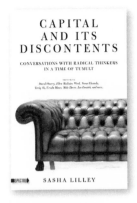

Capitalism is stumbling, empire is faltering, and the planet is thawing. Yet many people are still grasping to understand these multiple crises and to find a way forward to a just future. Into the breach come the essential insights of *Capital and Its Discontents*, which cut through the gristle to get to the heart of the matter about the nature of capitalism and imperialism, capitalism's vulnerabilities at this conjuncture—and what can we do to hasten its demise. Through a series of incisive conversations with some of the most eminent thinkers and political economists on the Left—including David Harvey, Ellen Meiksins Wood, Mike Davis, Leo Panitch, Tariq Ali, and Noam Chomsky—*Capital and Its Discontents* illuminates the dynamic contradictions undergirding capitalism and the potential for its dethroning. At a moment when capitalism as a system is more reviled than ever, here is an indispensable toolbox of ideas for action by some of the most brilliant thinkers of our times.

"These conversations illuminate the current world situation in ways that are very useful for those hoping to orient themselves and find a way forward to effective individual and collective action. Highly recommended."
— Kim Stanley Robinson, *New York Times* bestselling author of the *Mars Trilogy* and *The Years of Rice and Salt*

"In this fine set of interviews, an A-list of radical political economists demonstrate why their skills are indispensable to understanding today's multiple economic and ecological crises."
— Raj Patel, author of *Stuffed and Starved* and *The Value of Nothing*

"This is an extremely important book. It is the most detailed, comprehensive, and best study yet published on the most recent capitalist crisis and its discontents. Sasha Lilley sets each interview in its context, writing with style, scholarship, and wit about ideas and philosophies."
— Andrej Grubačić, radical sociologist and social critic, co-author of *Wobblies and Zapatistas*

Moments of Excess: Movements, Protest and Everyday Life

The Free Association

ISBN: 978-1-60486-113-6
$14.95   144 pages

The first decade of the twenty-first century was marked by a series of global summits which seemed to assume ever-greater importance—from the WTO ministerial meeting in Seattle at the end of 1999, through the G8 summits at Genoa, Evian and Gleneagles, up to the United Nations Climate Change Conference (COP15) at Copenhagen in 2009. But these global summits did not pass uncontested. Alongside and against them, there unfolded a different version of globalization. *Moments of Excess* is a collection of texts which offer an insider analysis of this cycle of counter-summit mobilisations. It weaves lucid descriptions of the intensity of collective action into a more sober reflection on the developing problematics of the 'movement of movements'. The collection examines essential questions concerning the character of anti-capitalist movements, and the very meaning of movement; the relationship between intensive collective experiences—'moments of excess'—and 'everyday life'; and the tensions between open, all-inclusive, 'constitutive' practices, on the one hand, and the necessity of closure, limits and antagonism, on the other. *Moments of Excess* includes a new introduction explaining the origin of the texts and their relation to event-based politics, and a postscript which explores new possibilities for anti-capitalist movements in the midst of crisis.

"More than a book, Moments of Excess *is a tool for 'worlding' . . . it speaks to questions that are crucial in creating a better world, all the while asking and opening more questions . . . Reading this book, I felt like a part of a conversation, a conversation that I didn't want to end."*
— Marina Sitrin, editor of *Horizontalism: Voices of Popular Power in Argentina* and (with Clif Ross) *Insurgent Democracies: Latin America's New Powers*

"Reading this collection you are reminded that there is so much life at the front-line, and that there is no alternative to capitalism without living this life to the full. The message is clear: enjoy the struggle, participate in it with your creative energies, be flexible and self-critical of your approach, throw away static ideologies, and reach out to the other."
— Massimo De Angelis, author of *The Beginning of History: Value Struggles and Global Capital* and editor of *The Commoner*

"Wonderful. Fabulous. The Free Association's work have been writing some of the most stimulating reflections on the constantly shifting movement against capitalism—always fresh, always engaging, always pushing us beyond where we were . . . exciting stuff."
— John Holloway, author of *Change the World Without Taking Power* and *Crack Capitalism*

The Angry Brigade: A History of Britain's First Urban Guerilla Group

Gordon Carr
with prefaces by John Barker
and Stuart Christie

ISBN: 978-1-60486-049-8
$24.95   280 pages

"You can't reform profit capitalism and inhumanity.
Just kick it till it breaks." — *Angry Brigade, communiqué.*

Between 1970 and 1972, the Angry Brigade used guns and bombs in a series of symbolic attacks against property. A series of communiqués accompanied the actions, explaining the choice of targets and the Angry Brigade philosophy: autonomous organization and attacks on property alongside other forms of militant working class action. Targets included the embassies of repressive regimes, police stations and army barracks, boutiques and factories, government departments and the homes of Cabinet ministers, the Attorney General and the Commissioner of the Metropolitan Police. These attacks on the homes of senior political figures increased the pressure for results and brought an avalanche of police raids. From the start the police were faced with the difficulty of getting to grips with a section of society they found totally alien. And were they facing an organization—or an idea?

This book covers the roots of the Angry Brigade in the revolutionary ferment of the 1960s, and follows their campaign and the police investigation to its culmination in the "Stoke Newington 8" conspiracy trial at the Old Bailey—the longest criminal trial in British legal history. Written after extensive research—among both the libertarian opposition and the police—it remains the essential study of Britain's first urban guerilla group. This expanded edition contains a comprehensive chronology of the "Angry Decade," extra illustrations and a police view of the Angry Brigade. Introductions by Stuart Christie and John Barker (two of the "Stoke Newington 8" defendants) discuss the Angry Brigade in the political and social context of its times—and its longer-term significance.

"*Even after all this time, Carr's book remains the best introduction to the culture and movement that gave birth to The Angry Brigade. Until all the participants' documents and voices are gathered in one place, this will remain the gripping, readable and reliable account of those days. It is essential reading and PM Press are to be congratulated for making it available to us.*"
— Barry Pateman, Associate Editor, The Emma Goldman Papers, University of California at Berkeley

The Floodgates of Anarchy

Stuart Christie and Albert Meltzer

ISBN: 978-1-60486-105-1
$15.95   144 pages

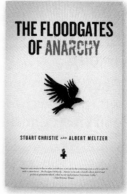

The floodgates holding back anarchy are constantly under strain. The liberal would ease the pressure by diverting some of the water; the conservative would shore up the dykes, the totalitarian would construct a stronger dam.

But is anarchy a destructive force? The absence of government may alarm the authoritarian, but is a liberated people really its own worst enemy—or is the true enemy of mankind, as the anarchists claim, the means by which he is governed? Without government the world could manage to end exploitation and war. Anarchy should not be confused with weak, divided or manifold government. As Christie and Meltzer point out, only with the total abolition of government can society develop in freedom.

"Anyone who wants to know what anarchism is about in the contemporary world would do well to start here. The Floodgates of Anarchy forces us to take a hard look at moral and political problems which other more sophisticated doctrines evade."
— The Sunday Times

"A lucid exposition of revolutionary anarchist theory."
— Peace News

"Coming from a position of uncompromising class struggle and a tradition that includes many of our exemplary anarchist militants, The Floodgates of Anarchy has a power and directness sadly missing from some contemporary anarchist writing. It is exciting to see it back in print, ready for a new generation to read."
— Barry Pateman, Associate Editor, The Emma Goldman Papers, University of California at Berkeley

William Morris: Romantic to Revolutionary

E.P. Thompson
with a foreword by Peter Linebaugh

ISBN: 978-1-60486-243-0
$32.95   880 pages

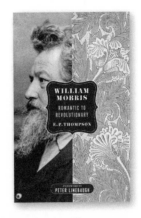

William Morris—the great 19th century craftsman, architect, designer, poet and writer—remains a monumental figure whose influence resonates powerfully today. As an intellectual (and author of the seminal utopian News From Nowhere), his concern with artistic and human values led him to cross what he called the 'river of fire' and become a committed socialist—committed not to some theoretical formula but to the day by day struggle of working women and men in Britain and to the evolution of his ideas about art, about work and about how life should be lived.

Many of his ideas accorded none too well with the reforming tendencies dominant in the Labour movement, nor with those of 'orthodox' Marxism, which has looked elsewhere for inspiration. Both sides have been inclined to venerate Morris rather than to pay attention to what he said.

Originally written less than a decade before his groundbreaking *The Making of the English Working Class*, E.P. Thompson brought to this biography his now trademark historical mastery, passion, wit, and essential sympathy. It remains unsurpassed as the definitive work on this remarkable figure, by the major British historian of the 20th century.

"*Two impressive figures, William Morris as subject and E. P. Thompson as author, are conjoined in this immense biographical-historical-critical study, and both of them have gained in stature since the first edition of the book was published... The book that was ignored in 1955 has meanwhile become something of an underground classic—almost impossible to locate in second-hand bookstores, pored over in libraries, required reading for anyone interested in Morris and, increasingly, for anyone interested in one of the most important of contemporary British historians... Thompson has the distinguishing characteristic of a great historian: he has transformed the nature of the past, it will never look the same again; and whoever works in the area of his concerns in the future must come to terms with what Thompson has written. So too with his study of William Morris.*"
— Peter Stansky, *The New York Times Book Review*

"*An absorbing biographical study... A glittering quarry of marvelous quotes from Morris and others, many taken from heretofore inaccessible or unpublished sources.*"
— Walter Arnold, *Saturday Review*

Damned Fools In Utopia: And Other Writings on Anarchism and War Resistance

Nicolas Walter
Edited by David Goodway

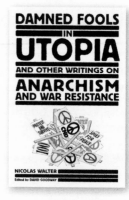

ISBN: 978-1-60486-222-5

$22.95   304 pages

Nicolas Walter was the son of the neurologist, W. Grey Walter, and both his grandfathers had known Peter Kropotkin and Edward Carpenter. However, it was the twin jolts of Suez and the Hungarian Revolution while still a student, followed by participation in the resulting New Left and nuclear disarmament movement, that led him to anarchism himself. His personal history is recounted in two autobiographical pieces in this collection as well as the editor's introduction.

During the 1960s he was a militant in the British nuclear disarmament movement—especially its direct-action wing, the Committee of 100—he was one of the Spies of Peace (who revealed the State's preparations for the governance of Britain after a nuclear war), he was close to the innovative Solidarity Group and was a participant in the homelessness agitation. Concurrently with his impressive activism he was analyzing acutely and lucidly the history, practice and theory of these intertwined movements; and it is such writings—including 'Non-violent Resistance' and 'The Spies for Peace and After'—that form the core of this book. But there are also memorable pieces on various libertarians, including the writers George Orwell, Herbert Read and Alan Sillitoe, the publisher C.W. Daniel and the maverick Guy A. Aldred. 'The Right to be Wrong' is a notable polemic against laws limiting the freedom of expression. Other than anarchism, the passion of Walter's intellectual life was the dual cause of atheism and rationalism; and the selection concludes appropriately with a fine essay on 'Anarchism and Religion' and his moving reflections, 'Facing Death'.

Nicolas Walter scorned the pomp and frequent ignorance of the powerful and detested the obfuscatory prose and intellectual limitations of academia. He himself wrote straightforwardly and always accessibly, almost exclusively for the anarchist and freethought movements. The items collected in this volume display him at his considerable best.

"[Nicolas Walter was] one of the most interesting left intellectuals of the second half of the twentieth century in Britain."
— Professor Richard Taylor, University of Cambridge